WHAT DO YOU DO WHEN:

—You take a grossly defective product back to the store and the manager says there's no warranty?

—You and your spouse want to separate or divorce?

—You and a friend want to start a business together?

—You need a power-of-attorney to help an ailing parent?

—You are fired for being too old?

—You are considering bankruptcy?

—You think a doctor or a hospital is guilty of malpractice?

You could, of course, go to a lawyer. On the other hand, you could save hundreds of dollars an hour by simply going to the best friend a legal consumer has today—this comprehensive resource.

REPRESENTING YOURSELF
What You Can Do Without a Lawyer

KENNETH LASSON is a professor of law at the University of Baltimore. His previous books include *Your Rights and the Draft, The Workers,* and *Private Lives of Public Servants.* **ALAN MORRISON** is one of the founders of the Public Citizen Litigation Group in Washington, D.C.

REPRESENTING YOURSELF

What You Can Do Without a Lawyer

SECOND EDITION

Kenneth Lasson

With Alan B. Morrison and the
Public Citizen Litigation Group

Introduction by Ralph Nader

A PLUME BOOK

PLUME
Published by the Penguin Group
Penguin Books USA Inc., 375 Hudson Street,
New York, New York 10014, U.S.A.
Penguin Books Ltd, 27 Wrights Lane,
London W8 5TZ, England
Penguin Books Australia Ltd, Ringwood,
Victoria, Australia
Penguin Books Canada Ltd, 10 Alcorn Avenue,
Toronto, Ontario, Canada M4V 3B2
Penguin Books (N.Z.) Ltd, 182–190 Wairau Road,
Auckland 10, New Zealand

Penguin Books Ltd, Registered Offices:
Harmondsworth, Middlesex, England

Published by Plume, an imprint of Dutton Signet,
a division of Penguin Books USA Inc.

First Plume Printing, July, 1995
10 9 8 7 6 5 4 3 2 1

 REGISTERED TRADEMARK—MARCA REGISTRADA

Library of Congress Cataloging-in-Publication Data
Lasson, Kenneth.
   Representing yourself : what you can do without a lawyer / Kenneth Lasson with Alan B.
Morrison and the Public Citizen Litigation Group ; introduction by Ralph Nader. — 2nd ed.
      p.   cm.
   Includes bibliographical references.
   ISBN 0-452-27451-6
   1. Pro se representation—United States—Popular works.   2. Attorney and client—
United States—Popular works.   3. Actions and defenses—United States—Popular works.
I. Morrison, Alan B.   II. Public Citizen Litigation Group.   III. Title.
KF8841.L27   1995
347.73'504—dc20
[347.307504]
                                                                              94-46383
                                                                                  CIP

Printed in the United States of America
Set in New Baskerville
Designed by Leonard Telesca

PUBLISHER'S NOTE: The information contained in this book is intended only to educate readers generally in selected areas of law and is not meant to substitute for legal advice applicable to specific situations. It is sold with the understanding that the publisher is not engaged in rendering legal or other professional service. For any particular legal concern or problem, the service of a competent professional person should be sought.

for Barbara, Tammy, Noah, and Jeremy

Contents

Foreword

Writing a law book for laymen runs the risk of being criticized for helping prove the notion that "a little knowledge is a dangerous thing." But the author's goals are simply to demystify the law by offering accurate information in understandable language, and to provide guidance to people perplexed by everyday legal problems. The reader's task is to recognize the wide variety of commonplace matters which can be handled without a lawyer—and to discern as well those matters where hiring a competent attorney may well be the best course of action.

This second edition of **Representing Yourself** has been completely revised and expanded to reflect changes in both the law and the way we look at it. Thus there are new chapters on alternative dispute resolution, getting the most out of government, and personal rights and liberties. The information provided is current as of early 1995.

The extent to which this book succeeds in avoiding both simplistic formulations of the law and overly complex or technical information is due in large measure to the lawyers, judges, and professors consulted on the various chapters that follow—all of whom were exceedingly generous with their time and expertise: thanks are thus due to Kenneth Breitbart, John Fader, Rebecca Korzec, Abba Poliakoff, Joseph Rosenblatt, Marcus Shar, Jane Schukoske, Walter Schwidetzky, Darrell VanDeusen, and William Weston.

The writer is also indebted to Ella Agambar for her expert word-processing; to Andrea Weisstuch for her diligent research assistance; and to Alan Morrison of Public Citizen, Inc., whose thorough and thoughtful comments throughout the editing process have contributed immeasurably to the book's clarity and usefulness.

—**Kenneth Lasson**

Introduction

by Ralph Nader

> They have no lawyers among them, for they consider them as a sort of people whose profession it is to disguise matters and to wrest the laws; and therefore they think it is better that everyman should plead his own cause, and trust it to the judge, as in other places the client trusts it to a counsellor.
>
> —Sir Thomas More, *Utopia*

That we do not live in a utopian society is often blamed upon our excess of lawyers. Even members of the profession itself—from Supreme Court justices to the vice-president of the United States—bemoan the fact that the United States is the most litigious country in the world. And indeed the presumption that grievances can best be redressed by going to court is encouraged by the very nature and training of American attorneys. It's no wonder that people are quick to quote Shakespeare: "The first thing we do, let's kill all the lawyers!"

The current criticism is so widespread, though, that perhaps we have become too quick to demean the hardworking attorneys who serve useful, important (and often absolutely necessary) purposes. Being a lawyer doesn't make one any less ethical than being a doctor, plumber, or bureaucrat. Compassion and integrity are reflections of one's character and upbringing much more than of one's education.

Nevertheless, there are good reasons why lawyers nowadays are held in such low esteem: the image of the legal profession—which should reflect an overriding concern for fairness, justice, and equality—has been tarnished by greed, complacency, and self-righteousness. The United States produces some forty thousand new attorneys a year and accounts for two-thirds of all the lawyers in the world (three times as many per capita as England, twenty-one times as many as Japan). Moreover, to put it bluntly, they need the work. The unfortunate truth is that lawyers often serve as needless middlemen in a wide variety of common legal problems—from the probate of wills (for which the British, as one example, seldom use attorneys) to the settlement of real estate transactions (which usually require little more expertise than simple common sense. Worse, lawyers often get in the way of resolving disputes amicably.

Practitioners like to say that the law is a jealous mistress; perhaps that's why lawyers are so expensive, and consequently tend to be utilized mostly by the well-heeled. In turn the rich are perceived as getting forever richer with the help of foxy tax attorneys paid hefty fees to find loopholes or lobby for their enactment. Law students are trained much more heavily in the technicalities of corporations, securities, creditors' rights, and commercial transactions than they are in consumerism, tenants' and debtors' rights, or the ethics and methodology of alternative dispute resolution.

In addition, despite the overabundance of lawyers, it's still hard to find one who will handle a low-paying case. In fact, until minimum-fee schedules and regulations against competitive advertising were ruled illegal in the mid-1970s (largely through the efforts of the Public Citizen Litigation Group), the consumer was even more a victim of the legal establishment's self-regulated monopoly.

But there are some very good reasons to pause before running to the nearest lawyer at the first mention of contract or blush of confrontation. Many businessmen insist they operate more effectively on handshake agreements than on written legal documents. Even when a contract is necessary, or simply judicious, it can frequently be drafted by the parties themselves.

Relatively minor arguments over rights, duties, and damages might better be settled after passions have cooled than through a heated "My lawyer will contact you in the morning!" In many cases, all that's needed is a cool-headed third party (a role that can also be played by an attorney). Indeed, a trend is developing toward the use of divorce counselors or mediators rather than lawyers in cases when both spouses seek a peaceful dissolution of their marriage. In short, with lawyers' hourly fees soaring into the triple digits and their professional image continuing to plummet, more and more Americans with legal problems wonder if there is an alternative to seeking an attorney. The answer is often yes. At the Public Citizen Litigation Group, a public-interest law firm we founded in 1972, letters arrive nearly every day from consumers unhappy with negligent, condescending, dishonest, or (most often) expensive attorneys. On several occasions Public Citizen has itself brought suit to establish principles that would make legal services available to more people at affordable prices. One of the first cases initiated by the Litigation Group was *Goldfarb* v. *Virginia State Bar,* in which the Supreme Court found that the bar's minimum-fee schedules for routine legal services violated federal antitrust laws. Public Citizen also participated in the suit in which the Supreme Court held that lawyers have a First Amendment right to advertise. Both decisions have served to increase competition among attorneys, encourage the development of legal clinics, and thereby reduce fees. Public Citizen likewise challenged the restrictions on non-lawyers who wish to help others pursue their rights. In Florida, the group represented a legal secretary who for several years had been helping husbands and wives prepare the forms necessary to obtain a divorce. In Virginia, it sued the bar on behalf of a title-insurance company which had offered low-cost house settlements to home buyers by hiring non-lawyers to do most of the simple work involved. In Wisconsin, one of Public Citizen's clients sued the established bar, which had sought to prevent an environmental activist from representing his group before state agencies on the ground that he was practicing law without a license.

In fact, many tasks that lawyers perform are routine, and reasonably intelligent citizens who have the time should be able to do things such as conduct their own house settlement, file for a simple divorce, or draft a plain will. This book demystifies the law, and details the many ways by which people can be their own lawyers. Its first edition was very well received, but this one is better in many ways. Chapters have been added on alternative dispute resolution and civil liberties; the text is even easier to read and understand; and, of course, it is current and accurate as of its publication date.

To be sure, many problems require an attorney. No one with a large estate should write a will without benefit of counsel; nor should one try to defend himself against a criminal charge. But a careful perusal of the pages that follow should help readers ask the right questions, get the best service, and—perhaps most important—decide whether they really need a lawyer at all.

CHAPTER ONE

Contracts

Make every bargain clear and plain,
That none may afterwards complain.
—John Ray,
English Proverbs

Contracts are the most common, yet most commonly misunder-
stood, legal transactions. Clients envision thick sheaves of heavy
paper filled with fine print and jargon: *parties of the first part, where-
fores,* and *hereafters.* Most people do not realize that practically
everyone makes contracts in everyday life, without ever using incomprehensible words or formally written documents.

Consider the following scenario: Phoebe telephones Virginia
late Monday evening. "Can you baby-sit for Willy on Saturday
night? Edgar and I want to see a movie."

"Sure," says Virginia. "What time?"

"Why don't we say seven-thirty? We'll pick you up."

"Okay. See you then."

Phoebe and Virginia have just made a contract. The terms of
their baby-sitting agreement were not spelled out in a written instrument, but they are reasonably clear to the parties who made
them. Virginia has agreed to sit for Phoebe and Edgar on Saturday night, forgoing other opportunities such as visiting with

friends or baby-sitting for someone else who might offer more money. Phoebe and Edgar, on the other hand, have obligated themselves to pay Virginia for her time, perhaps even if they decide to cancel at the last minute.

Most of the terms of this agreement are unstated. The only item actually spoken about was the time Phoebe would pick up Virginia. This is called an "express term." Everything else in the agreement is implied. For instance, no mention was made of a specific hourly rate. Yet both sides obviously had expectations as to what the figures would be, probably because Virginia has sat regularly for Phoebe and Edgar or because there is a "going rate" which all baby-sitters in the neighborhood receive.

There are other implied terms. Unless Virginia lives within walking distance, Phoebe and Edgar are obligated to pick her up and drive her home. For her part, Virginia must do more than just "sit"—she has to take care of the needs of the child, maybe even read him a story before tucking him in at bedtime. She also has certain unstated rights—to watch television when Willy is in bed, do her homework or read a book, have a glass of milk (but probably not a beer), and sample the contents of the cookie jar. All those implied terms are very much part of the contract, because they are part of the understanding that all people who enter into these kinds of agreements—baby-sitters and parents alike—accept as the operative rules.

Lawyers often use legalistic words in contracts that many people don't understand. The glossary at the end of this book should demystify the standard terminology.

The essence of a contract is an exchange of promises. Contracts must be mutually agreed upon. Thus, if someone offers to cut your lawn for ten dollars, you are not obligated to pay unless you accept the offer and the lawn is cut. A promise can also take the form of giving up something, such as not using your power lawn mower on Saturday morning, in exchange for the right to use your neighbor's pool on Sunday afternoon.

Regardless of the form of the contract, both sides must part with something of value for it to be valid. This is called *consideration.* Thus, if a janitor who is paid by a landlord to pick up trash tells a tenant he will empty his wastebaskets only if the tenant pays him an extra five dollars a week, the tenant's promise to pay would be unenforceable—because the janitor is already obligated to do the job without the additional payment.

Likewise, if promises are exchanged based on performance, payment need not be made until the work is completed. For example, you need not pay the person who has promised to cut your lawn until it is actually mowed.

The amount of consideration is generally irrelevant. If Sam offers to sell his 1954 Studebaker to Joe for $10,000, and Joe accepts—but then changes his mind because he thinks the price is too high—a court will probably not void the contract for lack of adequate consideration. That is, the court won't try to second-guess the parties about whether one gave up too much or received too little. (In other words, if you make a bad bargain, you are stuck with the results.)

One notable exception to this rule is the minimum-wage law, which is designed to protect those who are in a bad bargaining position and may need a job so much that they would be willing to work for less than what the law says is a fair wage.

Some contracts have to be in writing to be enforceable. The vast majority of contracts are simply agreed upon by an exchange of spoken words or a handshake, and not written at all. Make no mistake about verbal agreements, though: in many instances they are enforceable. Thus, if you go to the best restaurant in the city and order the highest-priced steak and the most expensive wine, you are legally obligated to pay for the meal even though you may have signed nothing.

However, there are a few agreements which can be enforced *only* if they are in writing and if you have signed a piece of paper accepting their terms. The most important of these are contracts for the purchase or long-term lease of land, a promise to pay someone else's debts, or a purchase of goods over a certain amount (anywhere from five dollars to a thousand, depending on your state's law). In addition, many contracts that require one side to perform a service or supply goods over a long period of time (generally a year or more) have to be in writing.

There are several reasons why the law requires these agreements to be in writing. Generally, they involve important matters such as the purchase of real estate, or they relate to items over which confusion often arises, such as whether your rich uncle really did mean to promise to pay your debts if you refuse to or can't.

But there is another reason why important contracts should generally be in writing: it greatly reduces disputes about who promised what to whom. People usually remember what's most favorable to them. Disputes often arise because people remember things they want to hear and forget those that may seem irrelevant to their circumstances. Putting an agreement in writing also helps ensure that the parties focus on each of its terms, considerably narrowing the potential for controversy. There will still be disputes, because no one can think of every contingency and few of us ever express ourselves as clearly as we would like. But putting it in writing helps.

Like almost everything else having to do with contracts, however, it's generally up to you to decide whether to insist that the agreement be written down. The best advice is to use common sense: if there's substantial money involved, or a number of special conditions, or if you've never dealt with the other person before, it's probably worth the time, trouble, and expense to write it down. On the other hand, in an everyday situation like a baby-sitting arrangement, demand for a written agreement would be out of place.

Note that it is never *illegal* to make a verbal contract for the sale of land, or to agree by handshake to shovel a neighbor's walk whenever it snows during the next three years for five dollars a year. Many such oral agreements are made and fully carried out every day. But if there is a dispute about the agreement, it's much easier to get a court to enforce the promise made by the other side if it is in writing and signed by both parties.

The terms of the contract are up to you. With few exceptions, the parties (not the law) dictate what will be in the contract. In our first example, Virginia was free to tell Phoebe that she would not baby-sit for less than five dollars an hour, and Phoebe could have said that she would pay no more than one dollar an hour. (The minimum-wage laws don't apply to casual baby-sitting arrangements.) If the parties had agreed on either rate, there would have been a contract; if they hadn't, there wouldn't. In other words, it's entirely up to you whether you wish to enter into a contract, and if so, on what terms.

Another example: the store where you bought this book was free to offer to sell it to you at a price higher or lower than was printed on the cover. You were free to accept that offer or (perish the thought) not buy the book. If the store refused to honor your check or credit card, but insisted on cash instead, it was up to you to decide whether that condition was satisfactory to you.

In short, there are virtually no contract terms forbidden by law, provided that both sides agree to them.

There are a few exceptions to this general rule. The law, however, will not enforce illegal contracts, such as a promise to pay $10,000 to damage someone else's property. Similarly, the courts will not help a winner in a card game collect the money that the loser borrowed, lost, and now won't pay back. The law also recognizes that in some circumstances the bargaining positions of the parties are so unequal, or the price exacted so high, as to be "unconscionable"; such promises will likewise not be enforced. (See Chapter 4 about defective products.)

Drafting a contract need not be difficult. Here are the basic items to include in a simple contract:

- a description of the document (e.g., "Contract" or "Agreement" or "Letter of Understanding")
- the names of the parties involved (e.g., "between Jack Armstrong and Mary Worth")
- operative language (i.e., what the parties intend to accomplish by the contract, and how they will perform their obligations under it, and when the agreement is to take effect)
- definitions of terms not commonly understood
- the date and signatures (preferably including witnesses or a notary)

The promises of certain categories of people are not enforceable against them. In order to enter a binding contract, you must have what is known as the *legal capacity* to do so. Certain groups of people, principally those who are judged not to have sufficiently sound judgment to decide important things for themselves, are protected by the law. Such people can sign contracts as they please, but the courts won't hold them to their promises.

The largest group of persons who generally are considered not to have the capacity to enter into binding agreements are minors—people under the legal age, which is usually between eighteen and twenty-one but varies from state to state. Agreements made by minors are not enforceable against them. That's why parents of minors are generally asked to co-sign a contract when, for instance, a teenager wants to buy a car. In that case, even though the minor cannot be made to pay, the parents can. Since laws relating to legal capacity are intended to protect minors and some others (such as the mentally unsound or the intoxicated), promises made by the other parties to the transaction are generally enforceable against *them* but not against the legally incapacitated.

On this issue, however, there is a notable exception to the general rule: that is, a minor who contracts for and receives necessities such as food and basic clothing may be sued for failure to pay (unless, of course, a parent or guardian comes forward who is ready, willing, and able to provide such necessaries). Thus a sixteen-year-old who refuses to pay for the meal he has eaten in a restaurant or a night spent at a hotel can be held liable for the cost of the food.

Beware of contract modifications. Modification of a contract is a change in its terms after both parties have agreed and (in the case of a written contract) signed. Sometimes modifications are no more than clarifications of ambiguities that the parties didn't recognize until after the contract was signed. In other instances, the change may be more basic, such as an increase in price on the work the carpenter promised to do in repairing your screen porch.

You don't need a lawyer to enter into a contract. If you did, life would grind to a halt, and we would spend all our time consulting with lawyers every time we bought a newspaper, ordered a meal, or got on a bus.

Nonetheless—especially when the agreement is complicated,

or when there is a great deal of money at stake—it is far preferable to have lawyers prepare certain kinds of contracts. Lawyers are supposed to have two important skills that laymen don't: they are trained to write clearly and precisely and to avoid ambiguities that can lead to later disputes, and they are accustomed to anticipating problems and assuring that all the essential elements of the agreement are spelled out.

For instance, you could enter into what seems like a perfectly straightforward written contract under which someone would paint your barn by the end of the next month for $500. A good lawyer would ask, "Who's going to pay for the paint?" The answer to that question may be clear if the other party is in the painting business, because in most places the custom is for the painter to supply the paint. But if the painter is a college student home on vacation, it's less likely that he would expect to supply the materials needed. In this case, anticipating the problem may mean that there will be no agreement, because each side wants the other to pay for the paint. But surely it is far better for that difference to be known before the work is done rather than after.

Bear in mind a few essential elements if you are writing your own contract. First and most important, keep it simple. Avoid legalese. If you don't know what a word means, don't put it in just because you saw it in some forms contract that you bought at the stationery store. Try to provide for all expected contingencies, but remember that even the best lawyers can't think of everything all of the time.

Be sure to put the date on the contract, particularly if there is more than one version or if there are modifications. If a dispute occurs later on, the dates may help explain what otherwise would be contradictions and may make clear what the final agreement was between the parties.

There is no one magic form for a contract. Anything will do which demonstrates that the parties have reached an agreement and which sets forth its essential terms. One of the simplest forms is a letter from one party to the other stating his understanding of the agreement. If the letter is signed by both parties, it is a contract. If you choose this method, enclose an extra copy of the letter and ask the other party to sign and return it, if the terms are acceptable.

When in doubt, have your lawyer look over the contract you've written. Lawyers can and often do prepare contracts for others. But since most lawyers charge more if they do more work, and since drafting a contract can be time-consuming, you may have to pay a lawyer a considerable amount of money if he actually *prepares* the document.

Lawyers can perform a very useful function—at a greatly reduced cost—if you simply ask them to look at your contract after you and the other side have agreed, but before you sign on the dotted line. This is especially important if the other side has a lawyer, or if the contract is on a printed form prepared by a bank or insurance company. Good lawyers can examine an agreement that has been prepared by someone else and let you know if they see any problems. Thus for a relatively small price you can have peace of mind, knowing that you have signed a reasonable contract or that you ought to consider changing it to add some protections or make some clarifications.

Again, though, if the contract is moderately complicated or a considerable amount of money is involved, hiring a lawyer might be a wise investment.

CHAPTER TWO

Landlord-Tenant Relations

A good lawyer, a bad neighbor.
—Benjamin Franklin,
Poor Richard's Almanac

Disputes between landlords and tenants are so common that in many jurisdictions they are resolved exclusively by special courts (often called "Rent Court" or "Housing Court"). But there is no special mystery about leases. They are basically like other contracts. The parties must agree on every term, and each provision is subject to modification. The fact that a typical apartment lease is on a printed form that requires a magnifying glass to read doesn't alter this principle.

Two things make leases a little different. First, they often include unfamiliar terms which over the years have acquired significant legal meanings that, unless changed, may seriously affect your rights. Second, in the absence of specific provisions to the contrary, the law often implies terms in a lease that do not appear anywhere in writing. Not too surprisingly, these two factors generally (but not always) favor landlords.

Condominium owners also have rights against management companies, but generally they are pursued by the condo owners' association. An owner can also sue the owners' association if he feels that his rights under the deed of purchase—essentially a contract—have been violated.

There are three basic kinds of landlord-tenant arrangements, called "tenancies." A *tenancy for years* is created by a written lease that expires at a specific date. The term of the lease is generally one year or longer, and when the term ends the lease expires automatically, without the need for either party to give notice.

A *periodic tenancy* is created when a lease runs from one period of time to the next (typically, month to month), until it is terminated by one party's notice to the other that he wishes the tenancy terminated. The time-period specified (day, week, or month) is generally the interval in which the rent is paid. The beginning date of such an arrangement must be specific, but the termination date is left open until the time that proper notice is given. The meaning of the term *proper notice* should be described in the lease, although it generally ranges from one week to two months, depending on the length of the period of the lease.

A *tenancy at will* (sometimes called a *tenancy at sufferance*) is an informal arrangement which either party can terminate without breaking any promises. Generally, there is no written lease. Under common law, neither the landlord nor the tenant had to give any prior notice of an intention to end the arrangement. The landlord could send the tenant a notice to leave the premises immediately; the tenant could likewise abandon whenever she wanted to.

Today most states have laws requiring the landlord to give some sort of notice prior to terminating a tenancy at will. Because state laws vary, the notice required is anything from a week to a month, although the required time seldom exceeds thirty days.

Your rights may depend on the type of tenancy you have. The kind of lease you have affects (1) the ease with which either party can terminate it without being liable for breach of contract, and (2) the manner in which a landlord can raise the rental payments. Unless otherwise provided, in a tenancy for years the amount of rent is assumed to remain unchanged during the life of the lease. In contrast, in a tenancy at will or a periodic tenancy, the landlord is generally free to increase the rent simply by giving the same notice as would be required to terminate the tenancy.

The type of tenancy also determines what effect, if any, the sale of the property to a new owner may have upon the tenant. In either a tenancy for years or a periodic tenancy, unless the tenant has breached the lease the new owner has no right to evict him until the tenancy expires or proper notice is given. Nor can a new owner single-handedly change the terms of an existing lease. The tenant has the right (and the duty) to perform his responsibilities under the lease to the new landlord, just as he would have done with the former one.

In a tenancy at will, however, the tenant has no such protection. Such tenancies terminate automatically, regardless of the intention of the parties, upon the sale of the property to a new owner. The new landlord, of course, is free to create new tenancy-at-will relationships with existing tenants if he so desires.

Your rent level depends upon whether the apartment is completely private, private but subsidized by the government, or public. In a few locations (such as New York City), specific state and/or federal laws may limit the amount of rent that can be increased at any one time. Your local housing-court clerk should be able to supply this information.

Read the lease carefully before you sign it. Check a lease for problems before you sign it, and negotiate new terms if necessary, rather than fight about it later in court. For this purpose a lawyer can be helpful, especially, if you do not understand a provision in the lease. The time it takes an attorney to warn of potential problems is usually much less—and less expensive—than the time you spend in court to resolve a disputed change.

Read the entire lease, even the small print. Anything you find confusing should be clarified. Handwritten changes on a standard lease form are usually valid when initialed by both landlord and tenant. On the other hand, verbal agreements (such as waiving a prohibition against pets) are often not enforceable. You may not wish to live under certain standard clauses, such as those which obligate the tenant to make repairs or which seek to regulate the tenant's conduct (for example, by forbidding pets or specifying hours after which a stereo cannot be played). Try to have such clauses modified to your satisfaction. Similarly, if you might be transferred to another area by your employer, you may want to make the lease flexible by securing the right to sublet, subject to the landlord's approval, "which may not be unreasonably refused." In any event, you should insist that your security deposit be placed in an interest-bearing account—as many states require—and that the accumulated total is returned to you at the end of the lease (assuming you have lived up to all your promises).

Both landlord and tenant have rights. The landlord has the right to receive rent, to enter the property for necessary repairs, and to recover the premises at the end of the rental term in the same general condition as existed when the tenant moved in (allowing for normal wear and tear).

Tenants have the right to use the premises undisturbed for the purposes for which they were rented, to have at least the common areas kept in good repair by the landlord, and to recover their security deposit if they have not breached the lease.

The typical residential lease contains standard terms, although sometimes you must look hard to find them. Most leases include the following:

- the full names of the landlord and tenant
- the address of the property
- the amount of rent, and details as to when it becomes due (either weekly, monthly, or yearly) and on what day of the month or week
- information as to which utilities, if any, are to be provided (and paid for) by the landlord, and which are to be the responsibilities of the tenant
- the length of the lease and its expiration date (in the case of tenancy for years), or the period of the lease (in a periodic tenancy)
- the amount and method of notice to be given prior to terminating a periodic tenancy

- the purpose for which the property has been leased (e.g., residential, office, or commercial)
- the rights and obligations of both the landlord and the tenant regarding repairs
- the amount of any security deposit, the conditions upon which it is to be retained by the landlord rather than returned to the tenant, and whether it bears (and who is entitled to) interest
- the tenant's rights (if any) to assign or sublease the premises
- the signatures of both landlord and tenant(s)

Commercial leases are generally much more complicated. Large buildings used for offices, manufacturing, or sales carry with them insurance obligations and legal considerations that are usually more complex than a simple residential dwelling. Such leases should be drafted by an experienced real estate attorney.

Your lease should state who is responsible for making repairs. Historically, landlords have been under no duty to repair leased premises. There were various common-law exceptions to this rule: common areas (which are under the control of the landlord) and hidden defects (unless the landlord pointed them out prior to the lease). In the past (and still, in many jurisdictions) the tenant has usually been responsible for all repairs to the premises unless the landlord promises otherwise.

In a few states and cities, however, the law includes an *implied warranty of habitability*. This standard is often defined in terms of meeting the important requirements of the local housing code. If the landlord won't correct the violations, tenants should report them to the proper authorities. If the property is not habitable, the tenant's rent may be reduced by a court to pay for repairs. Most states have specific statutes which forbid landlords from attempting to evict tenants because they have reported violations to the authorities.

You may be able to move out prior to the expiration date in a tenancy for years. First, carefully read the lease: some allow for early termination if a tenant is transferred to another location by her employer. Second, examine the lease for any restriction of your right to assign or sublease the premises. An assignment means that another party could move in and become completely responsible for carrying out the obligations of your lease until the expiration date. A sublease means that you are still primarily responsible to the landlord, and that if the sublessee doesn't perform one of his duties (like paying the rent on time), the landlord can still sue you.

No matter what the lease says regarding your rights of assignment and sublease, if you want to get out of your lease, ask your landlord. Offer to find a replacement tenant. The landlord may let you out of the lease if he thinks he can get more rent from someone else, or if he's tired of hearing you complain about the lack of heat. If there is no restriction in the lease, you have the legal right as a tenant to assign or sublet your interest in the property to another person. But the landlord may actually prefer to find his own substitute tenant—and his doing so makes life much simpler for you.

Unfortunately, most modern leases contain a restriction on the tenant's right to sublet or assign. If your lease does contain such a restriction, and your landlord does not agree to waive it, your rights are limited. Under common law, a tenant was responsible to pay rent to the landlord for the entire term of a tenancy for years—whether or not the premises were occupied. The landlord could refuse to let the tenant assign or sublease his interest to another person, and still sue the original tenant for the entire amount of rent.

Most states, however, now have laws obligating the landlord in such situations to negotiate damages—that is, to make a reasonable attempt to find another tenant. But if the landlord makes reasonable, good-faith attempts to find another tenant and is unsuccessful, the original tenant is still legally responsible for the rent until expiration of the lease. (Likewise, if the landlord can find a substitute tenant, but only at a reduced rent, the old tenant is liable for the difference between the reduced rent and the original rent.)

If your landlord claims to be unable to find a suitable substitute tenant, you should try to find one yourself—even if your lease forbids assignments or subleases. Be sure to explain to potential tenants that their tenancy is subject to the landlord's final approval—a requirement in most leases. Most courts would find the landlord to be acting unreasonably if he refused to accept a suitable tenant, and would release you from your obligation to pay future rent. But it's better to put a clause in the lease forbidding the landlord from unreasonably refusing to accept your subtenant.

If you are in the military service—even if it is only in the reserves—it would be a good idea to add a clause releasing you from the lease in the event you are transferred or called to active duty.

You may not have to pay anything if, because conditions in your apartment have made it unlivable, you are moving out prior to the expiration of the lease. If your premises have become unbearable for some reason for which you aren't responsible, and the landlord has failed to make corrections within a reasonable time of being requested to do so, the law recognizes a doctrine known as "constructive eviction." For example, if you abandon the property because there's no heat in the winter, or there's a large hole in the roof, a court would probably consider your lease terminated by the landlord's own inaction. The important thing to keep in mind before moving out is a potential court suit. Send certified letters to the landlord regarding the immediate need of repairs; where possible, take photographs. These items can provide documentary evidence to the court that the premises were indeed unlivable, that the landlord knew of the problems, and that it was the landlord and not you whose failure to act was unreasonable.

Certain steps should be taken when leased premises need repairs. If the landlord has expressly promised to make necessary repairs and hasn't done so—or the repairs are needed in a common area under the control of the landlord—your first step should be to contact him under the expectation that he will make the corrections promptly and thoroughly. If the landlord fails to take action in a reasonable period of time (from within hours to several weeks, depending upon the nature of the repair), of course, send a certified letter explaining the nature of the problem needing attention, and politely reminding him of his obligations under the lease. Such a letter indicates that you mean business and may be contemplating a court case.

If the landlord continues to be recalcitrant, you might want to make the necessary repairs yourself or have someone do them for you. In this situation it would be wise for you to take photographs, get a couple of estimates before hiring anyone, and take any other measures that would assure a court of the reasonableness of your actions should you ultimately sue the landlord for reimbursement.

Failure to pay rent can lead to eviction. Although withholding rent may seem to be the obvious way for a tenant to be compensated for making repairs, it could lead to eventual eviction. Because of a peculiarity of landlord-tenant law, the tenant's promise to pay rent, and the landlord's promise to make repairs, have always been considered by the law to be separate and independent. That is, the landlord's failure to make needed repairs has not been held in and of itself to be sufficient reason to excuse the tenant from the promise to make rent payments.

Thus the best way for the tenant to be reimbursed for making necessary repairs is either a suit against the landlord in small-claims court, or the use of the rent-escrow procedure (described below) in areas where it is available.

Rent escrow is designed to help the tenant. Although the law varies from state to state, rent escrow characteristically is a procedure whereby the tenant asks the court to establish an escrow account—one administered independently, out of reach of the landlord—because the premises have serious defects which the landlord refuses to correct. The tenant pays the rent regularly into a court account, but the landlord doesn't get the money until the repairs are done.

A judge will listen to both sides before establishing an escrow account, and can decide to do any of the following:

- terminate the lease
- dismiss the rent-escrow request
- order that the rent be reduced by a certain amount
- order the establishment of a rent-escrow account

Once an escrow account has been established, either the court, the landlord, or the tenant may request a second hearing. If the landlord can then show that the repairs have been made, the court will order that the rent be given to the landlord. If the repairs have still not made after a period of time has elapsed, the court can order that all or some of the money be given back to the tenant, the landlord, or a third party to make repairs; appoint a special administrator to ensure that the repairs are made; or order that some or all of the money in the account be given to the landlord to prevent foreclosure on the mortgage.

In some states, if the landlord still has not made a good-faith attempt to make the repairs after six months or so, the judge may order that the funds be given back to the tenant, who is nevertheless obligated to pay future rent into the escrow account. If the tenant does not regularly pay the rent into the court's escrow account once it has been established, the court can order that any existing escrow funds be turned over to the landlord.

A landlord must take certain steps before evicting a tenant. When the lease expires in a tenancy with an express expiration date, and it is not renewed, the tenant must move out. No notice is required from the landlord. If the tenant has breached some important term of the lease, such as failure to pay the rent when due, the landlord can consider the lease terminated before the expiration date and require that the tenant move out after reasonable notice. Such notice should be clear and definite, delivered to the tenant directly; it should contain an express request that the tenant "quit the premises and deliver up possession" to the landlord before a specific date. If a tenant responds to the notice by paying the amount of rent due and the landlord accepts the payment, he has abandoned the right to evict the tenant (unless of course the lease is breached again).

The landlord can begin legal eviction proceedings if the tenant fails either to pay the back rent or to move out of the premises. The court clerk should be able to supply the necessary forms. In a simple "failure to pay rent" case, the services of an attorney should not be needed.

Payment of back rent at any time prior to an eviction warrant—which must be signed by a judge—will stop the eviction process. In any event, there can be no eviction without a court hearing.

Explore the possibility that a law school in your area runs a housing clinic. Many law schools have excellent clinical programs that allow students, under close faculty supervision, to represent tenants or landlords on housing matters. The cost is minimal (or free), and the results generally as good as that achieved with a lawyer.

Prepare for housing court the same way you would prepare for small-claims court. (See Chapter 14.)

A tenant should know about security deposits. It is a perfectly legal and common practice for landlords to require security deposits. Many states, however, have laws designed to protect tenants from being defrauded by the landlord under the guise of such a practice. For example, some states require that the security deposit be not more than two months' rent or fifty dollars, whichever is greater. The landlord must give the tenant a receipt for the security deposit, although it may be included as part of the lease.

If you ask for it, you are usually entitled by law to a written list of existing damages within fifteen days of the date before you move in. This list protects you in case of a dispute over the property's condition when you move out—that is, from the possibility that the landlord will try to hold you liable for damages caused by a prior tenant. It is important that you check the list carefully to be sure it is accurate and complete.

When the landlord inspects the property for damages at the end of the lease, the tenant has the right to be present. Some state laws provide that the landlord may not keep any of the security deposit if she fails to inform the tenant of this right. In fact, many states have statutes which provide that a tenant is entitled to punitive damages should the landlord fail to tell him about his rights.

Finally, many states require that landlords place security deposits in an interest-bearing savings account, with the accumulated sum returned to the tenant within forty-five days of the tenant's vacating the premises. As a tenant, you should always insist upon such a provision in your lease; it's only fair, and never illegal.

The landlord may be entitled to keep the security deposit. Unless the terms of the lease provide otherwise, the landlord is generally allowed to keep all or part of the deposit if the tenant leaves owing unpaid rent, or having damaged the property beyond normal wear and tear. But if any portion of the security deposit is withheld to cover damages, the law in many states requires that the landlord send the tenant, by certified mail within thirty days after he vacates the property, a list of damages claimed and a statement showing the cost of the repairs. In these states, failure to provide the tenant this notice causes forfeit of the landlord's right to retain any of the security deposit regardless of damages.

Finally, in many states a landlord cannot unduly penalize a tenant for breaking the lease. Generally, even a tenant who breaks the lease or is evicted can recover all or part of the security deposit by giving the landlord written notice within forty-five days after the move and including a forwarding address. As mentioned before, the landlord must send such a tenant a written list of damages within thirty days of a request for one, along with a statement showing the actual repair costs. The landlord may subtract the actual repair costs or lost rent from the security deposit, but must return the rest of the money to the tenant.

Check to see if there's a tenants' association. A group of tenants can be much more effective than an individual in bringing to bear pressure upon a landlord to make needed improvements on the property or to keep rental fees within certain guidelines. If there is no tenants' association to which you can refer your problem before going to a lawyer, you might want to organize one. This can be accomplished in any number of ways, sometimes as easily as convening an informal meeting.

Many kinds of discrimination in housing are illegal. Various federal and state laws prohibit landlords from discriminating against tenants because of race, religion, sex, age, or national origin. If you feel that such discrimination has occurred, contact your local housing authority or equal-opportunity commission. Note, however, that in many areas landlords can legally discriminate against people with children, pets, unpopular hobbies, and the like.

CHAPTER THREE

Buying and Selling a House

Set thine house in order.
—*Isaiah 38:1*

Buying or selling a house—for most homeowners the largest single investment of their lives—can be a traumatic experience. But it need not be, as far as the law is concerned. The typical real estate transaction is actually quite understandable.

Neither a real estate agent nor a lawyer is required in the simple sale of a house. If you are the seller and have the time and energy to advertise and show the house yourself, you can pocket the commission an agent would normally charge. (Using the term *principals only* gives notice that you do not wish agents to inquire.) If you are a buyer and the house is already "listed," you have no such choice—unless you happen to become interested in a house before an agent is involved, and the seller agreed to have you specifically *excluded* from any subsequent agency contract agreement. Sellers are usually happy to do this, because it saves them the cost of a commission.

A lawyer can be helpful with the contract. The most useful service a lawyer can perform for both buyer and seller is to review the sales contract *before* it is signed. This document determines who pays the various costs involved, as well as what "non-fixtures" are to be sold along with the house. Your concern here should be to draft terms in your best interest; once the agreement is signed, even the best lawyer can't help you. In most states, real estate agents are allowed to draw sales contracts for others, usually by filling in blanks on standard forms; in a few other states, only lawyers may engage in this practice. (Check with your real estate agent or with the bar association in your state.) But even if the agent can't create the contract for you, you can always do it yourself; the rules against unauthorized practice of law only prohibit an individual from acting on someone *else's* behalf.

An agent is most useful to a seller. The major advantages of using a real estate firm are that agents advertise, screen buyers, help set an attractive asking price, advise as to whether to accept a lower offer, and assist in arranging various kinds of financing. If you decide to sell your house through a real estate agent, he will take a commission—a percentage of the selling price—as payment. An agent is familiar with the ins and outs of house selling, as well as the real estate laws, and should know the market in your area as to both property values and potential buyers.

The real estate agent is responsible to the seller and not to the buyer (although if your agent finds a buyer, he must operate in a fair manner toward both of you). The agent may be a solo practitioner working in your area, or may be a member of a regional or even national real estate firm. In any case, the seller enters into a contract with the agent, setting out the terms under which the agent will show and sell your house. These terms typically include:

- what type of listing you will have (explained below)
- how long the agent will be allowed to show your house to potential buyers (generally anywhere between thirty and ninety days, with provisions for extensions if mutually agreed upon)
- how much commission will be paid
- when the commission is payable

The contract can also include any other terms that you or the agent feel are necessary to be stated in your agreement. Similarly, it can be negotiated so that "customary fees" are reduced, especially when the real estate market is sluggish.

If you're a buyer, the agent must treat you fairly. Don't be misled by the friendliness of the agent. While of course it may be genuine, the agent is really acting on behalf of the seller, gets paid out of the proceeds of the sale, and is primarily interested in generating top dollar.

Remember that, unless you are dealing with someone who specifically operates as a "buyer's" broker, an agent's primary responsibility is to the seller. Buyers need not pay the agent any commission or other fees; the agent gets paid a percentage of the proceeds from the sale of the house.

On rare occasions a buyer will contract with a real estate agent to find a house. (In a market with fewer sellers than buyers, this practice may occur more frequently.) Like sellers, buyers cannot be discriminated against on the basis of their age, sex, race, color, or national origin.

Listing agreements take several forms. A house is "listed" when the real estate agent contracts with the seller to place it on the market. The most favorable agreement to the agent, as well as the most common, is the *exclusive-right-to-sell* contract. Under this arrangement, the agent you select is the only one who can sell your house—almost always for a fixed period of time such as sixty or ninety days. Even if you produce the buyer without the help of the agent, he gets a commission—unless the buyer has been expressly excluded in the agency contract. In other words, no one else has the right to sell your house during the term of the agency.

Under an *open listing* arrangement, you contract with an agent to sell your house for an agreed-upon commission, but you retain the right to sell the house yourself or to engage the services of another agent. This is the loosest type of arrangement, giving you the most flexibility and exposing the agent to the greatest risk of competition. An agency will likely spend less money to advertise under an open listing. Obviously, it is the least favored arrangement in the real estate industry.

A *multiple listing* service is an agreement among the real estate agents in an area to place the houses that they have contracted to sell on a master list, which in turn can be used by any participating agent. The fees are split between the agent originally retained and the one who actually finds a buyer. Agents who multiple-list have a much wider choice of houses to sell. If you don't want a number of different agents showing your house, you may request that it not be placed on a multiple list. Your chances of finding a good buyer, however, are thereby diminished.

In any case, you should read the agency contract very carefully to determine your rights and liabilities.

Commissions can be split. You do not have to pay any extra money when another agent is involved in the sale. Even if your house is multiple-listed, your original agent will often be the one to show your house to prospective buyers. If a buyer is brought to your agent's attention by someone from another firm, the commission is split.

Read your listing contract. Try to get the most flexibility in your listing contract. For example, try to have the agent allow you to sell your house independently if you can, although he may argue that your entry into the market will make it more difficult for him.

At any rate, make sure that you have told the agent if there are any possible buyers with whom you have already made contact—and that these buyers appear on the face of the listing contract as excluded. This is your protection that, even in an otherwise exclusive listing, you will be able to sell your house to a previously known buyer without having to pay an agent's commission.

Another way of maintaining flexibility is to contract for short periods of time with the agent. For example, you might agree to an exclusive listing for thirty to sixty days, and then open up the listing for other agents. You can always agree to extensions of the listing contract. Agreeing to representation for short periods of time will also make the agent more likely to concentrate on selling your house faster.

Don't be afraid to shop around for the real estate agent with the best terms and commission rates. Speak to several agents in your area before listing your house. *The main thing to remember is that, as with any other agreement (including the sales contract), all the terms in a listing contract are negotiable. This is true even if the terms are already spelled out on a printed form.*

Commissions are negotiable. Commissions usually run from five to ten percent of the sale price. Be certain you agree on an exact figure.

If you are selling your house under an exclusive agency listing, you will owe the agent a commission if your house is sold at any time during the course of the contract (or within a reasonable time after the contract has expired, if the ultimate buyer saw your house during the contract period). Don't think that because the contract has expired, you can sell your house to a buyer introduced by the agent without paying the agent's commission. Of course, if the house is sold to a buyer excluded by name in the listing contract, you need pay no commissions.

The contract of sale is critical to the transaction, for both buyer and seller. If you are listing your house with a real estate agent, he will prepare a contract of sale for you and the buyer to sign. If you are selling your house without an agent, you can use a form real estate contract—which is usually available from stationery or legal-supply stores.

The sales contract is a binding agreement between you and the buyer, setting out the terms under which the buyer will make the purchase. These terms include the settlement date for the property—when the transfer will be made (usually thirty to ninety days from the signing of the sales contract)—and the terms that the buyer and the seller agree to. It is the single most important document in any sale of property. Read it very carefully. If you have only enough money to pay a lawyer for one service, have him review the sales contract *before you sign.*

Again, all the terms in the sales contract are fully negotiable. In other words, try to make the best deal possible. As a seller, you would usually ask for some good-faith money to be paid at the signing of the contract (although perhaps held by the real estate agent), and assurances that you will be paid in full at the time of settlement. As a buyer, you might want to specify that you have the right to choose the title-insurance company or attorney who will make sure there are no outstanding claims against your house. (The title-insurance company that made the title search when the seller originally bought the house will generally give a better rate for an updated search now.)

If you are a seller, specify what extras come with the house—drapes, carpets, appliances, etc.—so there are no misunderstandings later. If you are planning to take your washer and dryer with you, for example, state your intentions.

As a buyer, you have the same right as the seller to make the best deal possible in the sales contract. You certainly would want the contract to be contingent on your getting acceptable financing for the house. This means that the contract will be terminated if you cannot find the financing specified in the contract. (For example, if the contract specified a fourteen-percent, thirty-year mortgage, it would not be enforceable if you were unable to get such financing within a designated time period.) Allow enough time to get the financing you seek.

If the seller has an assumable mortgage and you choose to assume it, specify that you should be entitled to any security deposit put down at the original transaction when the mortgage is ultimately paid off, and that you should have the right to choose both lawyer and title company.

The buyer would also want to make the contract contingent on the house passing various inspections, such as for termites. An inspection clause will protect you if the house is damaged in a way that is not noticeable to you. If the house fails to pass any inspections that you specify, you are not required to purchase it. If the house has well water, for example, you might specify in the contract that the property pass a specific test that measures the amount of water in reserve. Contact a local surveyor or the county water office for information on such tests.

Finally, make sure that you know what covenants and easements exist on the property. *Covenants* are agreements between the previous owners of the house that all the owners in the neighborhood agree to. These are the bylaws of the neighborhood, and although you were not party to their acceptance, they are generally binding on all subsequent homeowners in the area. For example, a covenant may restrict where garages or other buildings may be built, or set up binding rules such as how often houses must be painted and grass trimmed.

Easements are rights that other people may have in your property. Some may be written, but others may arise through continued use or may be otherwise implied by the law. For example, the electric company may have an easement to run power lines over your property. Other easements may not be so benign: a neighbor might have the right—purchased from a prior owner or by operation of law—to drive his car over your driveway in order to get to his house. Easements which concern your property and your neighbor's are said to "run with the land"—that is, they exist no matter who owns the house. Be sure you know what you are buying.

Inspections are sometimes required by law. Many states require that the seller of a house pay for inspections—for example, for radon or termites—and to repair or correct certain kinds of deficiencies, such as a leaky roof. Your local real estate board should be able to advise you about what kinds of inspections are required in your area.

An escrow agreement brings in a third party. Such an agreement is sometimes made in the sales contract. It appoints a neutral third party to handle the transactions at closing (settlement). An escrow agent is generally appointed by the buyer; sometimes he represents the title-insurance company or lending institution. Sometimes he is an independent third party such as an attorney. Houses financed through FHA or VA mortgages (discussed below) must be handled through escrow agents.

The escrow agent will handle much of the paperwork involved, make the necessary apportionment of the cost between the buyer and seller, and make sure the monies go to the right places. He is the stake holder who keeps the money during the closing transactions in order to make sure the right parties receive what they are due. The escrow agent applies the terms of the sales contract, and lists which charges are payable by the seller and which by the buyer. If there are unpaid real estate taxes, he makes the division—prorating it for the amount of time during the year the seller owned the house. (For example, if the seller owned the house from January to June, each party would be responsible for half the real estate taxes for that year.) The same divisions are made for utility bills and the like.

Credits are made for payments already made. There may also be an agreement that certain funds are to be withheld from the seller until he has performed a promised function, such as painting specified parts of the house or repairing a driveway. Both parties will want to set a convenient settlement date. If you are a seller moving to another house or an apartment, be sure that you won't have to move out of your present house before the new one is ready. You can protect yourself by providing in the contract that you will be entitled to rent your old house from the new owners, which will allow you to stay in the house as long as you need to.

The settlement sheet is prescribed by federal law. It must be prepared on a form printed by the Department of Housing and Urban Development (known as the HUD 1 form). There are two columns, listing the respective costs to be borne by the seller and the buyer. These terms reflect the sales contract, and are generally negotiable. They usually work as follows:

Transfer taxes are generally divided equally by the seller and buyer, as are *escrow* costs. The buyer is usually responsible for any *appraisals* necessary because of the loan or local law, and for the *points* payable to the lender. (See section on mortgages, below.) The buyer also pays the *legal fees* if any, as well as for a *report on his credit rating.*

The seller is usually responsible for *commissions* on the sale of the house, *document stamps* necessary for the deed of sale to be recorded in the local county or state office (see below), *notary fees* for signatures on the deeds, and *mortgage payments that are in arrears.*

Although the above division of costs is the normal practice, remember that all these fees are negotiable, and may be divided differently in the sales contract or the escrow agreement.

Title insurance guarantees a buyer's deed. Title insurance is intended to protect the buyer (and his mortgage holder) against the possibility that the seller does not in fact own the property, or that someone has placed a *lien* or other *encumbrance* on your new house. It is the function of the title-insurance company to search the official land records to determine if there are any such problems.

If the title-insurance company has found no encumbrances on the property, the title is said to be "free and clear" of all clouds on the title, or "merchantable." If an encumbrance is found, it is usually the present owner who is responsible for paying it off, or having it paid off as part of the settlement. Like other insurance, a title-insurance policy protects buyers against a future happening. The insurer warrants that there are no encumbrances on the property; if any are found later, the insurer will pay them off as long as you were not responsible. This protection lasts for the period you own the house and will further protect you should you want to sell your house later on.

Title to property should always be verified. It is possible to do it yourself (with the help of the records-office clerk), but searches can sometimes be tricky and it is probably best to pay someone with title-searching experience.

Most lenders require title insurance—or the opinion of a lawyer that there are no encumbrances—before giving a mortgage. But even if title insurance is not required, it is a good investment against what later might be a big bill.

There are different kinds of mortgages. Before you even sign the sales contract, it is a good idea to know the mortgage market in your area. You can't start looking too soon for possible means of financing.

Three basic types of financing are available.

Conventional mortgages come from commercial banks, savings and loan institutions, or mortgage brokers. A conventional loan charges interest based on the market rate, which is usually a small percentage over the prime rate (that which the bank charges its most favored customers). The bank is also likely to charge "points"—a fee equal to a percentage of the amount loaned. For example, if you are borrowing $100,000 and the bank is charging you seven points as a loan origination fee, it is getting $7,000 just for making the loan. Because this is money "up front"—that is, not part of the mortgage amount—it can substantially increase the amount you end up paying for the house. Points, like interest charges, are tax-deductible if they meet the following conditions: (1) they are not in the nature of a service fee; (2) if they are for a mortgage on the buyer's principal residence; and (3) if they are generally charged in your geographical area.

Federal Housing Administration loans are financed through banks or mortgage brokers, but are actually regulated by the Department of Housing and Urban Development. Such loans allow for a very small down payment. Anyone is eligible. Lenders may finance up to the appraised value of the house or up to a ceiling keyed to the local housing market. FHA loans, essentially insured by the federal government, are generally very acceptable to lending institutions. They are often for longer periods of time. There is no prepayment penalty. Because FHA loans can be obtained only on houses that have been FHA-inspected, they may not be approved until repairs are made pursuant to that inspection. Also, FHA lending institutions are limited to charging fewer points to the buyer; no regulations prohibit the assessing of points to the seller. (For further information about FHA loans, contact your local office of the Federal Housing Administration.)

Loans which are regulated by the *Veterans Administration* are also attractive. You must be an eligible veteran of the armed forces. Although VA loans are also made through commercial banks, a better-than-market rate is offered because the federal government guarantees a certain part of the loan in case of default (that is, if you are unable to make loan payments). VA loans are more easily assumable than FHA mortgages, and the period of time for payment is longer than those in conventional loans. But there is also no limitation on points and interest the bank can charge the buyer. A VA appraisal is also necessary. (For more information about VA loans, and especially for the eligibility requirements, contact your local office of the Veterans Administration.)

In recent years, various forms of creative financing have been developed, including "balloon" and "variable rate" mortgages. *Balloon mortgages* are those under which only the interest is due during the term of the mortgage, with the entire principle due at the end of the term (which is usually short). *Variable rate mortgages* are those which reflect the prevailing interest rates; in other words, they fluctuate over time. Because they are so risky, you should try to get the bank to agree to a ceiling of some kind—either a maximum rate over the life of the loan or a maximum increase in any one year.

A buyer should be assured of his mortgage rate. A lender (the *mortgagee*) is required by federal law to give each borrower (the *mortgagor*) a truth-in-lending statement. It shows the mortgagor exactly what rate he is paying on the mortgage, how much each payment will be—as well as the total cost.

Remember that the higher the down payment—the amount that is *not* financed—the lower the ultimate cost of the house. In order to make an informed decision, ask the lender to explain fully and clearly the various mortgage plans available. Do not sign anything before you are absolutely certain you understand the terms.

There are other ways to finance the purchase of a house. You can assume the mortgage of the current owners *if* the mortgage is assumable under its terms and the current mortgagor agrees. Obviously, lenders are not enthusiastic about letting a purchaser assume a low-interest mortgage if the current rates are much higher. But a bank may be amenable to "blending" a mortgage rate by setting an average annual percentage between the old mortgage and the newer rates. Try not to let yourself be intimidated by the bank. Remember that they are in business to attract and keep customers.

A bank does not always have to be involved in a mortgage. You may be able to arrange a private loan through a friend or relative and avoid the hassles of dealing with a bank. The terms can be more flexible than those in a standard bank mortgage or precisely the same. As in any contract, everything is negotiable. Still, it's a good idea to have a lawyer review the terms of a privately arranged financing agreement.

You can lose your house if you default. If you default under a mortgage, the lender has the power to take away your house. The mortgage is an agreement between you and the lender that, even though the house is titled in your name and you own the property, it is still subject to the lender's being paid.

A *deed of trust* is often just another name for a mortgage, except that in some states the property is actually titled in the name of the bank; when you have finally paid off the house payments, the deed will be transferred to your name. A deed of trust is an easy way for a lender to establish an interest in your house, without a formal foreclosure and retitling procedure after a default. Make sure you know the options legally available in your state.

A "Chapter 13" filing halts foreclosure. If a foreclosure has been initiated but the property has not yet been sold, a Chapter 13 bankruptcy filing (a formal proposal by the debtor to reorganize his finances) will suspend the foreclosure until the court approves.

The parties must agree upon a settlement date. The settlement date is the day specified in the sales contract on which the final transactions will occur—that is, the time the buyer will have to make the rest of the down payment and the lender will have to present a check for the balance. Some contracts of sale fix a date by which the settlement must take place, and the parties still have to agree on the actual time, date, and place. At that time the seller will sign over a deed to the buyer (or the mortgagee in a deed of trust), and the costs are allocated and paid.

If you understand what you've read so far, you probably don't need a lawyer for settlement. For the most part a lawyer will merely run through a checklist at the settlement, an exercise for which he often pockets a hefty fee—usually a percentage of the purchase price—for his minimal efforts.

Banks often require their own lawyer at settlement of houses they are financing (or at least to review the documents)—and charge the buyer for his services. Sometimes you can persuade the bank to waive either or both of these requirements.

Of course, in a complicated property transaction (not the usual buying and selling of a one-family dwelling), lawyers can be very helpful.

Both the deed and the mortgage must be filed. These documents are entered into the property records in your county or state depending on the local law. This step is required so that the buyer may have a good claim to his property and the bank a valid mortgage on it; the seller cannot do anything further (such as selling it again or making loans against it). Check with your state or county government to see what you must do (and what costs you must pay) before the records can be filed.

If you have any questions, the clerk at the filing office can help you. If an escrow agent or attorney is present at the settlement, he will usually file the documents for you—especially if the agent is the title-insurance company.

There are federal tax consequences to selling a house. If you are uncertain about what they are, you should see a lawyer or an accountant. Under current federal law, if you sell a house and do not buy another one for more than two years, you will be taxed on the entire amount of the gain from the sale; if you purchase another house within two years, you will be taxed only on that portion of the price of your old house which was not invested in your new house. There is also a one-time exclusion of $125,000 for house sales by people over the age of fifty-five.

Buying a condominium is about the same as buying a house. Most states apply the same basic law to condominiums as to regular houses, in all stages of the purchase proceedings. Check with your local government's housing agency for the rules in your area. Agreements regarding condominiums may be somewhat more complicated, and should be reviewed by a real estate agent and/or a lawyer.

Financing a cooperative apartment is sometimes easier. Cooperatives are generally corporations formed for the purpose of acquiring property. The shareholders are also lessees of the property. Their shares are inseparable from the leases, which are usually long-term (e.g., ninety-nine years and renewable).

It is sometimes easier to finance a cooperative apartment because more commercial money (and at better rates) is available for the purchase of a whole building as opposed to individual units. The entire property can be subject to one mortgage. Owners of units in a cooperative have the same tax benefits as owners of private homes or condominiums.

Cooperatives are managed by boards of directors who are responsible for maintenance of all the property. Because of the amount of money usually involved in buying into a co-op, a lawyer should be contacted at least to review the paper transaction.

CHAPTER FOUR

Defective Products

Caveat Emptor (Let the buyer beware).
—*Anonymous Latin proverb*

All too often we buy products that don't work when we open up the box, or that work for a while and then stop. Some people run to a lawyer when this happens. But perseverance, common sense, and a willingness to complain can often be as effective as a lawyer in getting a replacement or your money back, or in having repairs done at someone else's expense. Remember that most stores want your continual business; they are likely to try working things out to your satisfaction. But you are even more likely to succeed if you know your rights, and if you can make an informed judgment about whether it's worth your time and trouble to sue the department store over a bad ballpoint pen or a mousetrap that doesn't work.

All products have warranties. Almost every product available to consumers is required by law to meet certain minimum standards of quality (known as warranties). The various commercial codes in force in every state and the District of Columbia usually cover "goods"—products that can be moved at the time of purchase. In addition, there are several federal statutes which help protect consumers from defective products.

Under the Uniform Commercial Code, warranties are generally classified as either *express* or *implied*. The UCC has been adopted in some form by every state. Under the code, implied warranties automatically come with the product, regardless of any actions by the purchaser or the salesperson. Even if there is no written warranty, the law implies one. Two of the most common implied warranties are the implied warranty of merchantability and the implied warranty of fitness for a particular purpose.

An *implied warranty of merchantability* covers goods (such as appliances or cars—things movable at the time of sale—but not houses or plots of land) that are bought from merchants (people who are usually in the business of selling such goods). For example, an automobile dealer is in the business of selling cars; he is not a merchant with respect to the old desk he may want to sell from his office. The goods are merchantable if they can "pass without objection in the trade." This means that the product must be as good as similar products sold by other merchants. For example, the wood you want to buy from a lumber yard must be of the same quality sold by other lumber yards in your area. The product must also be "fit for the ordinary purpose for which such goods are used." A barbecue grill, for example, must be sturdy enough to hold enough charcoal for cooking. Additionally, the product must live up to any promises made on the package or in the literature included with it.

An *implied warranty of fitness for a particular purpose* arises when, for example, you tell a salesperson the purpose for which you need a product, or when the salesperson has reason to know how you are going to use it. If you are clearly relying on the salesperson's judgment and skill in selecting a product, an implied warranty of fitness for a particular purpose has been created. Thus if you told a salesperson at a paint store that you needed to cover a certain kind of masonry, his suggestion of a particular paint would carry with it an implied warranty that it is right for that use. If you tell an automobile salesman that you intend to tow a boat trailer with your car, his sale of the vehicle carries with it an implied warranty that the car is suitable to pull that load.

Express warranties are created when the salesperson or manufacturer of a product has stated or demonstrated to you a quality or characteristic of the product, and you buy the product because of that statement or promise. For example, if you are told that the radio you purchase is a stereo and in fact it is not, the salesperson has breached an express warranty.

An express warranty may also arise when you buy a product because of the models or samples you've been shown. Thus if you were buying storm doors for your home because you liked the ones on display, the seller has breached an express warranty if she delivers different doors that don't work properly.

Written warranties that come with a product are also express, and they must conform to federal law. The Magnuson-Moss Warranty Act states that a package warranty must be labeled as either full or limited. The difference between the two rests in the remedies available to the consumer, particularly in the amount of time during which the consumer can claim damages under the warranty. A full warranty obviously provides greater protection.

In addition, lawyers' fees generated by warranty complaints can be recovered (at the court's discretion) under the Magnuson-Moss Act.

Warranties protect the manufacturer as well. It is important to remember that warranties are often designed more to protect the manufacturer—that is, to limit its liability—than to protect the consumer. Artfully worded warranties give the opposite impression from their actual operation. Nevertheless, comparing warranties enables the careful shopper to choose wisely among similar products. One product may be covered under a warranty more comprehensive or longer-lasting than another. Under federal law, you have the right to ask the salesperson to show you a product's warranty before you buy it.

Services are usually not covered by warranties. Although you are not protected by way of an implied warranty, you still have a remedy for services that are inadequate. Those provided by professionals are regulated by various state boards which require practitioners to conform to certain standards of conduct. Besides doctors and lawyers, many different professionals must be licensed: home-improvement contractors, veterinarians, morticians, mechanics, real estate brokers, even landscapers may be licensed by state boards. Check with your state or county government to identify the board that regulates the service provider against whom you may have a complaint. Even if this provider is not subject to agency regulation, at the very least he is still obligated to perform his services in a workmanlike manner. If he hasn't performed as promised, try contacting your local consumer protection agency.

Be reasonable and use common sense. As with any dispute between people, your first step should be to let the seller or service provider know that you are dissatisfied with the product or service. Many businesspeople will go out of their way to correct your problem, even if they have no legal obligation to do so. Dissatisfied customers are bad business.

You should return a defective product as soon as possible after you discover the problem, and ask for a refund or an exchange. Many stores will cooperate, because they too can return the product to the manufacturer for a refund. Many sellers need authorization from the manufacturer to return the goods; if this is the case, allow the store enough time to obtain such permission.

If a service is involved, invite the service provider to inspect the work done. For example, if you are dissatisfied with how a painter painted your house, show him the work and suggest what you want as a remedy.

If you find that you are still dissatisfied with a product, contact the manufacturer. This might also be necessary if you have had the product for some period of time. The manufacturer's address should be found in any written warranty; otherwise, contact the store where you made the purchase. A growing number of manufacturers have toll-free telephone numbers which you can call for advice or to register a complaint. (To find a toll-free number, call the operator at 1-800-555-1212.)

When automobiles are involved and the dealer is not cooperative, contact the manufacturer's area sales or service representative. In most cases you will be asked to put your complaint in writing—a good practice anyway—so that all the facts about the grievance will be put down in writing. If the service provider is a member of a national or regional chain (such as a franchised auto or transmission repair shop), contact the chain's main office. Your state's department of motor vehicles may also be of help with automobile warranty problems.

Withhold payment for a defective product or poor service. Here is a good application of the old rubric "possession is nine tenths of the law." In many cases you'd be wise to withhold payment: if you keep the money, the burden is on someone else to prove a case. You should be certain, however, that the manufacturer knows why you are withholding payments; in some cases it may be entitled to return of a defective product.

The general rule is that you are not obligated to pay for products or services that are substantially deficient. Once you discover that the toaster you've bought will not toast, and your complaint to the seller goes unanswered or unsatisfied, do not hesitate to stop payment on a check or withhold future payments. You will usually get fast results. Similarly, if you have made a purchase by a credit card, notify the credit-card company of your complaint and (using the procedures prescribed) ask that all your other payments be made except in the one dispute. This is your right under the federal Truth in Lending Act—provided that the product or service cost more than $50 and that it was bought in your home state or within a hundred miles of your home.

You are in a more difficult position if you have already paid. Even then, though, you may reject any goods upon delivery, or you can "revoke your acceptance" within a reasonable time. To make certain that your rejection is effective, notify the seller immediately and do not use the product any longer. Even if you did not reject it when it was delivered or have used it for a period of time, you may still revoke your acceptance of the product if the defect impairs its value to you. There are technical aspects of these questions, however, which can better be answered by your state or local consumer-protection bureau.

Of course, you can always decide to contact a lawyer, especially if a substantial sum of money is involved. This course of action need not necessarily lead to court. Lawyers can be very effective at advocating your cause and negotiating a settlement.

Consider going to court only as a last resort. If all else fails, you can bring an action in court for the price of the product or service, and any other damages that have resulted from the inadequacy—such as if you had to buy a replacement item because the one you originally purchased was so defective as to render it useless. You can pursue these remedies in a small-claims court if the amount in controversy is small enough. (See Chapter 14.)

If you go to court, you are not limited to a refund of the purchase price. You might also claim consequential and incidental damages.

Consequential damages are damages that occur as a result of a warranty breach. For example, if your car has been improperly serviced and you need a car for work, you might be able to rent one and collect the cost of rental from the repair shop.

Incidental damages are those that occur more indirectly because of the breach. For example, if your car needs to be towed back to the shop because of faulty repairs, the towing charges could be claimed as incidental damages.

Warranties sometimes apply to used goods. A manufacturer's express warranty may have expired, or it may be applicable only to the first purchaser. You do not have any implied warranties against someone who is not a merchant dealing in such goods. And even if the product is covered by an implied warranty from the manufacturer, you may have only a limited period of time in which to bring a warranty claim. Some states allow four years or more after the product was sold to the original owner; others have no such time limit.

Many states require a used-car dealer to offer a minimum warranty, such as ninety days or six months. If in doubt, contact your state's department of transportation. Even with used cars, you might still be able to purchase an express warranty; check with the dealers in your area.

Consumer protection begins at home. You should be a wise shopper in other ways as well. That's what the law means by "caveat emptor"—let the buyer beware. Shop for the most reliable manufacturer. If the product is expensive or complicated, make sure you feel confident that the manufacturer will still be around if you need parts or services later on. (Studebaker and Edsel parts are not easy to come by.) Ask other people who have similar products how well they work. Read magazines that test common products, such as *Consumer Reports*.

Educate yourself as well by testing the product personally. If you are purchasing a car, drive it before you buy it. Request that the vacuum-cleaner salesperson give you a demonstration. Don't be afraid to ask questions. You can be firm without being offensive when dealing with salespeople; you need not let them act as if they are doing you a favor by selling you something.

Every state has a consumer-protection agency or its equivalent. Look in your telephone directory under state government. A consumer-protection agency can be an effective advocate on your behalf, especially if other people have had similar complaints about a particular product.

When there's an injury, see a lawyer. Any serious personal injury should be treated promptly and competently by a physician. Similarly, you'd be wise to contact a lawyer if you want to have a claim mediated or brought to court. The same is true for any substantial damage to your property. Most lawyers base personal-injury claims on contingency fees—that is, they take a portion of what the court awards; if there is no award, there is no charge. The law is quite favorable to plaintiffs injured by defective consumer products, a fact that is used to good advantage by attorneys who specialize in such cases.

CHAPTER FIVE

Debtors' and Creditors' Rights and Liabilities

Creditors have better memories than debtors.
—Benjamin Franklin,
Poor Richard's Almanac

Countless numbers of consumers get into trouble over their debts. Few people can manage a Cadillac lifestyle on a Chevy income. But if debtors understood the facts about credit, their lives would be much easier.

The debts you incur (or the credit you grant) almost always result from a contract that you have signed. Thus it is important to remember the principal point of Chapter 1: if you don't like the terms of a contract with eighteen percent interest or more—including the one that obligates you to pay that much or more interest per month on your average outstanding balance—don't sign it.

In fact, most credit contracts give you not only one chance to avoid problems but several. Just because you have a credit card or a charge account from your local department store doesn't mean that you have to use them, or that you are forbidden to pay the whole bill when it comes in the mail. Moreover, there are various laws that protect debtors from themselves by requiring creditors to make various disclosures, in order that borrowers truly understand what they are getting themselves into when they take out a loan.

Much of commercial law is concerned with the collection of debts. Legislation is in place at both the federal and state levels to protect the rights of both debtors and creditors.

Credit

Credit plans vary in their complexity and value. Credit cards are usually offered by banks and large corporations, which hope that consumers will make purchases beyond their immediate means (although within their credit limits)—and will thus borrow money at high rates of interest. Some stores extend credit without charging interest. There are also *revolving accounts* in which you must make monthly payments but can still buy items on credit), and *closed-end accounts* (in which you make a specific purchase or borrow a certain amount of money, and the account is closed until you have paid off that amount).

You need a few pieces of basic information—most of which are required by "truth-in-lending" disclosure laws—to be stated clearly in order to make intelligent decisions relating to credit transactions.

1. *Amount.* Before you make any credit purchases, it is a good idea to know exactly how much you may be borrowing. If a store is handling the financing, ask what the maximum cost could be.
2. *Terms.* Once you have signed a credit contract, you are obligated to pay according to the terms of the agreement even if you did not pay attention to the figures. Revolving credit accounts, which permit consumers to purchase goods or secure loans on a continuing basis as long as the outstanding balance on account stays below a certain limit, are most common. The loans are repaid and re-granted in a cycle. The atypical arrangement is for a lump-sum payment at the end of a specified time, or several monthly payments. Interest rates, of course, are very important. Do not be fooled by

lenders or merchants who advertise that they are not charging you interest. Rest assured that, except for the twenty-five or thirty days' grace period generally granted in standard billing, billing fees and interest charges are hidden somewhere in the price. By stating that they are not charging interest, merchants may be simply trying to circumvent disclosure laws. Be assertive. *Ask to compare the amount you'd ultimately pay under maximum interest charges with what the item in question would cost if you paid cash on the spot.* Remember that interest rates must somewhere be stated in terms of annual percentages. More often than not, you will be paying the highest rate allowed by the law of your state (see the discussion of usury laws below).

3. *Collateral.* Collateral is property that you promise to the lender if you fail to make payments on a loan. For example, the lender may insist that a car or other property you buy with the loan will serve as collateral to assure repayment—although you can still use the property exclusively if you remain current with the payments agreed upon. Make certain you know exactly what collateral (if any) you may be asked to put up in order to secure a loan.

4. *Default procedures.* Currently many states do not permit "confessed judgments"—whereby the borrower waives all rights to a court trial before a judgment is entered—for consumer loans. However, certain provisions that are helpful to the lender (such as clauses that cover the cost of collections, attorneys' fees, and court costs) may lawfully be included in a loan agreement.

Under both federal and state truth-in-lending statutes, the creditor must make all of these terms and procedures available to you in a written statement prior to your signing any financing agreement. Unfortunately, few consumers bother to read this piece of paper, and those who do often find it incomprehensible. It's frequently easier (and safer) to ask the lender to explain the terms in plain English. If there are additional charges (such as for insurance), these too must be included in the disclosure statement.

Whether the loan comes from a bank, merchant, or loan company, under the federal Fair Debt Collection Act the lender who does not give you the required disclosure statement can be subject to criminal penalties under regulations of the Federal Trade Commission or your state credit commissioner—not to mention civil remedies.

You can change the terms of a standard agreement. Simply strike out and initial any term you do not wish to accept. If the lender goes through with the transaction, he must abide by the terms as amended.

Most states limit the rate of interest a lender is allowed to charge. If a higher rate is applied, the lender is guilty of usury. Usurious loans are illegal and unenforceable. Under both federal and state truth-in-lending laws, banks and other lenders are required to state clearly their rates of interest—which in more cases than not are at the legal maximums. To determine the maximum rates allowed by your state, contact your local banking commissioner.

Debtors

Debtors are protected from abusive and unlawful behavior by lenders or creditors. Under both federal and state debt-collection acts, debtors must be treated fairly. They are entitled to "due process"—at the very least, notice of the claim against you and an opportunity to tell your side of the story to a neutral decision-maker—when taken to court.

You have the right to oppose the claim. You may assert that you do not owe the money, or disagree with the amount the creditor says you owe, or feel you never received the benefit of the money or goods in question. Even if your loan was transferred from the original creditor to someone else, you are entitled to the same defenses.

If you have difficulty paying a debt, try to reach an arrangement with the creditor that is mutually satisfactory. Ask the creditor for time to get your finances in order—for example, through a debt-consolidation loan available through your local bank or finance company. Or you can get in touch with a consumer credit counseling service run by your state or a local charitable organization, which will help you consolidate your debts and work out a payment plan. If you can prevent the creditor from taking you to court, you will avoid later difficulties in garnishments, attachments, or forfeitures of collateral—not to mention attorney fees, loss of time from work, and irritation.

Under federal law, a person may apply for bankruptcy or for debt adjustment when he feels that he is no longer able to pay his debts. In the traditional sense, bankruptcy means that your debts exceed your assets to the point that you must ask a court to intervene. Bankruptcy serves to discharge a person's debts by way of collecting those assets which are not protected under federal or state law. This is called a "liquidation of the assets." In turn the proceeds are distributed to creditors. Bankruptcy would either restructure your debts (protecting you temporarily, until you are able to pay them), or simply strike out all of your current debts (with a few exceptions such as, for example, those for alimony and child support, incurred through fraud).

Debt adjustment is similar to bankruptcy in that it is administered by the federal courts. It differs in that the debtor is allowed to continue to own most of his assets while paying his creditors what the law specifies he must pay them from his income. In many instances a person who files for bankruptcy would be better off had he sought debt adjustment under federal law.

For someone with a steady income and assets that are not exempt from the bankruptcy trustee, a debt-adjustment plan may be preferable. Declaring bankruptcy may be too drastic a step; the debtor may have gotten into some temporary financial trouble which can be resolved in time and with careful planning. On the other hand, if the debtor is at the end of his means and with little prospect of salvaging his finances, it may be that only a total discharge of his debts through bankruptcy can relieve him.

Both bankruptcy and debt adjustment are administered by federal courts. You may hear of bankruptcy liquidation procedures referred to as "Chapter Seven"; business reorganizations as "Chapter Eleven"; farm reorganizations as "Chapter Twelve"; and debt adjustments or wage-earner payment plans as "Chapter Thirteen." These references are to the Federal Bankruptcy Reform Act of 1978, as amended. Some state laws may apply through property exemptions—that is, property that the bankrupt person is allowed to retain in order to help with a fresh start.

Debt adjustment plans must be formally approved. Under debt adjustment, the debtor proposes to the bankruptcy court a schedule of payments that will satisfy his current creditors within a specified period—usually three to five years. During this time creditors must stop trying to collect their debts. The forms for filing for debt adjustment are available from the clerk of the local bankruptcy court, generally at the federal district courthouse or from an office-supply store.

Before filing for debt adjustment, you must demonstrate that you have a steady source of income. At one time, debt adjustment was available only to wage earners, but now any steady source of income will suffice. If you have pledged no collateral, you are limited to $100,000 in "unsecured" debt; if you have put up collateral, the limit is $350,000 on "secured" debt and $100,000 for the "unsecured" debt. Your plan for repayment must be submitted to the court in good faith, and the fees must be paid. Finally, the creditors must receive more than they would have in a Chapter Seven bankruptcy (an absolute liquidation of non-exempt assets).

The costs of administering a debt-adjustment plan will also be made a part of your payments. Every check you send to the trustee will include his payment, as well as the fee of your lawyer if you have one.

You do not need a lawyer to file a Chapter Thirteen proceeding. You may want to consult with an attorney to find out if Chapter Thirteen is the proper procedure for you, or you may want a lawyer to file the petitions and argue your case. But you can propose a plan to the court and represent yourself. This decision should be based solely on your confidence in your own capabilities. (Note that if you hire an attorney, he also becomes a creditor under the plan.)

You may also declare bankruptcy without the assistance of an attorney. Bankruptcy is the total discharge of your debts. It is subject to a few exceptions: for example, recent student loans and most taxes are not discharged. Thus, you are enabled to satisfy your debts by transferring non-exempt assets to creditors through an appointed trustee. Under federal law, exempt assets include a certain amount for your house; limited exemptions for the family car and the tools of your trade; unlimited household property valued under $200 per item; and certain insurance policies, pensions, and public benefits. State laws also exempt certain property from bankruptcy seizure. Although the exemptions fall into certain categories, in some cases you can shift and carry over amounts from one category to another. Check these exemptions carefully, because they change from time to time and may vary from state to state.

You can file for bankruptcy only if you have not received a similar discharge of your debts within the past six years. Once the petition has been filed with the court, creditors must stop trying to collect their debts or harassing you. Also, bankruptcy discharges are only for debts created prior to your filing, not for those incurred afterward. Likewise, a court will not grant a discharge from debts that it considers that you incurred in contemplation of bankruptcy. Thus you cannot go on a shopping spree, thinking that any debts can be erased through an impending bankruptcy. Nor are you permitted to give away your property prior to bankruptcy, or transfer it to another person to hide it from the trustee and from creditors. You may be able, however, to sell your property and buy exempt property.

Although you may declare bankruptcy without the assistance of an attorney, if your financial situation is complex you might be happy to have one. Keep in mind that if an attorney charges $500 for filing the papers, but saves you $700 in property that you would not have claimed as exempt, he will have been very cost-effective.

A number of forms are needed to file for bankruptcy. They are usually available through an office-supply store. The forms enable you to state your financial affairs clearly: your wages, tax payments, refunds due, bank accounts, safe-deposit boxes, property in your hands and held by anyone else, and transfers of property that you have made within the last year. You must also list creditors, the amounts and circumstances of the debts, whether they are secured or unsecured by property or other collateral, and if any liens on your property have been filed. In addition, you must note all personal and real property, as well as what you are claiming as exempt.

You will then meet with the creditors and trustees to make final the nature of your transfers to the trustee, and to determine what property you will be allowed to keep. For all of these steps, directions can be obtained from the bankruptcy-court clerk or from the trustee.

Bankruptcy should be viewed as a last resort. Declaring bankruptcy is a final and drastic step that should be contemplated only in dire circumstances. Under bankruptcy you are asking the courts to protect you from creditors. But bankruptcy also makes it virtually impossible to obtain credit for several years—even if you think you are able and ready to assume further credit obligations.

Creditors

Creditors also have rights. The law, of course, recognizes the right of a creditor to receive the money owed to him. If you are a creditor, your first step should be to notify the debtor that he owes you something. If he is recalcitrant, you can either continue negotiations, contact a debt-collection agency (which will probably take anywhere from thirty to fifty percent of the balance due), or go to court. There the object is to get the debt reduced to a judgment, which you then have to collect—often the most difficult part.

If the claim is substantial, you may wish to have a collection lawyer do the work. Once a judgment has been rendered, you don't have to prove anything except that the debt hasn't been paid. You also have a lot of time to collect—often as long as twenty years. (The time limitations differ from state to state). In most states judgments are renewable.

Before a judgment is rendered in your favor, however, be careful about how you go about collecting a debt. Under various federal and state laws, you cannot use unfair or abusive means to enforce your rights. For example, you cannot call a debtor on the telephone at unreasonable hours, contact the debtor's friends, neighbors, or relatives. Likewise, you cannot use foul or abusive language—or any forms that appear as if they have been issued by courts when in fact they have not. Nor can you threaten criminal actions if the only reason you are doing so is to collect the debt. In short, be careful not to do anything that may subject you to more liability than the debt is worth.

State laws generally afford debtors greater protection than do federal statues, which apply to less than two percent of the debts collected in the nation. In addition, state laws regulate a wider assortment of creditors and debt-collector organizations.

Once a judgment is entered establishing that you are legally entitled to collect a debt, you have several options. If your agreement with the debtor mentioned an item as collateral, you are entitled to take that property by way of "self help"—that is, you can take possession without judicial process, provided that you can do so without a "breach of the peace." You are also entitled to the property pursuant to an "attachment"—a judicial procedure by which, even before receiving a judgment against the creditor, you can take control of the collateral property and, once you win a judgment, you can sell the property in order to satisfy the debt (the judgment). If your loan is not secured by collateral, you might try to supply the court with the debtor's place of employment and ask for garnishment of his wages—that is, having the debtor's employer pay you directly a portion of the debtor's weekly pay check. Some states do not permit wages to be garnished; most place a limit on wages that can be garnished—often as low as ten percent. In any event, this action must be sought in court. None of these procedures requires a lawyer. Every state has different procedures and rules regarding attachments, forfeitures, and garnishments.

CHAPTER SIX

Marriage and Divorce

Litigious terms, fat contentions, and flowing fees.
—Milton,
Tractate on Education

For better or worse, the romance of marriage nowadays has increasingly given way to the drafting of premarital agreements concerning the rights of spouses and divisions of property. Likewise, the stigma once attached to divorce has been dissipated by the epidemic number of couples who split up. About half of first marriages end in divorce. People who learn from their experiences are much less likely to remarry without a premarital (antenuptial) agreement about division of property, custody of children, and many other spousal considerations.

There is nothing magical about a contract which specifies the rights and obligations of two people who are about to marry—the so-called "prenuptial agreement," which of course, need not be entirely formal. Similarly, your ability to handle your own divorce depends primarily on the complexity of your situation. If your differences are irreconcilable—and if you and your spouse can agree on how the property should be divided, the children supported and educated, and so on—you should seriously consider representing yourselves.

Agreements Between Spouses

Contracts between spouses can be written at any time. Contracts between husband and wife follow the same lines as do other contracts (see Chapter 1). The most common types of contracts between married persons are the *antenuptial agreement* (usually an understanding about property distribution in the event of divorce, signed before the marriage ceremony) and the *separation agreement* (also about property division, signed during the marriage in contemplation of separation or divorce). A similar kind of contract is the cohabitation agreement, drawn up by people in a relationship but disdaining the traditional bonds of marriage itself.

All three types of agreements are attempts to specify their expectations of and promises to each other. In the absence of such a document, the law would impose certain rules regarding support, division of property, and rights of inheritance. Courts generally uphold antenuptial agreements (assuming that the marriage has taken place) as well as separation agreements, especially if they are in writing and signed by both parties. Courts generally refuse to uphold cohabitation agreements.

The larger the assets, the greater the need for an attorney. Whenever there is a sizable amount of property involved, good legal advice could save tax dollars and prevent headaches later. Likewise, in any case that the parties' interests are adversarial, separate legal counsel is necessary—that is, each person should have an attorney whenever one is waiving more valuable rights than the other, or when one person is financially dependent upon the other. This may seem extravagant, but the fact is that antenuptial agreements are worthless unless a court is willing to enforce them. The existence of separate attorneys and a full financial disclosure are the most convincing evidence a judge could hear that the contractual provisions are really fair and should be honored by both parties.

Under certain circumstances, courts will refuse to enforce a written, signed cohabitation, antenuptial, or separation agreement. A court may refuse to enforce a cohabitation agreement if it finds that any part of the consideration was the provision of sexual services, or if the judge feels that honoring a cohabitation contract would encourage illicit relationships and thus offend public policy. A separation agreement will not be honored if the court fails to find a valid marriage in existence at the time the agreement was signed. Neither an antenuptial nor a separation agreement will be enforced if the court finds any of the following: that one of the parties did not fully disclose his or her assets; that the provisions are grossly unfair (or "unconscionable"); that one party signed the agreement because of fraud, duress, or undue influence; or that enforcement of the contract would be against public policy.

Courts will refuse to enforce spousal agreements by which a wife waived her rights to support or alimony when she clearly has no other means of supporting herself. The courts in such cases hold that spouses have no right to relieve themselves of the duty of supporting each other when refusal to do so means one spouse must become a public charge by receiving welfare. Courts may also refuse to enforce an earlier separation agreement if the parties have since reconciled and later separated again.

All cohabitation and antenuptial (premarital) agreements should be custom-made. Cohabitation agreements must be tailored to fit the couple involved. The contract could vary significantly—largely depending upon whether the couple views cohabitation as a temporary experiment, a trial marriage, or a chosen lifestyle. In particular, the financial provisions should differ according to whether a short-term adventure or a lifelong commitment is envisioned.

The most important provisions are those that reflect the couple's understanding about common expenses and household chores, and the division of property and money if and when the parties do divorce. If one person has agreed to perform household domestic services in exchange for support, the agreement should specify the duration of the support obligation, as well as the rights and obligations of the parties after their marriage ends. The couple should also consider including some degree of notice before one of them can unilaterally terminate the relationship.

Modern antenuptial contracts sometimes reflect the couple's

agreement regarding the wife's choice of a surname. Many couples also include provisions regarding the division of household responsibilities and expenses, and decisions about careers and changes of domicile. Most courts try to honor such provisions, although they may not be legally enforceable. In a second-marriage situation, when the couple wishes their individual estates to pass upon their death to the children of their first marriages, the antenuptial contract should include waivers of rights to whatever share of the other's estate are guaranteed by statute. Finally, the contract might contain the couple's understanding regarding the ownership of property that was acquired after the marriage, but primarily through the efforts of only one party.

There is little difference between the community-property and equitable-distribution methods of treating property acquired during marriage. In the community-property states (Arizona, California, Idaho, Louisiana, Nevada, New Mexico, Texas, and Washington), all assets acquired by either spouse during marriage are held as community property—that is, the property is owned by both and upon divorce is divided equally. A husband who buys stocks, bonds, houses, cars, and other property in his own name owns these items free of any claim by his wife upon divorce—unless the state's divorce statute allows a judge to order an equitable distribution. In common-law states with equitable-distribution provisions, the judge decides what will be most fair to the parties—without reference to who owns legal title.

A judge with powers to equitably distribute marital property generally has more discretion than a judge in a community-property state; the latter must divide the marital property in half, regardless of the fact that one party may have a far higher earning potential than the other.

A separation agreement should be particular. The document should specify the division of property when the divorce occurs, or state that the couple have already split the property between the two of them in a manner satisfactory to both. The contract should spell out the amount of alimony to be paid by one spouse to the other, or contain a clause indicating that both parties waive the right to any support. If there are children, which parent has primary custody? What rights of visitation are allowed to the noncustodial parent? How much child support will the noncustodial parent contribute? What about their education and medical expenses?

Separation agreements also usually contain a provision waiving any rights to claim against the other's estate. If the couple expect to petition under a no-fault ground of divorce, the contract should contain a clause stating that irreconcilable differences have arisen between the parties, and that they are now living (or intend immediately to live) separate and apart.

Divorce and Separation

No-fault divorce is increasingly common. Every state has different specific grounds for divorce. In all but Illinois and South Dakota, there is at least one ground for divorce in which neither party need be blamed for ostensibly "causing" the divorce. These no-fault grounds are most appropriate in situations where both partners have agreed to end the marriage, and recognize that placing blame or fault serves no useful purpose. There are a number of no-fault grounds for divorce (or "dissolution"—the euphemism for divorce used in some no-fault states), including "irreconcilable differences," "irretrievable breakdown of the relationship," "incompatibility," or simply mutual voluntary separation for a specific period of time.

There are numerous other grounds for divorce, which vary from state to state. Residency requirements range from six weeks to one year, although they are usually from ninety days to six months.

(For a complete list of grounds for divorce by state, see Appendix II.)

Divorcing couples do not necessarily need lawyers. In states that provide for a no-fault divorce, a husband and wife could easily file their own papers if they do not wish to contest the dissolution of their marriage—especially if there are no children involved nor much property to divide. Note, however, that a genuinely uncontested divorce without intervention of attorneys is rare. They generally occur when the marriage was short, the marital property is minimal, and both parties are self-supporting—that is, no alimony is necessary. Unless one of the parties is extraordinarily generous, the general rule is that the spouse who is going to need alimony should get an attorney to make sure that his or her financially vulnerable position is not exploited.

The couple seeking a lawyer-free divorce should sit down together and draft a separation agreement, outlining the details of property distribution, spousal and child support, visitation rights, etc. Then one party should call the clerk of the local court that handles divorces, and request an example of a properly drafted no-fault divorce petition. Many clerks are helpful, especially if you make it clear that you are just asking for a model. (Drafting a petition tailored to your situation might involve the giving of legal advice, which cannot be done without a license.)

You must file a divorce petition in the proper court. The clerk of the divorce court in your area of domicile (your legal residence) should be able to supply a sample form for you to follow.

After a properly drafted petition for a divorce decree has been filed, notice (called "service of process") must be given to your spouse—unless the petition is a joint one or the other spouse consents to its service. This is to enable the court to be assured the other party has been fully informed and can participate if it is felt necessary. The court clerk can tell you the different ways to provide proper notice. If your spouse has any objections to the proceedings, she must indicate to the court the need for a full-scale hearing.

Again, if an adversarial hearing is scheduled, it is generally wise to hire yourself an attorney.

If your spouse ignores the notice or indicates consent to the divorce, after some period of time (varying by state) the court will send both parties notice of a hearing date. A court appearance is not necessary in all states. Where it is, it generally consists of a simple proceeding during which the court may ask you a few questions about the matters covered in your petition. You may also need a witness to corroborate your residence or the basis for divorce (for example, that the parties are in fact living apart). Finally, the court will issue a divorce decree—which in some states may have an effective date months after your court appearance. This is important because you cannot legally remarry until your divorce decree is actually in effect, or else you might be guilty of bigamy. Be careful to avoid subjecting yourself to a "fault" ground for divorce—such as adultery—during the waiting period.

There are many ways to divide property without a fight. Here are some of them:

- The parties barter (each takes some items in exchange for others)
- Each spouse selects items from a list of all the marital property, without regard for their specific value
- One spouse divides the property into two lists, and the other chooses one of them
- One spouse places a value on each item of property, and the other chooses items adding up to half of the total value
- A third party values the contested items, and the spouses select alternately until the total value has been taken
- Some of the items are sold and the proceeds divided
- The spouses place secret bids on each item of property, and the one who bids higher gets it. When one spouse takes items exceeding half the total value, the other spouse receives a cash payment for the difference
- The spouses conduct a private auction in which they bid openly against each other. An equalization payment is made if one party wins more than half of the total value of the property
- The spouses agree that an arbitrator should hear arguments from both sides about the division of property and then render a binding decision
- The spouses select a mediator to help them reach an agreement on matters of valuation and division

If you think there is a possibility of reaching agreement with your spouse, consider mediation. In many cases husbands and wives may agree to an amicable divorce, but are unable to work out the financial matters or to arrange for custody and visitation rights regarding the children. Increasingly, couples are turning away from lawyers and toward mediators in order to resolve disputes either real or potential. This is largely because litigation is inevitably divisive, and often has particularly harmful effects on the children. In addition, mediation can produce innovative solutions that are impossible in a courtroom setting.

Mediation in divorce is a relatively new development. Briefly stated, a trained mediator (who may be a lawyer but usually is not) meets with the parties, tries to identify their needs, and helps them to find a solution that best suits all of their interests. The mediator does not take sides, but tries to encourage the parties to reach their own accommodations.

In many cases the mediator will strongly urge that the parties have their own lawyers look over any agreement they reach—but only after the basic terms have been reduced to writing. This precaution is generally money well spent, since lawyers can often spot places where an agreement is unclear or where they may be tax advantages to both parties were the deal to be structured a little differently. Some couples also use lawyers more as back-room advisers during the process than as active participants. This offers another benefit beyond that of reducing rancor: the attorneys' fees will eat up a far smaller share of whatever size pie the couple has to divide between them than if the lawyers are involved in full-scale litigation or even negotiation. (See chapter 13 for a fuller treatment of mediation.)

There are other ways to part. In certain circumstances a marriage may be ended by annulment, or by way of a suit for "separate maintenance." An annulment is a judicial determination that the marriage never really took place. This could be for a number of reasons: one of the parties induced the other by fraud or duress to enter into the marriage; a state law forbidding marriage between minors or certain close relatives was violated; one of the parties was insane, drunk, or under the influence of drugs so that he or she did not know the nature, meaning, or consequences of the marriage contract; or because one of the parties was still legally married to someone else. Generally, if a marriage is annulled rather than terminated by divorce, neither spouse is entitled to either alimony or separate maintenance. (There are exceptions to this rule; check your state's laws.)

If a married couple chooses no longer to live together as husband and wife, yet for religious or personal reasons they do not want a legal divorce, they can enter into a contractual agreement for separate maintenance. This is often called a legal separation by laymen. This kind of separation agreement spells out the rights and duties of the spouses to each other, their property, and their children. Although under the terms of such an agreement each party may live apart, free from harassment or control of the other, the couple is still legally married. In general, the separate-maintenance arrangement is merely an interim step on the way to eventual divorce. It is used on a permanent basis primarily in cases where both spouses firmly disapprove of divorce but can accept a separate-maintenance arrangement.

Alimony

Alimony is simply an amount a court may order one spouse to pay the other in financial support—either while the divorce action is pending or after it is granted. The former is called temporary alimony or alimony *pendent lite;* the latter is permanent alimony, although it may last for only a fixed number of years.

If the couple is unable to agree upon a figure between themselves, the trial judge will decide the amount. In this circumstance a lawyer is usually necessary in order to present the party's best possible case to the court.

The husband does not always pay the wife alimony. Alimony today is not the same as it was in the past. As a result of equal-rights amendments passed in various states and a recent Supreme Court decision, the party better able to afford alimony may have to pay. In addition, the spouse's attorney may have to be paid if the court so orders.

Pay attention to tax matters. The Internal Revenue Service publishes a document called "Tax Information for Divorced or Separated Individuals." (Ask for Publication #504.) A service called the
"Divorce Help Line" (1-800-359-7004) can also help. If you have a
lot of income and property, you should seek expert advice about
how to save on taxes.

Remember: alimony is treated as taxable income to the receiving spouse, and as deductible to the other—whereas child support is neither income nor deductible, but may determine which
parent can treat the children as dependents for tax purposes.

You can sue for nonpayment of alimony. If the spousal support
was part of a purely out-of-court separation agreement, you can
sue for breach of contract in a small-claims court. If the amount in
arrears is within the small-claims court's limit, you can claim it
yourself without an attorney. (See Chapter 14.)

But if a judge ordered alimony, or incorporated a separation
agreement, only that court can discipline the recalcitrant party.
In this case you should hire a lawyer and ask the court to award
attorney's fees as well. The court will order the nonpaying party
to appear to explain why payments were not made. Unless convincing extenuating circumstances can be shown, she may be
jailed for contempt of court until the court is satisfied that payment will be forthcoming.

Custody, Visitation, and Child Support

The best arrangements for custody, visitation, and child support are those worked out by the parties themselves. When the
spouses cannot agree, the court will decide based on what it feels
are the best interests of the children—regardless of what the parties themselves may think. Anyone who refuses to follow a court
order can be jailed for contempt.

More and more state legislatures and courts, as well as the
American Bar Association, are emphasizing mediation and other
alternative forms of dispute resolution to settle custody and visita-

tion problems. In many cases, even when divorcing parents are in agreement, courts will modify the terms if in their judgment to do so would be in the best interests of the children involved.

If you and your spouse cannot agree about what to do with the children, try contacting a reputable mediator. Divorce mediation is highly recommended when the parties appear to be stuck on a single issue; a growing field, it is likely that the community you live in has such service available. Even if you feel that mediation will be fruitless, give it a try. The time, money, and heartache saved by avoiding a public confrontation in court is often worth the effort. Besides, mediators expect to find strong differences of opinion and are trained to deal with them in a fair and reasonable way. Note, however, that even a successful mediation agreement should be reviewed by an attorney if the terms are complicated or you are unsure of their legality.

Get a lawyer if you cannot agree on matters involving the children. Unfortunately, unless the parties can agree about custody, visitation rights, and child support, they are best advised to hire good lawyers and prepare for battle. Although judges always make custody decisions on the basis of "the children's best interests," what they perceive to be in the best physical and emotional interest of the children can be colored by persuasive attorneys.

Visiting rights are usually granted. The noncustodial parent has a right to reasonable visitation rights, unless the custodial parent can prove that any such contact would be dangerous to the child's physical or emotional health. What is reasonable depends upon the circumstances—such as the parents' work schedules, the distance between the parents' homes, and the child's schooling.

Divorced parents can make private agreements regarding child support. Unlike alimony, child support is generally a joint obligation of the parents. Usually, though, the term *child support* refers to the amount of money paid by a noncustodial parent to help support the children raised by the parent with custody. Most courts will consent to any agreement made between the parents regarding child support as long as the judge is satisfied that the provisions are in the best interest of the child.

Since payments for child support are not taxable to the recipient—unlike alimony—make sure that your agreement clearly separates the two amounts. Otherwise, the lump sum will be considered alimony and taxed. Conversely, child support is not tax-deductible by the one who pays it, while alimony is.

Unlike alimony, the obligation of child support cannot be waived. Parents have the duty to support their children until adulthood. Thus even if the custodial parent had previously made the mistake of knowingly and voluntarily waiving the right to child support in a signed, written agreement, a court can still impose child-support duties upon the noncustodial parent if the court believes it is necessary for the child.

Child-support agreements should also specify each parent's obligations in the event either or both remarry, as well as when the children reach certain ages.

The custodial parent cannot deny visitation rights because an ex-spouse falls behind in alimony or child-support payments. Child support and visitation rights are independent of each other. Breach of either the duty to provide child support or the duty to allow reasonable visitation does not excuse the non-breaching party from living up to his or her part of the agreement. It is conceivable that *both* parties could be held in contempt of court—and either fined or even jailed—until they comply with the court order.

A custodial parent who has not received child-support payments can collect the money owed. Prepare a work sheet with information about your former spouse that may be helpful in obtaining payment—such as place of employment and residence, business contacts, current telephone numbers, etc. Keep this information in a safe and accessible place. If you don't have the court order specifying child support, get it. Then prepare a careful record of payments made and due. You can take all of this data to the court of record, and let the judge decide what your next step should be.

Residency is important. Keep in mind that if the other spouse is not a resident of your state, a court in your state cannot order the payment of alimony or child support unless your spouse consents to jurisdiction. (Your state court can, of course, attach property that is under its jurisdiction.) The alternative—to sue where the other spouse lives—is likely to be expensive and inconvenient.

CHAPTER SEVEN

Adoption and Changes of Name

I cannot tell what the dickens his name is.
—Shakespeare,
The Merry Wives of Windsor

Adopting Children

Adoption is the act of taking someone else's child into your family, as if it had been born to you, and giving it all the rights and duties of a blood relative. A legal adoption is the procedure which establishes that relationship, and terminates the rights and duties of the natural birth parents. In short, an adoption creates real parents by law.

Children can be adopted by a stepparent, privately, or through an agency. A stepparent adopts a spouse's child from a prior marriage. This is technically called a "step-adoption." The other method for adoption is when the birth parents give up all rights to the child to an appropriate agency, which then tries to place it with suitable adoptive parents, or through an intermediary like a doctor or lawyer. Some would-be adoptive parents advertise in newspapers and make direct contact with the birth parents.

You must be an adult to adopt. State laws vary, but the general rule is that any person over the age of eighteen can adopt a child. Many states require that the adopting parent be at least ten years older than the child, although such a provision does not generally apply to stepparents.

Although many adoption agencies look primarily for married couples, legally you don't have to be married in order to adopt. It is no longer as difficult as it used to be for a single adult to convince either an agency or a court that such an adoption may well be in the child's best interest. But if you are married, all states require that the adoption petition be made jointly, or at least (in the case of stepparents) be consented to by the other spouse.

Adults themselves can sometimes be adopted. All state laws provide for the adoption of minors, ordinarily defined as a child under twenty-one years of age. Adult adoption—generally done for reasons involving inheritance—is permissible in most but not all states.

Where adult adoption is allowed, it is generally a simple procedure in view of the fact that the stringent provisions designed to protect vulnerable minors are often eliminated. Publication is usually required, however, so that creditors are advised of possible name changes.

Do-it-yourself adoptions are feasible. When both birth parents consent to adoption of their child by stepparents, the procedure generally involves little more than the drafting and filing of a few papers. In such cases non-lawyers could easily arrange an adoption by themselves.

If there is any difficulty obtaining consent from both birth parents, you're probably better off hiring an attorney because adoption is often complicated and emotionally charged. The expertise of a knowledgeable lawyer is likewise important in an agency adoption.

Birth parents who change their minds also need an attorney. Similarly, any birth parent who has surrendered a child to an agency or otherwise consented to an adoption—and then has a change of heart—should immediately consult an attorney familiar with such matters. Timing is of the essence, because once a final adoption decree is issued by the court, it will probably be too late to regain custody.

Be aware that adoption laws are changing. With more and more states concerned with baby selling, restrictions on adoption are increasing. Courts are careful to make certain that money other than for medical expenses is not changing hands.

In addition, the new Interstate Compact on the Placement of Children requires approval when a baby is being taken across state lines. A private interstate adoption may be denied if the adoptive parents have taken custody of the child before their fitness as parents has been certified. The compact requires that both the sending state and the receiving state approve the proposed interstate placement.

There are various formalities involved in adopting a child. Once the prospective parents have in mind the child they wish to adopt, the legal process consists of five basic steps:

1. Obtaining the necessary consents
2. Filing an adoption petition in court (the clerk sends notice of the adoption to the state's register of vital statistics, usually within a week after the adoption is finalized)
3. Giving appropriate notice to interested parties
4. Having an investigation done (if required by the court)
5. Participating in a hearing

Consent is generally a prerequisite. Although state laws vary, most require that children and natural parents consent before an adoption is approved by a court.

Children, of course, cannot give binding consent unless they are of a certain age. A few states allow ten-year-olds to consent, but most have the minimum age at fourteen. As a practical matter, you should always try to gain the consent of any child who is old enough to know what is going on—since nothing is lost even if such consent has no legal significance. Both natural birth parents must approve unless they have previously surrendered the child to an agency, or their parental rights were terminated in a prior court proceeding. Some states, however, now give natural parents the right to withdraw their consent within a specified time period. If the whereabouts of one of the birth parents is unknown and efforts to locate him or her have been unsuccessful, the adoption may be granted without that consent. If both natural birth parents are dead or cannot be located, the court will likely require the consent of a guardian, next of kin, or state-authorized agency.

Natural birth parents relinquish their right to withhold consent once they surrender the child to an authorized agency. The rights of birth parents are considered voluntarily terminated if they have given their child over to an adoption agency. As long as the agency itself approves, the child may be adopted by others without the birth parents' consents or even their knowledge.

Likewise, if it has been determined in a prior legal proceeding that the birth parents have persistently neglected or abandoned their child, or are unfit for some other serious reason, their parental rights may have been involuntarily terminated.

Consent forms need not be complicated. The consent can be as simple as a signed statement that is witnessed and dated. In a simple case the following statement would be legally adequate:

I, John Doe, hereby consent to the adoption of my minor daughter, Mary Doe, by Henry Smith, and to the changing of Mary Doe's name to Mary Smith. I hereby voluntarily join in the adoption petition and waive any requirement that I be given further notice of these proceedings.

If the consent has to be "verified," add another sentence:

I do solemnly swear and affirm under the penalties of perjury that the contents of the foregoing document are true and correct and that my consent is given of my own free will and volition without any promises or coercion whatsoever.

Sign and date the document in front of a notary public, unless the court clerk has assured you that notarization is unnecessary.

An adoption petition is a formal document. It is filed by the adopting parents in a proper court, setting forth information about the child and its natural and adopting parents. Generally, it reflects the fact that all parties capable of consenting have done so (attaching copies of the consents is advisable); announces which if any of the parties has waived further notice; requests the court to approve the adoption; and, ordinarily, asks the court to authorize changing the child's name.

State laws are usually specific in indicating what information must be included in an adoption petition. Usually required are the name, sex, residence, age, race, and religion of all parties; the date and place of birth of the child; any property the child owns; the marital status of both birth parents and adoptive parents; the length of time the child has resided with the adoptive parents and how it came into their home; and, if the child is in the custody of an agency, a statement of how such custody was acquired.

In many states, if the birth mother is unmarried she need not disclose information regarding the birth father. But under the Uniform Parentage Act of 1973, if the identity of the father is unknown the court must make a reasonable effort to ascertain it; if that effort fails, the father's rights may be terminated. The same is true when the father is known but shows no interest in the child. On the other hand, if the father wishes to have an adoption decree blocked or set aside, he can do so by proving his paternity and demonstrating an interest in the child. The paternity action must be filed within the time allowed by the state's statute of limitations.

If you are a stepparent wishing to draft and file an adoption petition, and spousal consent is not a problem, you should call the clerk of the court that handles adoptions. He can instruct you how to buy the appropriate form or can show you a properly drafted adoption petition. Once you have a model to use, adapting it to your own situation should be easy. The clerk will also be able to tell you how much it costs, whether the consents and waivers of notice must be notarized or witnessed, as well as about other technicalities.

Some states permit adoption by a third party over the objection of the natural parents. When a court in these states finds that the natural parents' consent may have been withheld against the best interests of the child, it may waive the requirement. This usually occurs where the child has been abandoned or abused.

Proper legal notice is a very important and often highly technical requirement. Generally, the same parties who must consent to the adoption are legally entitled to notice—that is, to be told when and where the court proceedings will take place—unless a waiver of notice was included in the consent form. But each jurisdiction has different rules. The court clerk can inform you who must receive notice and how to go about giving it.

The court does not always order an investigation. In cases of an uncontested stepparent adoption, the court may decide that an investigation is unnecessary. In other cases, the judge will usually ask the appropriate agency to provide detailed information regarding the adoptive parents and the surrounding circumstances, in order to make certain that adoption by the petitioning parties is in the best interest of the child.

In some cases there is no court hearing. A court hearing may be waived when stepparents are involved and all the parties have been notified and have consented to the adoption. Otherwise, after proper notice has been given and an investigation made by the appropriate state agency, a judicial hearing will be held.

The hearing is frequently informal. It is often held in the judge's chambers. The prospective adoptive parents must be present, as well as the child if he is old enough to give consent. The judge will interview the parties and consider the investigative report. Although the court is not bound to accept the report, its recommendations generally carry weight and are seldom ignored. The court may also hear witnesses and generally ask questions to satisfy itself as to the advisability of the adoption. The court's primary concern is for the welfare and best interests of the child.

Adoptions from foreign countries usually do not require local investigation. Many adopted babies now come from South America and

Asia. American courts often accept the investigative data supplied by the foreign agency.

Decrees are not always final. After the hearing, if the court approves the adoption it will issue either an interlocutory (temporary) or a final decree. With an interlocutory decree, the court has issued conditional approval of the adoption, and will reconsider the application at a later date, generally six months to a year in the future.

During this intervening period the child lives in the home of the prospective adopters. Usually there is some sort of appropriate agency supervision, often involving visits to the home to see how the child is getting along. Interlocutory decrees may be revoked at any time during the trial period, either by the judge on his own or at the request of the birth parents, the adopting parents, or the supervising agency.

If all goes well during this trial period, however, the court will issue a final decree approving the adoption—with or without another hearing. Many states do not explicitly provide for an interlocutory decree, but achieve a similar effect by requiring that the child must have lived in the adoptive parents' home for a specified period of time before a final decree will be approved. This requirement is often waived by the court when there is good reason to do so, such as when stepparents are involved.

Birth parents can sometimes regain custody. In the majority of states, a parent can regain custody of a child put up for adoption within a fixed period of time—usually ranging from six months to one year after the surrender—during which no final adoption decree can be issued. Some states allow the birth parent an absolute right to regain custody at any time before a final decree has been issued—unless their parental rights had been involuntarily terminated in a prior legal proceeding. Other states, however, never allow a surrender to be rescinded unless there was evidence of fraud or duress that made the surrender involuntary.

Once a final adoption decree has been issued by a court, it is virtually impossible for a birth parent to regain custody.

The law makes it difficult for an adoptee to learn the identity of his natural birth parents. Although it is never illegal for an adoptee to try to learn the identity of his birth parents, the law in most states hinders rather than assists the adoptee's search. As of 1992, the only two states that did not automatically seal all adoption records were Alabama and South Dakota.

In the rest of the states, sealed-record statutes prohibit the inspection of records which would disclose the identity of the adoptee's birth parents, except in special circumstances. In some states the court can open an otherwise sealed adoption record if medical information is needed or if the birth parents are contacted and give consent. In others, registries have been created that enable adoptees to be united with their birth parents if they both indicate their desire for reunion.

It should be noted that there is a growing national movement to make all adoption records open. An adult adoptee (or a birth parent) interested in searching should contact a search group such as Adoptees' Liberty Movement Association (ALMA). Based in New York but with branches in almost every state, ALMA also maintains a nationwide registry—the only one of its kind. (ALMA's telephone number is [212] 581-1568.) People in such groups are usually far more knowledgeable about how to conduct a search than the average attorney.

Adoption agencies generally encourage birth parents to provide updated information (especially medical information) which will be given to any adoptee who requests it. In addition, most agencies will release non-identifying information—genetic and medical data, and sometimes a description of the circumstances which led the birth parents to surrender the child for adoption—to adoptees who request it.

Changing Names

It has always been the common law that a person may change his or her own name without resorting to legal proceedings—provided that there is no intention to defraud, that no one else is adversely affected, and that the proposed name would not be against public policy. A change of names can be legally accomplished by usage and habit—that is, if you use a new name consistently and exclusively, it becomes your legal name for all purposes—just as though you had carried it from birth or it had been provided by court order.

A change of name may also be obtained from a court. Although this method is no more legal than the common-law method explained above, it does have the practical advantage of providing an official record, and is often demanded by governmental agencies before they will issue a new Social Security card or driver's license, or change names on a deed or voter's card.

Courts do not look kindly, however, upon frivolous switches: for example, they have refused to change a man's name to a number, or a feminist's name from Zimmerman to Zimmerwoman.

A woman's surname is not automatically changed to that of her husband after marriage. If the woman adopts the custom of taking her husband's surname, and uses his surname as her own consistently and exclusively, the change of name is accomplished by the common-law method of usage and habit. This practice is so established that governmental agencies generally honor a woman's request to have their records reflect her name change without demanding a court order. However, if the woman consistently and exclusively uses her maiden name after marriage, the recent legal trend is to accept the rather obvious conclusion that the wife's name was not changed by the simple fact of her marriage.

Three kinds of court orders can change names. They are adoption decrees, divorce decrees, and change-of-name decrees. Since the first two orders are discussed elsewhere in this book, only the third will be explained here.

The change-of-name procedure is so simple that a layperson should easily be able to handle it. You do not generally need an attorney to obtain a court order changing your name unless there is an adversarial proceeding.

Although state requirements vary, in general there are three parts to the process of changing your name by a court order: (1) the petition; (2) publication (or notice to show cause why a name should not be changed); and (3) the court's decree.

Under normal situations, you should be able to purchase a petition-to-change-a-name form from the clerk of the court that handles such proceedings. Just as every state has a statute prescribing the procedure by which a person may change his name, so does each specify the information that must be contained in the petition addressed to the court.

Generally, the petition must be in writing and signed by the person seeking the name change. In most states it must specify the former name, the date and place of birth, and the reasons for the name change; the current age and address; and the proposed new name. In some states you must say whether you have ever been convicted of a crime or declared a bankrupt, and whether there are any judgments or liens or court proceedings pending under the old name. It is wise to include a statement to the effect that this change of name is not for fraudulent purposes or to avoid creditors.

When you call the clerk of the court to ask about buying or seeing a petition to use as a model, also ask whether the petition has to be verified and/or notarized. Verification is done by adding a statement to the effect that the petitioner swears that the facts contained in the petition are true, and if necessary the petitioner is prepared to testify to them under oath or prove them through documents.

Publication is usually required. Publication is the act of giving some type of notice to the general public of the petitioner's intention to change his name. Anyone who objects to the name change (for example, a creditor or a person with the same name) then has the opportunity to make such objections known to the court, which will try to balance the competing interests.

Publication is generally accomplished by placing a notice in a local newspaper. The clerk of the court will be able to give more specific details about the procedure followed in your jurisdiction. It might also be useful to ask the clerk under what circumstances publication by newspaper can be waived and some other less expensive method used in its stead. In many states, newspaper publication may be dispensed with if the name change involves a minor and both parents consent to the new name, or if the name change is requested by an adult who has been known by the "new" name all of his life and whose "old" name was never used except on the child's birth certificate.

The court decree makes it official. If sufficient time has elapsed after publication of the notice of the petitioner's intention to change his name, and no one has objected (certainly the usual case), the judge will issue a decree stating that the name requested is now the petitioner's legal name for all purposes. Once you have the court decree, you can get your name changed on your driver's license and Social Security card simply by showing the decree to the appropriate agency.

CHAPTER EIGHT

Guardianship and Powers of Attorney

Guard us, guide us, keep us, feed us,
For we have no help but Thee.
—James Edmeston,
Sacred Lyrics

Although guardianships are generally assigned for either persons or property, there are some other more limited guardianships for specific purposes as well. Different states have different rules concerning the rights, duties, and responsibilities of guardians. Sometimes a guardian has complete power; sometimes she must apply to a court for most actions on her ward's behalf.

Guardianships are sometimes required for minors to obtain insurance proceeds, and for regulating the use of monies obtained by virtue of legal or medical malpractice. Guardians may be also be appointed when adults are unable to care for themselves because of physical disabilities, although most adult guardianships are created because of mental incapacity.

With an increasingly older population, such guardianship activity is on the rise. Questions often arise as to the authority of a guardian to withhold or withdraw life-sustaining medical procedures. States which have statutes providing for "living wills" recognize the right of those who hold powers of attorney to advise relatives and/or guardians of the desires of incapacitated individuals.

Guardians are usually appointed out of necessity. Since the parents are considered the joint natural guardians of their minor children, there is generally no need to provide a child with a guardian unless both parents are deceased. But it is wise to appoint a guardian for minor children in your will, in case your spouse dies before you or you both die in a common accident. As noted above, guardians are also appointed for persons who are mentally incapable of handling their own affairs.

No special terminology is required. Simply be certain that the proposed guardian is clearly identified, and that his or her authority is clearly expressed—that is, whether the guardian is to be given custody over the child's person, property, or both. It is also wise to provide an alternate or co-guardian. Since most states require those acting in a trust capacity to post a bond (in order to insure honest performance), it would be a convenience and consideration to your chosen guardian if you explicitly waive any bond requirement otherwise demanded by your state. It is also wise to include instructions regarding the care, maintenance, and education of the child, and the conditions under which the guardian should consider his duties terminated, such as when the child reaches age eighteen.

Some states (e.g., Maryland) do not consider will-appointed guardianships to be binding, but courts generally honor such appointments. Guardianship is heavily regulated. State statutes are designed to protect the rights and interests of the physically disabled or otherwise incompetent persons from those who would try to take advantage of their vulnerability. Except by way of a last will and testament, being appointed a guardian is a complicated process involving consents, physicians' approvals, and proper notice prior to a judicial hearing during which the judge decides whether to approve the petition for guardianship. Such appointments are probably best handled with the assistance of a competent attorney.

Powers of Attorney

If adult children wish to take care of their elderly parents, a far easier solution is to obtain a power of attorney while the parent is still of sound mind. No court approval is necessary prior to acting under a power of attorney given by someone who is considered mentally capable. Likewise, anyone who wants to have her affairs administered by someone else (as, for example, where geographical distance is a problem) can do so by means of a document called a "power of attorney." Having a power of attorney has nothing to do with being a lawyer—although a lawyer may be given a power of attorney.

A power of attorney is simply a written legal paper in which one individual (called "the principal") gives another ("the agent") the authority ("power") to act in his behalf. The principal can also be an individual, a partnership, or a corporation. The power can be *general* (extending over the principal's person and all her property), or *specific* (limited, for example, to the handling of a particular transaction such as the sale of a certain house).

The power may take effect at the time the document is signed (a "presently exercisable" power) or at some future time—for example, when the principal becomes incompetent (a "springing" power). The principal can grant his agent the power to borrow money, pay bills, collect debts, manage a business, or sell property.

No court approval is necessary prior to acting under a power of attorney given by someone who is considered mentally capable. Thus, if adult children would like to be able to take care of the affairs of their elderly parents, a far easier solution is to obtain a power of attorney while the parent is still of sound mind.

Any adult of sound mind can grant a power of attorney. An adult who can communicate rational decisions (usually those concerning health or financial affairs) can create a power-of-attorney relationship. Conversely, if a person is so mentally or physically disabled that such communication is impossible, it is too late to create a power-of-attorney relationship. (In such a case it might be wise to consult a lawyer to determine whether non-consensual guardianship proceedings are necessary or advisable.)

The power of attorney should be precisely drafted. Traditionally the document creating a power of attorney begins with the phrase "Know All Persons by These Presents." But those words are hardly essential. The instrument should set out the name and address of both principal and agent. It should indicate the date or specific event (such as illness or disability) upon which the power of attorney is to take effect. Care must be taken when it is the alleged incompetence of the principal that will cause the agent's power to "spring." Unless the power of attorney contains a provision specifying precisely who is to determine the principal's competence, you might end up in court asking the court to decide. A typical enabling clause might provide that the family physician make the decision.

The document should expressly outline the exact powers given to the agent. Even with a general power of attorney, failure to be precise might invalidate the document. Language that is too general (e.g., "my agent can do anything . . .") will usually present a problem. The power of attorney should also explain what effect disability or death of the principal will have, as well as the date or event (if any) upon which the agent's power of attorney is to be terminated.

A power of attorney that continues after the disability or incompetence of the principal has ceased is called a "durable power of attorney." The elements of a durable power of attorney include:

1. Words stating the principal's intention
2. Appointment of the attorney, his or her name and address, and a description of his or her powers
3. Words stating that the powers will survive the principal's disability or incompetence
4. Signature of the principal, and date of the signing
5. Notarization
   The principal should make a copy of the signed document (for his own records) before delivering it to the agent.

The person named attorney does not have to sign the document. Likewise, no formal transfer of the principal's title or assets is necessary. The document should be clearly legible, kept in a safe place, and with a copy sent to the person named as attorney. If the attorney may buy or sell real estate, the power should be recorded.

Check your state's filing requirements. Some states have special filing/recording requirements for durable powers of attorney. Thus it may be a good idea to have the document reviewed by a lawyer.

Examples of general and specific powers of attorney can be found in Appendix III.

The power of attorney document should be notarized. It is in the agent's interest that the document creating a power of attorney be notarized, even though that step is not legally necessary for the authorization to be valid and binding. Notarization may be of some protection against a subsequent claim that the agent exerted undue influence over the principal, or that the principal was not of sound mind at the time the power was created.

In addition, if the powers granted concern the conveyance of real estate by the agent on behalf of the principal, the formalities associated with the making of a valid deed may apply. That is, the power of attorney may have to be witnessed, acknowledged, and recorded. If you are in doubt, call the clerk of the land-records office where the property is located, and ask what measures should be taken.

A power of attorney is not permanent. A power of attorney can always be revoked by its author—even if he or she is no longer of sound mind. In some states a power of attorney automatically terminates when the principal becomes disabled or dies, unless the principal has provided otherwise. A well-drawn document creating a power of attorney should include the date or event, if any, upon which the power is to be terminated. Notwithstanding such a provision, however, it is always best to end a power-of-attorney relationship formally by means of another signed written document, again delivered to the agent himself. If there is any concern that the agent might continue to hold himself out to others as if he were still acting on your behalf, it is a wise precaution to send notice that the relationship has been terminated to all those who might be affected.

CHAPTER NINE

Health Matters

To protect . . . their inalienable rights . . .
not only as equals before the law,
but also in their health . . .
—Samuel Gompers, 1898

Determining whether you need a lawyer in a wide variety of health matters is facilitated by knowledge of your basic legal rights— concerning everything from access to medical records to protesting a bill for fees or services. It's also important to be assertive. The medical establishment can be extremely difficult to penetrate.

Access to Records

Medical records are kept in a variety of places. Your medical records are those kept by your private doctor, clinic, or hospital of visits, tests, forms that you may have signed, billings and payments, and other personal information.

The Joint Committee on Accreditation of Hospitals, a voluntary organization to which most hospitals belong, has developed guidelines for which records must be kept on each patient. They include any consent forms you have signed, your medical history (supplied either by you or your doctors), records of physical examinations, laboratory reports, doctors' orders, and the record of your treatment and progress in that hospital. The contents and the completeness of these records are also regulated by state laws.

Your medical records should be important to you. As a patient, you should be aware of your condition and the progress you have made under treatment. This information should be useful in discussing your problems with doctors or hospital staff, and to allow you to make informed choices about treatment. You can also evaluate the quality of the care you have received—as well as protect your legal rights if any procedure has been done that you have not approved. A review of your medical records can also help you determine if you have been properly billed for the services rendered.

Once you decipher the horrendous handwriting for which doctors are notorious, medical records are not difficult to understand. You may need a medical dictionary or glossary of terms relating to your specific condition.

You do not own the records themselves. The paper on which your records actually appear is owned by the health-care provider (the hospital, doctor, or clinic). So too are the X rays taken by the radiologist his property. But you have a right to know what information is contained in those documents, as well as the right to inspect and copy them if you wish.

It is not always easy to copy or inspect your records. Unfortunately, many states do not allow patients easy access to their medical records. Such jurisdictions take the position that you do not have any rights to your X-ray films because they were ancillary to your medical treatment: you did not commission a photographer (but rather asked a medical professional for an opinion about your condition) and the physician took the pictures as an aid in making a diagnosis.

In these states your medical records may be obtained only through a subpoena or court order. The hitch is that you must sue your doctor or hospital before the court will order them to produce your records. This situation prompts the filing of many needless malpractice suits against doctors and hospitals. Many of these providers will relinquish your records, if requested, in order to avoid a lawsuit.

Other states allow access to your records if you ask for them in writing. You may be charged a fee for locating and copying them.

You can avoid the problems related to gaining access to your records by having your doctor agree ahead of time that you will be entitled to keep your X rays or other pertinent data or at least have access to them.

If the hospital is operated by the federal government, or by a state with its own freedom-of-information law, you can get access to your records more easily. Ask to see the hospital's Freedom of Information Act officer for details on how to initiate the process.

If you are a government employee, consult the applicable federal or state statutes and regulations. Federal employees' records are often held in a federal facility or by the Department of Defense, as are the records of employees exposed to harmful agents and residents of a long-term care facility or participants in a federal drug- or alcohol-abuse program.

Your state's medical society can also be helpful. Some states have an office that handles complaints from people having difficulty getting their medical records. The American Health Information Management Association ([312] 787-2672) can direct you in this regard. You might also get assistance from the American Medical Association's office in Washington, D.C. ([202] 789-7400).

The Public Citizen Health Research Group publishes a useful handbook called "Medical Records: Getting Yours." Write to 1600 20th Street, N.W., Washington, D.C. 20009.

Confidentiality

Generally, your records are confidential. If they are doctor's records, only the doctor and his staff should have access to them. If they are hospital records, only hospital personnel who have cared for you are entitled to access—not nurses or other aides who happen to be on the floor.

Some types of records are open to certain officials or health agencies. For example, all treatment received for bullet or knife wounds, or injuries sustained in an automobile accident or under other violent circumstances, must be reported to the local police. Suspected child-abuse cases are referred to state or local social-service agencies. Records of some contagious diseases and birth defects, as well as drug abuse, are sent to state or local health agencies.

When you tell someone something with the understanding that it will not be repeated, you have created a confidential relationship. Medical records and other information about your health are considered to be confidential. Under the Hippocratic oath taken by all physicians as well as the American Medical Association's Principles of Medical Ethics, a doctor is forbidden to disclose any fact that has come to his attention by virtue of his professional relationship with a patient unless a court orders the disclosure. A physician who violates your confidence could face professional disciplinary action, as well as a lawsuit brought by you. Hospitals and other health-care providers are under a similar legal duty.

Confidentiality applies to information about your spouse or other relative. You do not have an automatic right to medical information regarding your spouse or other relative. However, they may grant you permission to see their medical records, or to have you included in any discussion with the health-care provider.

The primary exception to this rule, of course, is the right of parents to information about their children. Parents are generally responsible for making decisions about the health of minor children—those under eighteen or twenty-one, depending on the state laws. However, children can seek certain medical procedures, because a confidential relationship is established which cannot be circumvented by the parents. A health agency in your state or county may be able to help you determine what rules of confidentiality govern a given medical situation.

There is little difference between confidentiality and the courtroom's doctor-patient privilege. Basically, the doctor-patient privilege that may be invoked in court is the same as the confidentiality rule. The testimonial privilege belongs to the patient, not the doctor. If a doctor is asked in court to tell about the patient's condition, the doctor must refuse unless the patient has previously authorized him to testify.

But the law in this area differs from state to state, and there are certain exceptions to the privilege, such as if the patient has put his condition or treatment in contention by a suit against the doctor, or if the legality of a document signed by the patient is in question. Again, though, the privilege is always the patient's and not the doctor's.

Informed consent is necessary before you are treated. In the matter of consenting to treatment, the law does not allow a doctor to substitute his own judgment for that of the patient. To the contrary, the law requires that (except in certain situations noted below) you grant your consent before any medical procedures are performed on you. Not only must you consent, but you must do so willingly and must understand the possible consequences.

If your doctor says that you need a certain operation, he must first tell you the risks involved, the alternative therapy available, and the possible adverse results of that operation—for example, a slow recovery or possible chronic illness or disabilities. Anything less will fall short of the required informed counseling. A doctor operating without informed consent is liable to both professional discipline and a lawsuit (for battery or malpractice).

Consenting to treatment is your right, and the law does not allow a doctor to substitute his own judgment for that of the patient. It is important that you be able to make a clear and intelligent choice. Do not be afraid to ask questions until you are satisfied with the answers. Read all consent forms provided by the doctor or hospital before signing them. A conscientious doctor will not pressure you into any operation before you know the risks involved. Listen carefully; when necessary, take notes.

Informed-consent procedures must be followed in all cases where the patient is of sound mind and is conscious. But if the patient cannot consent to a procedure because of mental incompetence or some other disability, a court must appoint a guardian who, after having the procedure explained to him, decides whether to consent. If there is no time for such an appointment, such as in the case of emergency treatment, informed consent is implied. Even in that situation, though, there are standards that cannot be exceeded. For example, if a person is brought into an emergency room unconscious and needing stomach surgery, no further surgery (such as appendectomy) can be undertaken.

There are other situations as well when the court may be asked to appoint a guardian. If, because of religious or other beliefs, a parent refuses to consent to a blood transfusion to save a child's life, the court can appoint a guardian who has the power to consent to the transfusion. The same is true if an elderly person needs an operation and is not of the proper mind to make a clear and rational decision. Depending on your state's law, the guardian may have to be a relative.

There are several exceptions to the informed-consent requirement. The doctor need not obtain the patient's consent if a "nonmaterial risk" is involved. For example, the possibility that a minor and temporary rash will result from treatment of a life-threatening condition might not be considered a material risk which the doctor is duty-bound to disclose. Even material risks need not be revealed to the patient who is mentally incapable of giving consent, or if he has specifically requested that he not be told of any risks involved in treatment. Similarly, the doctor's duty to disclose is suspended in emergency situations when obtaining the patient's consent for treatment would be impossible or impractical.

Before agreeing to medical treatment or surgery, know all the facts. Try to confirm your illness or condition by way of a second opinion, and if possible in an unpressured environment. What are the most likely consequences if you decide not to undergo treatment? Is alternative therapy possible? Who will conduct the recommended treatment or surgery? What will it cost?

You have a right to a second opinion. You have every right to tell your doctor that you wish to get another opinion before consenting to any form of treatment. A good physician, who feels he has properly diagnosed your problem, should have no qualms about your seeing another physician to verify his opinion. Do not think that you are insulting the doctor by asking for time before giving your consent. Doctors should understand your concern; some even *expect* you to ask for a second opinion on major operations.

Some health insurance plans *require* you to get a second opinion before they pay for health claims resulting from major medical treatments. Check with your insurer before committing yourself to a course of treatment.

There is a Patients' Bill of Rights. The American Hospital Association has developed a "Hospital Patients' Bill of Rights," which should be given to you when you are admitted to a hospital. (Ask for a copy if you haven't been provided one.)

Most hospitals are members of the AHA, and thus you should insist on these basic rights while you are under their care:

- to accept or reject any visitors
- to refuse medication if you so desire
- not to be disrobed for longer than necessary
- to have present at any physical examination a staff person of your gender (a right that should also exist in the doctor's office)
- to consent to physical examinations (or while in a teaching hospital, to refuse to be examined by medical students or groups of interns)

These rights are augmented by some state laws.

Bills

Talk to your doctor if you have a question about the bill. As with any other dispute over fees or costs, you should first bring your complaint to the attention of the health-care provider who has billed you. Try reasonably to come to an agreement with the provider, such as by compromising between his claim and what you think you owe him. With hospital services there are often charges by individuals with whom you have had no direct contact. Do not feel intimidated from asking for justification of specific items on your bill.

If you are being treated by a clinic and have a billing problem, rather than discussing your dispute with the collection office (which often has no authority to reduce or modify bills), go to the administrative officer of the clinic, or if at a hospital to the chief financial officer.

You may also want to contact your local office of Medicare or Medicaid and ask for a listing of the charges that it allows for the specific services you received (although they will often be lower than most doctors' fees). Similar lists are maintained by other health insurers.

If you are still dissatisfied, contact the state agency that licenses hospitals or medical professionals in your area. A number of states have a dispute-processing center for just this problem.

Pay what you think is fair and justified, recognizing the risk that the health-care provider may sue you for the balance. In court, of course, you can ask to have your records produced and require the provider to justify its billings.

Note that you cannot refuse payment simply because you have not been cured: neither doctors nor hospitals warrant that their treatment will cure.

Health Insurance

For most people, health insurance is an absolute necessity. Without it the costs of unexpected medical bills can devastate a family's budget. There is an infinite variety of health plans available for purchase. You should be careful to get the coverage best suited to your needs and circumstances.

There are various levels of premium payments. The basic coverage generally pertains to a certain percentage of hospital and medical costs incurred by either you or your family. But not all policies are family-coverage plans—so read the policy statements carefully to see who is covered and how reimbursements are made. Some policies pay the doctor or provider directly; others reimburse you for expenses after you pay the provider.

Other policies reimburse greater percentages of your hospital bill, and may also cover you and your family for dental care or eye examinations. Because such policies are more comprehensive, they are more expensive. Do not assume that you are covered for anything. Read the policy carefully before you purchase it.

You might also choose to sign up with a clinic or "health maintenance organization" (an HMO), which generally cost less but offer a more limited choice of physicians. Your state's insurance commissioner should be able to answer questions about local health insurers.

Some payments go directly to the doctor. "Assignments" are payments that the doctor or other health-care provider agrees to accept directly from the health insurer—in full satisfaction of your bill. For instance, if the insurance company will pay eighty percent of your care bill, you can ask your doctor if he will accept that amount in full payment of your claim; if he does, you will owe him nothing more. Many doctors will agree to such an arrangement to encourage confidence and goodwill in their patients, as well as to assure prompt payment.

The government often helps. Almost all states have some type of medical assistance programs to help individuals unable to afford health insurance themselves. Some are called "Medicaid," some "Social Services." You can find out about the state program in your area by looking in the "government" section of your local telephone directory.

Medicare is the federally funded and administered program that pays for certain items of health care for persons over sixty-five, or persons with certain disabilities, regardless of financial need. *Medicaid* is available only to those who can demonstrate extreme financial need.

Medicare covers basic health and hospital needs. Part A Medicare Hospital Insurance provides basic coverage for inpatient stays, post-hospital nursing facilities, and home care; it requires a yearly deductible. Part B Medicare Medical Insurance pays eighty percent of what it considers to be "reasonable" charges for doctors, laboratory work, therapy, medical equipment and supplies. You can ask your health-care provider to accept what Medicare determines the "reasonable" costs to be so that you can avoid the twenty percent co-payment.

Be aware that although Medicare pays for much of the cost of hospitalization, there are many expenses that are not covered at all. For example, Medicare does not pay for any drugs; nor will it cover equipment or devices not approved by the Food and Drug Administration, medical services using such drugs or devices, or experimental procedures not considered safe and effective. Nor will Medicare ordinarily pay for custodial care or visits from a doctor. For more information about Medicare, contact the Health Care Financing Administration or Social Security office in your area.

You must file a written application for Medicaid coverage. To obtain Medicaid coverage, you must file a written application to the state agency designated to handle this insurance. You will be interviewed by a Medicaid eligibility representative, who will assist you in filling out the application. Within several weeks (by law within forty-five days), you will receive a decision on your eligibility. If you're eligible and have already incurred medical bills, Medicaid may still pay for some of them; such retroactive coverage is limited to the beginning of the third month prior to the date you filed your Medicaid application.

The duration of your Medicaid coverage depends on your financial situation and medical costs. Medicaid coverage is reviewed at least once a year.

The Right to Die

Some states have legislated a "right to die." In some states, critically ill people are granted the option of having life-sustaining procedures withheld or removed if they are in a coma and have a minimum chance of recovering. Life-sustaining treatment is that which is necessary not to cure an individual, but merely to keep him alive through mechanical and chemical means. The most prominent legal issue is whether physicians can refuse treatment to such an individual: in some jurisdictions, doctors can be criminally charged and subject to professional discipline if they allow such patients to be taken off life-sustaining treatments.

In states that allow for a right to die, the patient or his guardian must sign a specific document to permit or prohibit any treatment. When a guardian is involved, the restrictions are stringent. To fully understand the procedures that exist in your state, call your health agency, board of medical examiners, or doctor.

Malpractice Suits

Medical malpractice is not easy to prove. It might be easier to understand what is *not* medical malpractice. Doctors (as well as hospitals and medical labs) do not have a duty to cure patients; therefore they cannot be sued for failure to cure. To recover, some level of fault or negligence must be proven. A physician is generally held to the standard of care and skill expected of a reasonably prudent doctor under similar circumstances. If a specialist is involved, the standard of care reasonably to be expected of a specialist in that field—generally a higher standard—is applied. If the doctor does not perform up to that subjective standard, and you have been damaged as a result, you can bring suit against him for your damages. Some states have voluntary arbitration procedures in these cases; others may require arbitration of all claims over a certain amount.

You usually need a lawyer for a malpractice suit. This is because of the complexities of medical malpractice and the different standards that apply from state to state. Medical malpractice cases are hard to prove, and are sometimes even more difficult because doctors are often extremely reluctant to testify against a colleague.

In addition, there are usually questions involving a specific *statute of limitations*—that is, how long a period of time you have in which to bring a suit. A lawyer should be consulted on such matters.

There is a wealth of information available about representing yourself in health matters. For starters, see the Bibliography at page 315.

CHAPTER TEN

Wills and Probate

When there's a will, there's a way.
—George Bernard Shaw,
Fanny's First Play

Distributing the assets of an estate can be a complex legal experience. Long ago, laws were adopted to spell out the rules for dividing property when one died without a will. More recently, the laws have been made even more complicated by the government, in its efforts to share in the spoils. Creditors have always wanted to be paid off as well. The law has thus developed a pecking order for distributing an estate where there is no will—with the heirs usually at the bottom.

There are several reasons to have a will. Most important, if you don't state your desires as to how much your spouse should get (beyond the minimum the law requires), the law will make the decision for you—a determination that may well not reflect your wishes. Moreover, the law never provides for small gifts to friends or to other than immediate relatives.

You should also remember that many statutory requirements, such as posting a bond for the executor or appointing special guardians for your minor children, can be avoided if you declare in your will that you want to eliminate them. In the absence of a will these "protections" are mandatory, and can cost your heirs both time and money.

But the fact that you need a will doesn't mean that you can't draft one yourself. In most cases you can, and if you choose to have a lawyer quickly peruse it when you're finished, you will usually be well ahead of the game.

Your estate includes everything of monetary value or personal significance. Your estate consists primarily of your home and other real estate; bank accounts, cars, silver, valuable jewelry and dishes, and other personal property; personal papers; hobby collections and art objects; investment portfolio; and certain rights under your pension plans. Almost all adults have a personal estate. Even housewives who have never worked outside the home have estates if title to any property or bank account is in their name, or if they have inherited anything of value. Nowadays, some seventy percent of American households earn two incomes—thus there is generally more property to distribute than in the past.

Intestate estates are divided according to local law. People who die without a valid will are said to have died "intestate." Their estates are distributed in accordance with the laws for the state in which they maintained their principal residence (in legal terms, where they were "domiciled") at the time of their death. In short, people who die without a valid will have allowed the state legislature (rather than themselves) to determine how to distribute their estate.

Intestate laws vary from state to state. Usually the surviving spouse will receive from one-third to one-half of the estate, with the balance going to children if any, to the surviving parents, or to brothers and sisters and other kin. The result may be a distribution completely at variance with the wishes of the decedent and the needs of those dependent upon the estate.

Even if the intestate distribution is the same as the decedent would have wished, there are still advantages to having a will. Intestate procedures are generally more cumbersome, time-consuming, and expensive than those involved in the approval of a will (called "probate"). A court-appointed personal representative is required to post a bond, which is paid by the estate, to assure honest performance. In a will, the one who makes the will (the "testator") can appoint his or her own choice of personal representative, determine the guardianship of any children, and give up ("waive") the sometimes expensive requirement of posting a bond.

Keep in mind also that a court-appointed personal representative must often file petitions and secure court approval before taking even the most sensible and necessary actions on behalf of the estate. Personal representatives appointed by a will are not subject to such burdens as long as they act reasonably and prudently.

You can make your own will without hiring a lawyer. Under certain circumstances a reasonably intelligent person can write a will as well as many attorneys can. When the assets are relatively small and little property is involved, the clerk's office can often be as helpful in protecting the estate as a lawyer.

If your estate does not involve complicated holdings, and if you don't expect any of your heirs to be disappointed enough over their share to make a fuss, it can be a relatively easy matter to make your own valid bequests. If, on the other hand, your estate could benefit from tax planning, or if there are ex-spouses, stepchildren, or children from a prior marriage, you would be better off having a good attorney draft your will. Likewise, if you are considering a trust, or leaving your estate to your grandchildren rather than your children—or if you can foresee that your intended distribution might create a stir among your heirs—you should definitely hire an attorney.

A simple estate may be one which consists primarily of life insurance payable to a first beneficiary, backed by a second beneficiary; bank accounts with rights of survivorship; a house and car held as community property (or in a joint tenancy with rights of survivorship, or as a tenancy by the entirety); and furniture and other personal property of negligible monetary value.

Tenancy by entirety **is a particular form of ownership available only to married couples.** It means that each spouse owns an undivided half of the property, and if one dies the survivor inherits the entire holdings. It is just like a joint tenancy except that neither spouse can sell her share without the other's permission.

The major difference between a joint tenancy and a tenancy by the entirety is that the former can be changed by either spouse during her lifetime; the latter can be terminated only by death, divorce, or mutual agreement. When you purchase property you can specify the form of ownership you prefer, or you can change it later by a separate deed.

Determine how large your estate is before you decide to hire a lawyer. If your entire estate is going to your spouse, no matter how large, it may be that there is no tax involved. If, however, your assets are going to be divided, and the total value of your estate (including the equity you have in your house) exceeds the amount exempt from federal estate and gift taxes (currently $600,000), hire an attorney experienced in estate planning. When there may be state or federal estate and gift taxes payable, the services of a knowledgeable lawyer could mean substantial savings that far outweigh the legal fees charged. Similarly, if there are children from former marriages or stepchildren, advice from an experienced attorney could prevent dissension in the family—or worse, a will contest.

Finally, if you are interested in creating a trust (in which control over certain property or funds is given to one party who must act for the benefit of other designated parties), or in giving a life estate to one person regarding certain property (so that upon his or her death ownership would automatically be transferred to some other designated person)—or any other scheme that might be complicated or controversial—the drafting of such provisions should be attempted only by a competent lawyer.

Every will should include certain items. Even simple wills should contain the following:

- the full name and "domicile" (permanent address) of the testator
- a declaration that this document is the testator's last will and testament, and revokes all former wills and written amendments ("codicils")

- a brief description of all the real and personal property that the testator wishes to bequeath
- specific gifts of personal property ("bequests"), gifts of real property ("devices"), and gifts of sums of money ("legacies"), including gifts to charities or friends
- where the residue (remainder) of the estate should go, with several alternatives listed in case some of the beneficiaries should die first
- the names of guardians for one's minor children upon the death of both parents
- appointment of an "executor" (a personal representative) to handle the probate of the estate (often the surviving spouse, and sometimes including others as well)
- an express statement that it is the testator's intent that the state-imposed bond requirement be waived for the personal representative
- the signature of the testator at the very end of the document, in the presence of witnesses
- signatures of the required number of witnesses under the state's laws after the testator's signature, along with an attestation clause (such as: "The foregoing instrument was at the date thereof signed, published, and declared by the said [testator's name] as and for his last will and testament in the joint presence of us, who, at his request and in his presence, and in the presence of each other, have subscribed our names as witnesses")
- the date that the signatures were affixed
- the witnesses' permanent addresses

Trust clauses should also be specific. If you wish to leave money, personal property, or real estate to someone but only when that person reaches a certain age, you can establish a trust on his or her behalf. The individual who will manage the assets until the beneficiary reaches the specified age is called the "trustee." The trust clause should name the trustee; note his or her general powers; list the names of the beneficiaries; provide specific instructions as to the management of the trust; and state exactly when distribution of both interest and principal is to take place.

Trust clauses can be tricky. When you draft them yourself, it would be advisable to have them reviewed by an attorney.

Oral wills are generally not valid. A few states have laws that allow oral wills in certain very limited situations—for example, when the will was made during the testator's last sickness. In these circumstances two (in some states, three) people must have been requested by the testator to bear witness to the contents of his will, and they all must have heard the contents of the will at the same time in each other's presence. In addition, such witnesses must have reduced what they heard to writing within a certain number of days, and the resulting will must be offered for probate within a certain number of months afterward. Even then the amount and kinds of property that can pass by oral will is usually limited. Similarly, in most jurisdictions the oral wills of soldiers in active military service and of sailors at sea are permitted for their personal property.

If there is any question as to the validity of a will, oral or written, consult an attorney.

Handwritten wills can be valid. In some states wills that are handwritten, dated, and signed by the testator—called "holographic wills"— are valid without attestation or the other formalities of execution. In other states, however, formal attestation is required regardless of whether the will is handwritten, typed, or printed. And some states will recognize a will that is valid according to the laws of the jurisdiction in which it was made. There is nothing that requires a will to be typewritten as long as the other formalities are met.

Twenty-four states currently allow unattested holographic wills. As of 1993 they are Alaska, Arizona, Arkansas, California, Colorado, Idaho, Kentucky, Louisiana, Michigan, Mississippi, Montana, Nevada, New Jersey, North Carolina, North Dakota, Oklahoma, Pennsylvania, South Dakota, Tennessee, Texas, Utah, Virginia, West Virginia, and Wyoming.

Making a proper will means following certain steps. First, you should select as your witnesses stable adults who have no direct or indirect interest in your estate. This means that your beneficiaries, heirs, personal administrators, and trustees, as well as their close relatives, should not witness your will. Wills executed in Connecticut, Georgia, Maine, Massachusetts, New Hampshire, South Carolina, and Vermont must have at least three witnesses. In all other states except Louisiana, the attestation of only two witnesses is sufficient. (The laws of Louisiana are heavily influenced by French civil law, rather than the British common law which forms the legal basis of the other states. Residents of Louisiana should consult a lawyer in making wills.) To be safe, have three witnesses sign your will, none of whom are beneficiaries.

Second, you should personally sign and date the very bottom of the will. Any provisions added after the signature of the testator will not be considered by the probate court, and may possibly invalidate the entire will.

Third, the witnesses should sign the will under an attestation clause. Since some states demand that witnesses be in one another's presence when they sign, this is the better practice. The witnesses do not have to read any of the will. They need only be able to testify that the testator signed the document in their presence, declared it to be his last will, requested the proper number of witnesses to attest to the execution of the document as a will, and that they did so. The witnesses' addresses should also be noted in the will.

(A frequent and substantial mistake is to assume that a notary's verification is sufficient to validate a will. Notarization alone does not satisfy the state's legal requirement for attestation.)

Finally, it is a good idea for both the testator and the witnesses to initial or sign each page of the will—which should also be numbered, to discourage later attempts at substituting pages. On the last page, each signature should be accompanied by printed names and addresses.

If the testator is elderly, sickly, or otherwise incapacitated, be certain that his signing is personally observed by the witnesses. Even after all that is done, there should be at least one extra copy that is signed and attested.

Certain legal requirements must be met before a probate court will validate a will. The testator must have been of legal age—generally eighteen years old—mentally competent, and not acting under any undue influence at the time of making the will. He must have had the intention to make a will. He must not have revoked it prior to his death. The specific provisions of the will must not violate any statutory requirements of the state in which it was executed, or go against public policy. (For example, the probate court might decide that public policy is offended if a testator left all his property to an animal and none to his children. Likewise, in most states courts will not permit a spouse to be disinherited.)

Finally, the will must not have been "revoked by law" because of significant changes in the circumstances of the testator that occurred since the time of the will's execution—occurrences such as marriage, divorce, the birth of a child, or perhaps the death of the principal beneficiary.

When an insurance policy conflicts with a will provision, the policy usually controls. Ordinarily a beneficiary named on an insurance policy cannot be replaced by someone else named in a will. (The theory is that the proceeds of the insurance policy are not considered assets of the insured's estate.) In some jurisdictions, however, the testator's clearly expressed intention to change a beneficiary by way of her will might be honored by a probate court.

When a will specifies creation of a guardianship, it is important to create a specific guardianship estate. More often than not, insurance companies paying proceeds and other individuals want the protection of knowing that anyone representing the estate has been duly recognized by a court. Therefore the testator should make sure that his designation of a guardian is specific enough for the court to be able to implement his desires.

Similarly, it is important to make a specific designation of a pension-plan beneficiary. If the testator has not specifically named a beneficiary of his Social Security or other pension payments, federal law allows the agency to make its own designation.

You cannot later change your will by crossing out or erasing provisions. Never try to change an operative will (one that has been signed and witnessed) by erasing or crossing out provisions or names or amounts. Attempts to do so will be considered defective because of the lack of the proper formalities of execution. Most probate courts disdain attempts to alter the will in such an informal manner—and could even invalidate the whole document.

You do not have to make a new will every time you want to change a provision. A new will is not necessary every time a change is desired. By use of a *codicil,* a testator can make limited changes without having to revoke and rewrite the entire document just because, for example, you want to increase a specific bequest or add a charitable gift. A codicil is a supplement or amendment adding to, deleting from, or modifying the terms of a will. In order for it to be valid, it must be executed with the same formalities as a will. It should specifically identify the will to which it should be attached, mention previous codicils if any, and affirm those portions of the will and former codicils that it does not seek to modify.

Consider modifying your will when there is a major change in your life. The necessity or desirability of a codicil—or even a new will—should be considered any time there is a change in the testator's life. Such events include the birth of a child; marriage, divorce, or the death of a spouse; any significant increase or change in the value or nature of one's property; or when a selected personal representative or trustee dies or otherwise becomes unable to serve.

Revocation of an existing will or codicil should always be accompanied by the execution of a new will or codicil. Tearing or burning a will with the intent to revoke it may be a legally effective method of revocation—but when done in the privacy of one's home, the gesture may go unrecognized. Moreover, a probate court could consider the destroyed will as being lost, and accept a signed copy provided by the drafting attorney (or even one of the beneficiaries) in substitution. In short, if a will is to be revoked without a simultaneous replacement, there should be a paper affirming the revocation placed where the will itself would have been.

Do not keep your will in a safe-deposit box. Your most recent will should be clearly marked as such, and kept wherever you keep important documents in your home. Your spouse and children should be told of its location. Many lawyers think it is better not to keep your will in a safe-deposit box—which is temporarily sealed in many estates when the bank is notified of the testator's death, and may thus be less accessible than a location in your home. Some people ask their lawyers to keep the original in their office safe, or to file it in court, where that is allowed.

Probate is not always necessary. Probate is the process by which the authenticity of a will is proven to the proper authorities, usually before a probate court. Any property that is held in joint tenancy automatically transfers to the survivor upon the death of one tenant, and therefore eliminates the necessity of probate (although not necessarily the necessity for paying estate taxes).

Note, however, that under the Economic Recovery Act of 1981, all assets can be passed tax-free to a surviving spouse. Note also that a bequest which blindly passes all assets to the spouse will not accomplish the optimal tax savings available but may be desirable for other reasons; an automatic unlimited gift wastes the current $600,000 exclusion provided by the federal estate and gift tax laws. This makes no difference, of course, unless your estate is quite large. (See the latest edition of *How to Avoid Probate*, by Norman F. Dacey, available in most public libraries.)

Even when there is probate, a lawyer is not always required. If the remainder of the estate involves a relatively small amount of money, and no one is contesting the provisions of the will, a lawyer is often not necessary. A designated personal representative can usually obtain the necessary legal forms to be filled out from the office of the probate-court clerk. These papers should include a petition for probate; a statement from the personal representative consenting to her appointment; a notice of appointment and notice to creditors; appraiser's reports; and requests for bond if necessary. Once the court confirms the appointment of the personal representative, it will issue "letters testamentary," a document which gives the personal representative permission to transact any matters on behalf of the deceased's estate.

The personal representative (executor) has specific responsibilities. Initially, the personal representative should submit to the probate court any will that has been found. Ultimately, the personal representative is responsible for gathering all the assets of the estate, and investing, disposing of, or preserving them; paying all valid debts from these assets; and then distributing the remainder as the testator directed. The distribution is according to the terms of the will, if any, or according to the law of intestate succession if there was no valid will.

The personal representative is also responsible for the preparation and filing of any federal estate tax return, any state inheritance tax returns, the fiduciary tax return, and any income tax returns required as a result of the death, as well as for paying those taxes from the assets of the estate. This must be done within the legal time limit and before final distribution of the estate. All these actions are done under the supervision of the probate court, and are part of what is called "probating a will."

Living Wills

Among the many personal rights enjoyed by American citizens, perhaps the least known is the right to refuse medical treatment. The difficulty arises when you are unable to assert that right because of the nature of an illness or injury. The use of living wills and advance directives solves the problem.

Living wills and advance directives accomplish the same purpose, but in different ways. The living will takes effect under certain circumstances—incapacity due to illness or injury—and communicates your desires with respect to medical treatment. An advance directive appoints an agent to make health-care decisions for you (in most cases according to your instructions) and can take effect immediately or be delayed until certain conditions exist. (Unless otherwise stated, the discussion in the remainder of this chapter applies to both living wills and advance directives.)

The right to refuse medical treatment must be affirmatively asserted. Even though you have the right to refuse medical treatment, you will be unable to express your desires if you are unconscious or otherwise unable to communicate. By law and ethical codes, health-care providers must continue to administer life-sustaining procedures unless the patient asserts a contrary wish.

Living wills are recognized by law. Most states today recognize living wills by statute. Typically, they take effect only when the patient's condition is terminal or death is considered imminent (Arkansas, Ohio, Oregon). Some states apply special restrictions regarding the cessation of artificially supplied nutrition and hydration (Kentucky, Missouri, North Dakota); others also restrict the implementation of living wills if you are pregnant (Delaware, Michigan, Oklahoma, South Carolina, Utah).

A living will is evidence of your wishes. Most state laws require evidence of an incapacitated patient's "clear and convincing" desire to refuse medical treatment. By executing a living will and providing copies to relatives, close friends, and your physician, your wishes regarding continuation of life-support systems will be known.

The living will may contain specific instructions. Some statutes allow you to spell out health-care instructions (in the event you are unable to make an informed decision yourself) that specifically decline artificial life-sustaining procedures such as the administration of nutrition and hydration.

You must designate a "health-care agent." Nearly all states recognize the concept of a "health-care agent" (also referred to as a "health-care power of attorney," "health-care proxy" or "health-care surrogate"). You simply name someone as your agent, with authority to make decisions concerning your health care if you are unable to do so. Several states (Florida, Iowa, Illinois, Maryland, and Texas) provide for a surrogate in situations that a patient cannot make informed decisions regarding his health care even if no living will was executed. The candidates are typically ranked in a prioritized next-of-kin order.

The health-care agent's power can be effective immediately or upon some condition. If you designate someone as your health-care agent, you may have that person's power take effect immediately (at the time you execute the document) or upon the occurrence of a specific condition (for example, in the event you are unable to make an informed decision yourself). In the latter case, the document might state that your attending physician and a second physician must agree that you are unable to make an informed decision regarding your health care.

Like a will, how you execute a living will is important. The state's law will specify its requirements for executing a valid living will. Typically, two witnesses and/or notarization is sufficient. Be careful to follow the rules precisely as they are set forth in the statute.

A living will executed in one state may not be enforceable in another. Only about half of the advance-directive statutes recognize the validity of out-of-state documents—even if they were executed in compliance with the law of the state where executed. And of these, most say only that they recognize a valid execution—but do not guarantee the enforceability of a document that may contravene their own state law.

Be careful about using a living-will form found in a form book. Given the nature of a living will, it should be a personalized statement of your wishes after considerable thought and discussion with those close to you. Using a form provided by a form book may be a good way to get started, but should be used primarily as a guide and not as the finished product.

The Patient Self-Determination Act (PSDA) requires that health-care providers give patients certain information. This federal law (which became effective in December 1991) applies to:

- the individual rights of patients under state law to control health-care decisions, including the right to have an advance directive
- information on the facility's policies on advance directives

Under the PSDA, health-care institutions must also:

- ask the patient if she has an advance directive and document the directive if she does
- educate their staff and the community about advance directives
- comply with state law regarding advance directives and not discriminate on the basis of whether a person has an advance directive

More information on living wills and advance directives is readily available. For current information about living wills and advance directives, you may want to write to the Society for the Right to Die, 250 West 57th Street, New York, NY 10107.

CHAPTER ELEVEN

Employees' Rights

O, how full of briars is this working-day world.
—Shakespeare,
As You Like It

For a variety of reasons, in the field of employment the law is frequently stacked against the average worker. Consequently, an employee with a grievance can often obtain better results by organizing with other employees to form a union than by having a lawyer pursue a particular remedy. In addition, because of the numerous procedural pitfalls which line the path to justice in this area, an employee is often best advised to use attorneys (such as government lawyers) who can be obtained free of charge.

The more you know about your legal rights, of course, the less you need to rely on lawyers at all.

Your rights begin when you apply for a job. Often the first contact you have with a prospective employer is through his advertisements. Under federal and many state laws, employers are not permitted to discriminate in the way they recruit and hire employees. They cannot advertise for employees of a particular race, color, national origin, religion, sex, or (as of July 1992) disability—or for an employee who is not a member of such a group—unless those qualifications are considered necessary to perform a specific job. (For example, if an employer wanted a women's room attendant, he could legally require that she be female. This exception is called a "bona fide occupational qualification.")

Certain kinds of discrimination are permitted. As long as federal or state laws do not prohibit employers from discriminating against or in favor of a particular personal trait, such discrimination is allowable. For example, if an employer wants all his employees to have brown eyes, he can legally refuse to hire people with blue eyes. (But if he chooses only people who have blue eyes in order to exclude a race in which no one has blue eyes, the law will intervene.) In states where marital status itself is not a protected category, an employer might even ask whether the candidate is married, if the question is job-related—if, say, he does not want a single person to manage a computer-dating service.

Employment agencies are likewise restricted. You should understand that employment agencies are also prohibited from discriminating in their advertising, their practices, or in any agreements made with prospective employers.

When using an agency, inquire about whether its fee is to be paid by you or the future employer. Ask if the fee is payable even if you don't stay with the employer very long. States generally establish maximum fees which can be charged, and the conditions under which their fees may be imposed. If in doubt, check with your state's commissioner of labor or its equivalent agency.

An employer may check your background and credit. Generally, employers are permitted to make reasonably thorough background checks on prospective employees—as long as the information sought is related to the position being applied for. The degree to which an investigation may go likewise depends upon the job in question. A background check for a bank teller, for example, would be more stringent than that for an assembly-line worker. In any event, the investigation may not be used as a means to unlawfully discriminate against you.

An employer may also check your credit rating or determine if other employers have checked, but only under the strict guidelines set by the Federal Credit Reporting Act, as well as the credit-reporting acts of some states. You are entitled to know the name of the agency that supplied a credit report, as well as to correct any errors. Call the nearest office of the Federal Trade Commission for instructions. If the federal act is violated, the employer is subject to both civil and criminal penalties, and you may seek both actual and punitive damages, as well as attorney fees.

An employer may test you. Generally, an employer can use any "professionally developed ability test" as long as that test does not discriminate against your race, color, religion, sex, or national origin. Again, such tests must be job-related. If you feel that a test was discriminatory or not job-related, contact your state labor commissioner or the local office of the federal Equal Employment Opportunity Commission (EEOC).

Do not lie on an employment application. Remember that any incorrect or false statement in an employment application is sufficient grounds not to hire you—or to fire you if the employer finds out later that the answers were false.

Federal law now prohibits the use of a lie detector or polygraph test in connection with any employment activities, except in a few specific instances. Check with your state labor department, or your union if you belong to one.

You should probably sign any waivers or releases requested to allow distribution of information from your former employer. Employers who ask for such waivers usually intend to use them. Although you certainly may refuse to sign them, if you don't get the job the employer can reasonably claim it was because you were uncooperative or were trying to hide something in your past (unless, of course, you can show that the request was discriminatory).

An employer can require pre-employment medical examinations. A medical exam can be required in order to assess your capability of performing job-related functions. The Americans with Disabilities Act protects handicapped people against post-hiring medical examinations unless they are job-related, and this applies to both private and public employers. Screening for the current illegal use of drugs is generally permitted.

In certain situations an employer can ask for information which you might feel is discriminatory. It is not a violation of the law for employers to ask you to identify your race, sex, or national origin—if the data are used solely for reporting to government agencies that regulate various employment-practice programs. Such information, however, cannot be used for hiring purposes.

You cannot be discriminated against because of your age. If you are forty or older, the federal Age Discrimination Act prohibits an employer from arbitrarily discriminating against you because of your age. Employers covered by this act are those in the private sector who have twenty or more employees, federal or state governments (regardless of the number of employees), employment agencies, and labor unions with twenty-five or more members. If you feel that you have been discriminated against because of your age, contact your local office of the Equal Employment Opportunity Commission (EEOC). Some states have their own age-discrimination laws. Check with your state labor commissioner for information.

Women cannot be discriminated against on the basis of pregnancy, childbirth, or any related condition. Under Title VII of the Civil Rights Act, pregnant women employees who need to take time off from work must be treated the same way as employees who are absent for other medical conditions. (This protection includes women who need to take time off from work to recover from an abortion.) On the other hand, a pregnant woman who wishes to and is able to work cannot be required to take a leave of absence; nor can she be forced to take time off after giving birth.

Veterans are specially protected. The fact that you are a veteran cannot be held against you. If a veteran has a thirty-percent or more disability, he can be protected throughout his working life.

Information about this program, and which employers are covered under it, can be obtained from the Veterans Administration, or from your local office of the federal Department of Labor.

Employees with disabilities are protected by federal law. In July 1992, the Americans With Disabilities Act (ADA) became law for all employers with twenty-five or more employees. In July 1994, employers with fifteen or more employees will be covered. The ADA affords significant new rights for millions of American workers, and imposes major obligations upon employers.

No federal law prohibits discrimination on the basis of sexual orientation, but many states and cities do. As of 1993 discrimination against homosexuals is illegal in Connecticut, Hawaii, Massachusetts, Wisconsin, and the District of Columbia. At least eighty cities have similar laws on the books—including Atlanta, Austin, Boston, Buffalo, Chicago, Columbus (Ohio), Detroit, Hartford, Iowa City, Milwaukee, Minneapolis, Portland (Oregon), Sacramento, Seattle, and Tucson.

Your specific rights as an employee depend on a variety of circumstances. It all depends on where you work, whom you work for, what type of work you are doing, and what additional rights are in your contract. If you work for a private employer and are not represented by a union, your relationship with your employer is more under his control. Nevertheless, it is still subject to various state laws, and if it employs more than a certain number of people (specified by statute), or has government contracts, or the business is in interstate commerce, it may also be subject to federal laws. Statutes (both federal and state, and in some cases, even city and county) may regulate your wages and hours; assure you of nondiscriminatory treatment in employment, promotion, and pay; and guarantee a safe work environment and pension rights. Unions (including those for government employees) often enhance these basic rights by gaining employer concessions for medical and sick benefits, pensions, grievance procedures, strike clauses, and the right not to be fired except for just cause.

Even if you don't belong to a union, you have basic rights. Assuming that you work for a small company, you have rights specified by the state law—usually the right to work in a safe environment, for a minimum wage, and for a maximum number of hours—and those especially contracted for. The latter are the trickiest, because many employment "contracts" are unwritten agreements which can be terminated by either party for no reason at all ("at will") and, in most cases, for reasons you might consider unfair. This type of contract generally arises when, after an interview, you and the employer "shake hands" on your "agreement" to accept the job based on the salary and benefits that you have discussed. The terms of your contract may be listed in a letter to you from your employer, but most often they are merely evidenced by the wages you are paid and the benefits you receive or have been promised. Because very little has been committed to writing, many rights or benefits to which your employer may have agreed orally may be difficult to secure if he later chooses to ignore or deny them. The best advice, therefore, is to get as much in writing as you can, and ask questions before problems arise.

If you work for a larger company, you might receive a manual explaining what is required of you as an employee, as well as the benefits to which you are entitled. Many employers go so far as to require that you sign a form indicating you have read and agreed to the information in the manual. Depending on state law, this may create an agreement binding on both you and the company. Any disputes that arise can probably be decided under the manual, so read it carefully.

In addition, some courts have declared it public policy that employment contracts must include an implicit, unwritten term of "good faith and fair dealing" toward employees. Thus they have forbidden companies from firing employees for improper reasons, such as because they have filed worker's compensation claims or have refused to cover up illegal activities.

Union contracts are generally comprehensive. If you belong to a union, your rights are generally better than if you were not represented by one. Unions have generally negotiated a written contract covering your employment, which often gives you greater protection. You should have a copy of that contract so that you know exactly what your rights are. Although it usually doesn't specify your personal rate of pay, it may place you in a class of employees with a graduated pay scale based on the number of years on the job and the type of work you do. Wage and salary increases are also specified, as well as health benefits and pension plans.

Union contracts also generally include a grievance procedure so that you can complain through the union to your employer if, for example, the terms of the contract regarding break time or sick leave are not being met. In fact, the contractually established grievance procedures must ordinarily be followed whenever you assert your contractual rights. The union normally pays the cost of the grievance procedure, which works much faster than a lawsuit.

You can resort to court actions, however, if you think the union is acting arbitrarily, or undemocratically, or otherwise not fairly representing you with regard to your complaint. To do so you may have to take your complaint to court quickly after losing a grievance or learning of the union's improper conduct. Such actions are generally difficult to win, and usually require a lawyer to handle.

Your union membership cannot be restricted. If you belong to a union or want to organize one among the workers in your company, you have certain protections under federal law. Various statutes protect the rights to organize, to participate in union activities, and *not* to be represented if a majority of your fellow employees agree.

You also have the right to vote in union elections without management (or union) interference, and to engage in activities with other employees—through a union or independently—for mutual aid, benefit, or protection. Your employer cannot interfere with or discriminate against employees who exercise such rights. Neither can employers discriminate against anyone who files a complaint with the National Labor Relations Board (NLRB), which protects employees whose rights have been infringed. You are equally protected against unfair restraints placed upon you by either unions or employers.

Enforcing National Labor Relations Act rights need not be complicated. If you feel you are not being treated fairly by an employer or union, you must first file a charge with the NLRB stating an unfair labor practice. Charges must be lodged within six months of the alleged violation at the NLRB's regional offices. (Look in the phone book, under "U.S. Government.") If the NLRB agrees that your employer or union is subject to federal law and that you are a covered employee—that is, neither an employee of the federal or state government, nor a supervisor, and not subject to other federal laws like the Railway Labor Act, which covers rail and airline employees—it will investigate your charge.

You can get a charge form from your regional NLRB office. It must be truthfully filled in, sworn to or affirmed under oath, and filed. Your union can also file a charge on your behalf. The other party will be notified of your complaint, and an investigation will be undertaken by the regional NLRB office. If the agency concludes that a violation has occurred, it will issue a complaint. Even if it concludes that there was no violation, you cannot be fired for filing a complaint in good faith.

If the regional office concludes that your charge lacks merit, you can appeal to the NLRB's Office of Appeals in Washington, which can direct that a complaint be issued. If a complaint is filed, a hearing will be held before an administrative law judge who will issue proposed findings, which are in turn reviewed by the NLRB in Washington. If an unfair-labor practice is found, the board will issue an appropriate order—for example, one that requires immediate corrective action, including back pay if appropriate. If the union or employer fails to obey the board's order, the NLRB will seek to enforce it in court.

Although the NLRB's regional legal staff will represent you in the matter, you should nevertheless be active in preparation of your case. You may also have your own lawyer if you wish.

Complaining to EEOC is similarly uncomplicated. If you feel your employer has discriminated against you because of your race, color, religion, sex, or national origin, you should take your complaint to the local EEOC office within a hundred and eighty days. In many areas, state or local counterparts have been created to handle such complaints.

The procedure is similar to that followed with regard to the

NLRB. You must fill out a complaint form. The EEOC will investigate. If it finds merit, it may order a hearing. If a hearing is ordered, the employer will be asked to justify its conduct. Initially, the EEOC acts as an intermediary with your employer, but if an act is considered discriminatory, it may choose to pursue the employer for you as if it were your own private counsel.

If the EEOC determines that your complaint lacks merit, it will be dismissed and your employer will be so informed. In this case, or if the EEOC has simply been unable to process your claim within one hundred eighty days, you are entitled to receive a "Right to Sue" letter. You will then have ninety days in which to file an action for discrimination in a federal district court, or risk losing your action completely. (More detailed instructions can be obtained through your local EEOC office.)

Preparation is important. If you think trouble is coming, keep a notebook to document your case. You can decide to retain counsel to assist you in organizing your complaint, or proceed to represent yourself. Either way, the key to success is good preparation. Find others who are aware of the allegedly discriminatory action at work, and ask them to corroborate your complaint. Their written statements should be sworn before a notary public; you can get the necessary forms from the EEOC or NLRB office.

Before you prepare your case, make certain that you are covered under the law by making an inquiry to the information officer at the NLRB or EEOC. You might find books in your public library or union office to assist you in understanding the intricacies of labor law.

Do not hesitate to see a lawyer if you are unable to understand the law or what you can do to protect your rights. In a successful EEOC case you will be awarded attorney fees. (This right does not ordinarily apply to NLRB cases.)

Check the state law too. As long as state regulations have not been superseded by federal law, states may control employer-employee relationships or judge the fairness of employee discharges under common-law or public-policy principles.

States often have their own laws for minimum wages and overtime, maximum hours, the health and safety of the work environment (e.g., noise, dust, and fume levels, or exposure to toxic chemicals and asbestos), and child employment. Many federal laws exist in these areas also, but state laws that are more stringent are also generally enforceable. For example, many states have their own prohibitions against sexual harassment and other discriminatory practices in the workplace.

Other employee rights are protected not by statute but by state courts applying "public policy." Thus a court may set aside a discharge if it came about because the employee was fired for serving on a jury instead of coming to work, voted in a manner contrary to his employer's wishes, or refused to do something illegal, unethical, or dishonest—even for reporting a fellow employee to a supervisor or to a governmental authority for wrongful acts. Such "whistle-blowing" is protected by statute if you are a federal employee, as well as in a number of states.

Public servants are sometimes more vulnerable and sometimes better off. State employees are generally not covered by federal statutes, and are sometimes not even protected by state laws that apply to private employers. This is due to the unique role of the state as both an employer and a regulator. But unlike private employees, government workers have protections from both state and federal constitutions which are not applicable to private employers, and an employment contract written by the state cannot be changed by state law.

Many government employees belong to unions, receiving the benefits and protection afforded them in the union contract, but most government employees are prohibited from striking and can be fired for doing so.

For more information about the rights of state employees, check with your personal commissioner or union representative. Federal employees are regulated by the policies of the Office of Personnel Management, and their unions come under the jurisdiction of the Federal Labor Relations Authority.

In many jurisdictions you have the right to a smoke-free work environment. Numerous states and municipalities have laws that restrict smoking in both public and privately owned workplaces. (On the other hand, a number of states make it illegal to discriminate against employees who smoke during non-working hours.)

If you live in a state without antismoking laws and have severe health problems made worse by secondary smoke, your best solution might be to ask your employer to find a smoke-free workplace for you. If such a space is unavailable, you may quality for worker's compensation or unemployment insurance benefits.

Sexual Harassment

Learn to recognize the kind of sexual harassment that can be legally challenged. Sexual harassment occurs whenever any sexually oriented behavior that is unwanted creates a working environment detrimental to the victim. You can often get relief from sexual harassment without going to court simply by confronting the offender and threatening to report him to management's personnel department. You can also file a complaint under Title VII of the Civil Rights Act, which covers both sexual harassment and other forms of employment discrimination.

Title VII covers "quid-pro-quo" sexual harassment. Quid-pro-quo sexual harassment exists when a supervisor demands sexual favors in exchange for tangible job benefits. Sexual harassment of this sort exists when (1) the victim—whether male or female—has been subjected to unwanted sexual advances; (2) the harassment complained of was based on sex; (3) submission to the unwelcome advances was an expressed or implied condition for receiving job benefits; or (4) refusal of the unwelcome advances resulted in a tangible job detriment.

Title VII also covers sexual harassment in a "hostile" or "abusive" working environment. When sexually offensive words or actions adversely affect the victim, a hostile or abusive working environment exists. This type of sexual harassment is more difficult to prove. Different from the quid-pro-quo variety, an abusive working environment can exist when there is any unwelcome sexual harassment. A "reasonableness" standard is used: if a particular person is oversensitive to merely juvenile or insensitive comments made on the job, it may not be "harassment." The harassment complained of must have affected a term, condition, or privilege of employment. The victim must show a detrimental effect sufficiently severe or pervasive so as to alter working conditions and create a discriminatorily hostile or abusive environment.

In 1993 the Supreme Court reaffirmed this standard, adding that all circumstances are examined in determining whether a hostile or abusive work environment exists. Courts are now guided by these relevant factors: the frequency of the discriminatory conduct; its severity; whether it is physically threatening or humiliating, or a mere offensive utterance; and whether it unreasonably interferes with an employee's work performance. While each of these factors may be considered, no single one is required.

The complainant must prove that the employer knew (or should have known) about the harassment and failed to take the proper remedial action. In hostile-working-environment cases involving sexual harassment, the employer is given a chance to correct the problem before being subjected to liability to the victim for damages. Proper remedial action not only must be reasonably calculated to end the alleged harassment, but must also be of a disciplinary nature.

In addition to a complaint under Title VII, there are various state antidiscrimination laws that apply as well. If you choose to hire an attorney, not only can you take action either under federal law or state antidiscrimination laws, you may seek redress by filing a personal-injury lawsuit based upon a tort theory. Several such actions in tort are available to the victim of sexual harassment, the most popular being intentional infliction of emotional distress. Others are abusive or wrongful discharge, assault and/or battery, tortious interference with a contractual relationship, defamation, and invasion of privacy.

CHAPTER TWELVE

Beginning a Business

Anybody can start something.
—John A. Shedd,
Salt from My Attic

The courage and hope that go into starting a small business are as integral parts of the American psyche as the businesses themselves are of the economy. There are close to five million small businesses in this country, employing over half the nation's workers and representing the great majority of all firms. New businesses start (and many fledgling ones fail) every day.

Would-be entrepreneurs need not have a lawyer to begin. It is not difficult to understand the three basic forms that a small business can take: sole proprietorship, partnership (general or limited), or corporation.

A *sole proprietorship* exists when the person operating a business goes it alone or with a spouse. He or she is the boss, although the authority to make decisions can be delegated to an employee. The sole proprietor is entitled to all the profits generated by the business—but is also personally responsible for all debts and losses incurred. The laws concerning sole proprietors are basically those applied to any individual. Thus this chapter will deal primarily with partnerships and corporations, although most laws (e.g., minimum-wage regulations) apply regardless of the form of organization.

Partnerships

Partners share in profits and losses. A partnership is a voluntary association between two or more persons who intend to share profits (and losses) from the operation of a business. The partners' intentions and expectations should be set out in a written partnership agreement, but partnerships can and do exist that are based on purely oral agreements. They can even result solely from the acts of the parties toward themselves and others (that is, a court can find a partnership existed when the parties acted as if they were partners).

There are several drawbacks to operating a business as a general partnership. One major disadvantage of an ordinary general partnership is the unlimited personal liability of each of the individual partners for the firm's debts and losses. Another is that one partner's act can bind the partnership: as a rule, the other partners are fully liable for the actions of any one of their partners. Moreover, if the partnership incurs debts and there are not sufficient assets in the firm to pay for them, each partner is individually liable. Creditors can even choose which partner to proceed against, because the debts do not have to be allocated proportionately.

There is one major exception to the foregoing general rule. When one partner's acts are obviously not in the ordinary course of the business, the other partners are not bound. For example, if your partner in the shoe-repair business takes a trip to Hawaii "to look for customers," you aren't required to pay for his airplane ticket. Likewise, when the partner in fact has no authority to act for the partnership in a particular matter and the third party with whom he is dealing knows about this limitation, the partner's acts are not binding on the others.

You do not need a lawyer to create a partnership. But keep in mind that the services of a knowledgeable attorney or certified public accountant is generally a sound business expense. Partnership agreements and similar business contracts are not mere formalities drafted for show or to impress potential creditors. They should be useful documents, outlining the genuine expectations of the parties as to how the business should be created, operated, and dissolved; they should also govern the relationships, investments, and profit-sharing agreements of the partners—and they have tax consequences.

A good lawyer can be invaluable in deciding all of these issues. If you and your partners do not have a clear understanding about such operational rights and responsibilities, you are headed for trouble. (Note that an unsigned or unwritten understanding is not illegal—it is just useless for most purposes.)

Various items should be included in an ordinary partnership agreement. Every such agreement should contain at least the following provisions:

- the name and address of the business
- the purpose of the partnership
- the date the partnership is to become effective and the date or events upon which it will expire
- the names and addresses of the partners
- the percentage interest of each partner in the assets of the partnership, and how profits and losses are to be shared
- the capital (money, services, supplies or equipment) each partner is contributing
- the salaries or rights to withdraw capital allowed to each partner
- the duties and authority of each partner in operating the business (especially the division of decision-making, the power to sign checks, to make loans, to buy goods, or to enter into contracts and leases)
- if and how a partner's interest can be transferred
- how and under what circumstances additional persons can become partners
- how partners can withdraw (and the right to continue the business should a partner withdraw)
- who is responsible for the preparation of financial statements

- how the partnership can be dissolved
- how any profits or surplus should be distributed upon dissolution
- whether the business is to continue should a partner die or become mentally incapacitated—as well as whether the legal representative of an incapacitated or deceased partner should have access to books and records of the firm

Partnerships don't last forever. Unless the partnership agreement provides otherwise, the partnership automatically ends if a partner dies, becomes bankrupt, or is no longer competent. If one of the partners wants to retire, or if another person wishes to join the partnership, the old agreement should be amended to reflect the consent of all the partners. When a partner retires, he usually remains liable to creditors for the debts of the partnership incurred prior to his retirement. The incoming partner is not liable unless he assumes such an obligation.

Liabilities of a dissolved partnership are distributed according to a prescribed order. When a partnership is formally dissolved, liabilities of the business are paid out of its assets in the order of those due:

- to creditors other than partners
- to partners for loans or other debts from the firm to them (a partner's capital investment is not considered a debt fitting into this category)
- to partners for their share of the capital investment and the profits

Limited Partnerships

A limited partner differs from a general or ordinary partner. Even a limited partnership requires at least one general partner, that is, one whose liability for the debts of the partnership is unlimited. The rest of the partners can be limited partners.

A limited partner is one whose liability for the debts incurred by the business is usually limited to the amount of his investment in the partnership. If the partnership agreement does not specify otherwise, a limited partner has no further obligation to the other partners or to creditors—unless funds were distributed to him at a time when they were needed to pay creditors.

Unlike a general partnership, a limited partnership can be created only if specifically allowed by state law. It may be formed only upon compliance with the laws of the state in which it is formed. Most states require filing with their department of taxation or other such agency a certificate that contains at least the following information:

- the name of the limited partnership
- the address of its principal office in the state and the name and address of its resident agent
- the name and the business, residence or mailing address of each general partner
- the latest date upon which the limited partnership is to dissolve

Of course, the document can contain any other matters the partners decide to include in the certificate. Some states require much more information, similar to that listed above with respect to general partnerships. Check with your state agency or a knowledgeable attorney as to the requirements.

Furthermore, although the certificate forms the entity, it does not necessarily describe all of the terms of the relationship among the partners. These terms are normally set out in a limited partnership agreement, which likewise contains much of the same type of information as for general partnerships.

Limited partners give up the right to manage the business or to exercise control over the limited partnership. Instead, these rights and duties are vested in the general partners. A limited partner who engages in the management or control of a limited partnership is likely to lose his limited-liability protections. The theory behind this rule is that a limited partner is merely a "silent" investor in the business and not an active participant. Limited partners may, however, vote on certain extraordinary matters affecting the limited partnership, such as mergers.

Corporations

A corporation is an artificial legal entity. It is created under the authority of state (or in some cases federal) law, and has the legal powers to do almost anything an individual or partnership can do, such as operate a business, lend and borrow money, own property, sue and be sued.

An individual can own a corporation. A business operated as a corporation can be formed and owned by a single person or many individuals or even other corporations or partnerships. The number of owners is irrelevant, since the law regards the corporation itself as having a personality and existence distinct from that of its shareholders. In fact, corporations are considered to have the attribute of *perpetual existence.* This means that a corporation continues forever, despite any changes in the people who own it. These individuals are known as the stockholders or shareholders because they have contributed capital (anything of value: money, property, or services) in exchange for shares of the corporation's stock.

Why incorporate? The great advantage to creating a corporation is that its owners (i.e., the stockholders) have no liability for debts and losses. The corporation itself is responsible for its financial status; it is considered separate and distinct from its owners. Although the owners may earn profits in proportion to the stock they own, their losses are limited to their investment—that is, the money and property they contributed in exchange for a share in the business. In contrast, those who operate a sole proprietorship or a general partnership are fully liable for the losses of the business extent of their assets including their personal property. Thus, a corporation is the most protective form of business. In addition, a corporation can provide a wide range of fringe benefits to its employees (including directors and executives), and deduct the cost as a business expense.

The tax consequences of incorporation are tricky. It is best to consult a lawyer or accountant concerning the corporation's tax liability.

Likewise, if you are interested in obtaining corporate financing by selling shares to outsiders, good professional advice can save you dollars, headaches, and possibly painful lawsuits.

Follow certain steps when incorporating by yourself. First choose a name that you like for your business. Then call the agency that handles incorporations in your state (see Appendix III) to make sure that your business name has not already been taken. Include the designation "Incorporated," "Inc." "Company," or "Co." to indicate your business's status as a corporation. ("Limited" is the British term and can generally be used in this country only as part of a trade name.) The law usually requires that this form of notice be given to those doing business with a corporation so that they know that its liability is limited, unlike a sole proprietorship or a partnership.

Then file for your certificate of incorporation. (Check Appendix III to find the agency in your state that handles incorporations and request that it send you model forms. You can also buy certificate-of-incorporation forms at most commercial stationers.) Make sure that your purpose clause is worded broadly enough for you to conduct the affairs of the business. Send the agency the completed certificate of incorporation, together with a check for the proper amount. After you receive notification of approval from the state, order a set of corporate records and a corporate seal from a commercial stationer. It may take a couple of weeks, but they are required by law. The simplest corporate-record set is a loose-leaf binder which contains stock certificates, a stock-transfer ledger in which the shareholders' names and addresses are recorded, pages to which you attach the filing receipt and a copy of the certificate of incorporation, and sample minutes of meetings and bylaws so that you can simply fill in the blanks. Every corporation must go through this paperwork; even if the company is completely owned by you, you must issue stock certificates to yourself, enter the issuance in the corporate record book, and place the certificates in a safe-deposit box.

Next, apply to the Internal Revenue Service for an employer identification number—you will not be able to open a corporate savings or checking account without it. The application for an employer identification number can take up to six weeks for IRS to process.

You will probably want to set up both a savings and a checking bank account once you have an employer identification number and a corporate seal, although neither account is required by law. Meetings *are* generally required by law; they are advisable in any event, if for no other reason than to periodically verify the existence of the business.

Finally, on the day that you begin your corporation, transfer the capital, assets, and liabilities of your business into your corporation. You can then begin your business (and bookkeeping) as a corporate entity.

"S" corporations are taxed in a manner similar to partnerships. Under Subchapter S of the Internal Revenue Code, stockholders in a small corporation can elect to have its profits taxed to them individually in the proportion of their percentage holdings in the corporation. This is desirable because it avoids double taxation— on both the corporation's profits and the amounts distributed to its shareholders. An S corporation can have up to thirty-five stockholders, all of whom must be individuals. Neither a partnership nor another corporation can be stockholder in an S corporation, which itself cannot have any subsidiaries.

All corporations must have certain officers. Every corporation must have directors, a president, a secretary, and a treasurer. The number of directors required varies from one jurisdiction to another, but all states have adopted the Model Business Corporation Act (which you should consult before setting up your corporation).

Remember to comply with related laws. Contact the IRS to assure yourself that the corporation is in compliance with laws related to workman's compensation and withholding taxes. To comply with minimum-wage laws, contact your state's department of licensing and regulation or the Department of Labor, which regulates federal minimum-wage laws.

CHAPTER THIRTEEN

Alternative Dispute Resolution

Discourage litigation. Persuade your neighbors to compromise whenever you can. . . . As a peace-maker the lawyer has a superior opportunity of being a good man. There will still be business enough.

—Abraham Lincoln, "Notes for Law Lecture"

For the most part lawyers are trained to be part of an adversarial process: instinctively, their first response to a dispute is to think in terms of initiating litigation by filing a complaint. Their goal is to win the case for the client.

Likewise, many non-lawyers think that the way to solve problems is by bringing suit. America is easily the most litigious country in the world, and its civil courts are clogged to the point that cases are sometimes postponed for months and years. But even when one party has been clearly wronged, his best remedy may not be litigation. Not only is it time-consuming to bring suit, it can be very expensive as well.

The logic of lawyering does not always dictate going to court. There are numerous extra-judicial remedies available, most of them involving a third-party intermediary. Such solutions are especially appropriate when both sides have good factual arguments to support their positions. The parties may choose to avoid the time and expense of litigation by submitting to conciliation, negotiation, mediation, arbitration, or a combination of those processes—in which lawyers can (though they don't necessarily have to) play the roles of advocates.

Alternative methods of dispute resolution are easy to understand.
Conciliation is simply a sincere attempt by two parties to a dispute to resolve their differences amicably, without resorting to lawyers or courts or third-party mediators. Once the parties vent their grievances face to face, the problem can sometimes be resolved quickly and to their mutual satisfaction; adjudication will firmly favor one side over the other, but it can often leave the parties bitter and unreconciled.

The parties may *negotiate* the terms of a settlement, either directly or through their lawyers. Usually (but not always) negotiation is initiated by the defendant, who generally has the most to lose in money damages—particularly if his misconduct has been intentional or clearly negligent. The plaintiff may welcome a fair settlement in order to avoid protracted litigation.

Mediation is the most common form of alternative dispute resolution. It requires an independent mediator acceptable to both parties, who meets with them in a non-adversarial setting and attempts to formulate an agreement between them. The goal is a fairly balanced compromise. Nothing is binding on either side unless they both agree, at which time the compromise takes the form of a contract.

Arbitration is binding mediation. That is, the parties mutually agree upon an independent arbitrator to hear their case and render an opinion. Arbitration clauses are often placed in employment contracts and other commercial agreements; under them the parties agree in advance that should any dispute arise over the contract, it will be resolved by way of arbitration rather than court adjudication.

Newer dispute-resolution processes involve variations or combinations of those mentioned above, such as "med-arb" (if the mediation fails, it will trigger arbitration); "rent-a-judge" (the parties hire a retired jurist to hear the facts and render a decision); and "mini-trials" or "summary jury trials" (a jury hears the facts, usually presented by a lawyer, and arrives at a nonbinding verdict).

Negotiation

Negotiation is a bargaining process by which the parties attempt to reach agreement about a current or potential dispute. Whether the goal is to open or close a transaction or to sever or cement a relationship, many people—particularly those in business or real estate—instinctively negotiate without the benefit of a lawyer. Lawyers are sometimes trained in negotiation skills, but usually bargain from an adversarial posture.

Negotiation is at the foundation of many alternative dispute resolution processes. It need not be simply intuitive, however: how to bargain, develop strategies, and close deals can be learned by the layperson.

The great majority of all civil and criminal cases are settled through negotiation. Most lawsuits never get decided in court. Lawyers and judges alike recognize the importance of relieving clogged dockets by way of settling civil cases and plea-bargaining criminal ones. The time and expense involved in trying a case are often disincentives for clients. Moreover, most lawyers will tell you that a far greater percentage of their cases are settled than are tried.

Negotiations are used to close transactions or settle disputes. "Transactional negotiation" brings the parties together to plan for a future event, such as drafting a contract or lease or licensing a copyrighted work. The issues are generally resolved by the parties themselves, sometimes with the help of their attorneys. "Dispute negotiation" usually involves the resolution of a problem that has already occurred, such as a broken contract, an infringed patent, or a personal injury. The issues are often more easily resolved through the intervention of someone else who may help discover facts and identify issues; when the parties themselves cannot reach agreement, the intervenor can be asked to mediate the dispute.

The negotiators can take an adversarial or problem-solving approach. Before alternative dispute resolution processes came into vogue in the 1970s, most negotiation was adversarial. Nowadays there is a growing recognition that "principled negotiation" or a "problem-solving" approach may be more efficient and satisfactory.

The primary goal of the adversarial negotiator is to maximize individual gain. A particular position is adopted, and all discussion centers on how to come closest to achieving that goal. The adversarial negotiator may be either competitive or cooperative. Competitive negotiators make high opening demands and allow few concessions; their goal is to maximize their (or their clients') profits (or fees) and to outmaneuver their opponents; they are often perceived as aggressive, arrogant, tough, and threatening. Cooperative negotiators also have their own (or their clients') best interests at heart, but seek to achieve them by way of establishing and maintaining a good personal relationship with their opponents.

A problem-solving negotiation focuses on opportunities for joint gains. The negotiator perceives the transaction or dispute as a mutual problem that can be best resolved when the parties are mutually satisfied. The goal is for both parties to win. At some point in all negotiations, the parties recognize that the resources to be divided between them must be fixed. The problem-solving negotiator attempts to bring about that recognition at an early stage, to balance the power between the competing parties, and to achieve an agreement that is mutually satisfying.

It's always a good idea to plan ahead when you are negotiating. You don't necessarily have to know what the result of the negotiation will be, or even what your "bottom line" is, but you must be prepared to deal with the other party's proposals as they are made.

Planning ahead can be done by way of a simple checklist:

- Learn all of the underlying facts in the dispute
- Ascertain the strongest and weakest points of your case
- Determine your goals
- Decide upon an initial bargaining strategy, including what information you are willing to give the opposing party at the outset
- If possible, plan to be flexible

Listening is an important skill to master. Lawyers often interrupt by making legal arguments. The most successful negotiators (lawyers or others) are able to resist this urge.

Even passive listening—looking the talker in the eyes but not saying anything—can be very effective in convincing the other party that you take his position seriously. Active participation in the discussion—for example, by summarizing positions once the opposing party has stopped talking—can also be a useful technique.

Concessions are an integral part of the negotiating process. It is important not to reveal ultimate positions at the outset, but to reserve them until you see where the opposing party is headed. Thereby you can offer concessions in good faith.

Of course, it is equally important to be truthful. Although candor may seem antithetical to the competitive negotiator, you can be truthful without necessarily disclosing your ultimate bargaining position. Deliberate lying about factual matters, on the other hand, may give rise to a charge of fraudulent misrepresentation if the other party relies upon the misstatement.

Mediation

Mediation is an extension of the negotiation process. Disputing parties who have been unable to reach an agreement make use of a neutral third party (the mediator) to assist them. Mediation is not a new technique. In many cultures it remains the dominant mechanism for resolving disputes—having to resort to a court is viewed as a shameful last resort. In the United States mediation has been used for more than a century, ever since the beginning of governmental intervention in railway labor disputes.

The advantages of mediation are clear. The mediation process saves time, money, and energy. Besides being procedurally simpler than having a case adjudicated, mediation is private—an important consideration for parties who do not want to undergo the intense scrutiny that a public trial often entails. Moreover, mediation need not be viewed as a last resort; it is not binding on the parties unless they wish to make it so.

Certain types of cases naturally lend themselves to mediation. The parties themselves may be neighbors, friends, or relatives and thus predisposed to settle. Or they may have mutual business goals. Or the dispute may appear to be a short-term one (like the time of day that blasting at a building site will continue). As in other cases, the legal outcome of a case may be highly uncertain, and the parties might not want to risk a lengthy and public trial. Mediation is particularly effective in resolving disputes arising out of divorce, which involve complex issues of property distribution, child support, alimony, and custody.

The mediator's role may be easily defined. The mediator first reviews the case to determine if it can be resolved by way of an out-of-court mediation—or if the parties and their positions are so firmly entrenched that mediation will likely be a waste of everyone's time.

Once mediation has begun, the mediator explains the process to the parties, encourages them to air their grievances and exchange information in good faith—with a minimum of open hostility. The mediator assists them in bargaining fairly: helping to frame the issues, isolate points of agreement and disagreement, generate options, and suggest compromises.

If an accord is reached—and a surprisingly high number of mediations are successful—the mediator assists the parties in drafting an agreement which often takes the form of a written contract.

Disputes between neighbors are common. Neighbors often have disagreements over trees, boundaries, easements, and noise. Try contacting your neighborhood association, which should have knowledge of relevant ordinances or codes and probably a means for sending a polite letter to the offending party.

In addition, many communities have free neighborhood mediation centers; lists of such centers are often available from the local libraries, police station, or courthouse.

Mediators often meet with the partners separately. These meetings are called "caucuses." The mediator will attempt to ascertain how far the parties will go in order to compromise their differences, underscoring the idea that by submitting to mediation they have implicitly agreed to a give-and-take process.

Everything said at a mediation is confidential. The mediator cannot be ordered to testify at a subsequent trial about what transpired during an unsuccessful mediation. Nor should the mediator disclose to the other party what he has learned at a caucus without permission to do so.

Arbitration

Arbitration is the most formal of the alternative dispute resolution processes. It involves the appointment of a neutral third party to hear the evidence and render a decision, which both parties agree will be binding on them.

Like mediation, there is nothing new about arbitration as a means of solving disputes—particularly in the context of organized labor.

There are many advantages to arbitration. It is generally considered more efficient, much quicker, and less expensive than litigation. Arbitration also offers greater flexibility in the choice of a neutral third party, as well as in procedure and the production of evidence. Arbitrators themselves usually have more expertise in specific areas (e.g., construction contracts) than do judges. They also have more latitude in rendering decisions, because in some situations they are not bound by prior cases—and are often not even required to give reasons in support of their awards.

Traditional arbitration is a voluntary process. Either before or after a dispute arises, the parties can agree to substitute arbitration for formal judicial proceedings. Most often arbitration clauses are written into labor contracts, in recognition that employment disputes are inevitable and should be anticipated. They are also very common in contracts between stockbrokers and their customers.

Certain types of arbitrations are compulsory. These include public-sector, court-annexed, and medical-malpractice arbitration in some states. To prevent strikes by critical employees—such as policemen, firefighters, teachers—a majority of states have enacted legislation requiring compulsory arbitration as the final step in negotiating the terms of collective bargaining agreements.

A growing number of jurisdictions have adopted court-annexed arbitration systems to reduce the delay and expense associated with civil litigation. Like mediation, court-annexed arbitration is particularly popular in resolving domestic disputes, such as child custody and property settlements. In some states such arbitration is mandatory, in others it is optional; where it is mandatory, the parties often have the right of appeal if they disagree with the arbitrator's decision.

Similarly, the rising costs of medical malpractice suits has spawned legislation requiring compulsory arbitration of such disputes. Some states compel "mandatory nonbinding arbitration" (which in truth is mediation) as a prerequisite to bringing a case to court. Other states provide for voluntary but binding arbitration clauses which patients sign before they submit to treatment.

Arbitrators are selected by the parties. Usually one arbitrator is chosen, although it is not uncommon to have a panel of three— two of whom would be chosen by the parties and the third appointed by the first two chosen. The qualities to look for in an arbitrator are honesty, integrity, impartiality, and expertise in the subject matter in dispute.

The arbitration hearing is similar in many respects to a trial. Although the forms differ from state to state, both parties generally make opening statements and present their case to the neutral third party. Witnesses may be called and evidence introduced. The parties often make closing statements.

The arbitration process differs from litigation in several ways. Ordinarily the fact-finding process is less formal, and the record of the proceedings may not be as complete. Likewise, the rights of discovery and cross-examination are often more limited than they would be in a trial. And the arbitrator is not required to provide detailed reasons for his decision.

Arbitrators sometimes act under special formulas. In personal-injury cases, for example, "high-low-binding" arbitration is popular with both plaintiffs' attorneys and insurance companies. Plaintiff and defendant agree to arbitrate as follows: each party sets the dollar figure it wants, without telling the arbitrator; arguments and evidence are presented; the arbitrator decides what he thinks is fair and equitable. If the arbitrator's figure is lower than that set by the defendant, the latter becomes the award; if higher than that set by the plaintiff, likewise.

The so-called "baseball formula" is patterned after player-management arbitrations under major-league baseball rules. Each side presents the arbitrator with a dollar figure and arguments on its behalf. The arbitrator decides in favor of one party or the other, and is bound by either figure chosen; he cannot make any other award.

Arbitration awards cannot usually be appealed. Courts will generally not review arbitration awards even when errors of fact or law have been made. An arbitration award can be vacated, however, if it was procured by corruption or fraud; if the arbitrator was guilty of misconduct (such as a clear conflict of interest); or if the arbitrator exceeded his power or failed to make a final and definite disposition of the case.

Other Processes

New alternative dispute resolution processes have been developed over the past several years. They include the summary jury trial, private judging, the mini-trial, and a hybrid called "med-arb."

The summary jury trial facilitates settlements. The summary jury trial is a process by which lawyers present a brief synopsis of their cases to a jury, which then renders a nonbinding advisory decision. Lawyers and their clients are thus given an advance assessment of what a jury might do if the dispute were submitted to full-scale litigation. After participating in a summary jury trial, the parties try to reach an agreement, which in turn is reduced to writing.

Retired judges are often hired to hear cases. This process is commonly known as "Rent-a-Judge." It is similar to an arbitration, but the parties have a great deal of flexibility in creating their own ground rules for decision-making.

The mini-trial is a structured settlement process. It blends various components of negotiation, mediation, and the adversarial techniques common to traditional litigation. A neutral adviser usually presides. Counsel for each side makes an abbreviated presentation of his client's best case before senior management executives on the other side who have full settlement authority. Following the hearing, they make a recommendation as to settlement. The process is private and voluntary.

"Med-arb" is a combination of mediation and arbitration. The disputing parties agree to undergo mediation and, if that process does not yield a positive outcome, to have the dispute submitted for binding arbitration. The same neutral third party serves as both mediator and arbitrator. This is considered a more efficient process than a mediation followed by an arbitration before a different person, because the intermediary need not be retold the stories and arguments of either side.

CHAPTER FOURTEEN

Small Claims

The good have no need of an advocate.
—Plutarch, *Lives*

If you have suffered a personal injury or property loss because of the negligent or intentional acts of someone else, you deserve to have your grievance redressed. Unreasonable people may refuse to submit the dispute to mediation. But even among reasonable people, differences occur every day that are often over relatively minor matters. Many of them can be resolved in small-claims courts, sometimes called people's court or district court—see Appendix V—where lawyers are not only unnecessary but frequently unwelcome.

Cases Handled by a Small-Claims Court

Many different kinds of cases are brought before a small-claims court. The most common suits are those compelling people to pay money agreed to in a contract (including separation agreements and promissory notes) and getting compensation for services performed. Others include suing a landlord for the return of a security deposit (or tenants for rent due and damages); seeking compensation for defective merchandise and any resulting damages; bringing an insurance company to court when it fails to pay for claims on homeowner, medical, or automobile policies; suing someone who performed poor or unnecessary repair services; asking a court for property damage in automobile-accident cases; bringing an action against municipalities and their agencies; asking compensation for intentional damage done to you or your property; or trying to recover missing goods that were entrusted to someone else.

Some of these disputes (like separation agreements and landlord-tenant cases) may be handled exclusively by special courts (like divorce or housing courts) in large jurisdictions.

Not all small-claims courts are the same. There are variations from state to state, as well as within a particular state. But all have relatively informal procedures. Lawyers are usually permitted, but most small claimants represent themselves.

Certain types of cases must be filed in other courts. In general, you can't go to small-claims court when you want to obtain a divorce, an adoption, a division of property, or a court order against illegal conduct. Some states have special courts which handle all landlord-tenant disputes. But if all you want is to be compensated for losses caused by another person, and you are unable to reach or unwilling to mediate a settlement, small-claims court is the right place to go.

The maximum amount you can hope to win in small-claims court varies from state to state. If the amount you wish to recover is in excess of the small-claims limit, you have two choices: you may sue for the maximum amount allowed by the small-claims court and forgo the balance of your claim, or you may sue for the full amount in a higher court where the jurisdictional limit is greater. Because the services of an attorney are practically mandatory when suing in a higher court, in many cases it is wiser to sue for the maximum amount possible in the small-claims court and save the fee you would otherwise pay an attorney. You should check with the clerk of your local small-claims court as to the current applicable limitations. The jurisdictional limits are often revised (usually upward) by state legislatures. (See Appendix V.)

Courts will generally not let you split claims by dividing a lawsuit in order to avoid the jurisdictional limitation. "Forum shopping"—picking the court most likely to be favorable—is also frowned upon. States usually demand that the person being sued either reside or do business where the small-claims court is located, or that the events which gave rise to the suit occurred in that jurisdiction. The general rule is that you can sue a defendant in the county where he resides or where he is maintaining a place of business, and in most states you can sue in the county where the injury or property loss occurred. In many states you can also sue a defendant wherever he was supposed to have carried out an agreement with you. The rules regarding where to sue a given defendant likewise vary from state to state. The best way to ascertain the local rules is to contact the clerk of your nearest small-claims court, describe whom you intend to sue and over what, and ask where you may file an action.

Most small-claims courts do not have jury trials. Some state and federal laws permit jury trials if claims are in excess of $500. That means if you (or your opponent) want a jury trial, you may have to file in a different court.

Use common sense in deciding whether your complaint is serious enough to take to court. Virtually any grievance that can be resolved by money damages can be addressed by a small-claims court, but a judge will not take kindly to what he considers a frivolous complaint. Use your best judgment. If you feel your problem is genuine and treat it seriously, you're likely to get a fair hearing.

In some states a corporation cannot sue in a small-claims action. The theory is that if a business receives the advantages of being incorporated, including limited liability in certain matters, it should not be permitted to use a simplified procedure to collect small claims. On the other hand, corporations can be sued as defendants: once sued, they may be allowed to bring a counterclaim against the plaintiff (even if they ask for more than in the original suit), and in some places they can even seek more money than the small-claims limit.

There are several disadvantages to suing in a small-claims court. The major drawback is the jurisdictional limitation on the amount you can recover. Also, in most jurisdictions once you file a small claim you waive any right you may have had to a jury trial. Finally, appeals from the judge's decision in a small-claims case are somewhat restricted (and generally unsuccessful). Practically speaking, your only day in court is at the time of the original hearing.

Settlements

Don't file a small claim before trying to work out a settlement with your opponent. On the other hand, one should always be wary of the defendant who tries to avoid liability by pretending to be engaged in good-faith negotiations, while in fact he is trying to divert the potential plaintiff from filing his claim until after the statutory limitations period has run out.

Even if mediation has failed, it is often wise to precede the filing of even a small-claims suit with a well-thought-out, neatly typed settlement letter sent to your adversary. The letter should be civil, polite, and to the point—not sarcastic or antagonistic. It should state your grievance (that is, the factual situation and the monetary losses you have suffered), demand compensation, and say that you are prepared to sue for damages if you don't receive satisfaction within a specified time. The letter may intimidate its recipient to the point of negotiation, but even if it doesn't, it serves two other important functions. First, it satisfies the requirement of some states that a person make a demand upon his adversary for payment prior to filing a small-claims case against him. Second, the letter may be useful as evidence in the small-claims court, where it should serve as a summary of your case to which the judge can refer when he or she is tying together the pieces of your claim. An appropriate deadline for response is generally two weeks. Keep at least two exact copies of the letter you sent—one for use in court and one for your personal file.

Send the letter by registered mail, return receipt requested. This method will provide you a post office slip to offer as evidence to the court that you made a mailing to your adversary on a specific date, as well as the further evidence of a return postcard to prove your opponent received the envelope.

Once your suit is filed in the small-claims court, keep in mind that a settlement is still possible. If the logic of your settlement letter or the actual notice that he is being sued belatedly puts your adversary into a negotiating mood, it still shouldn't hurt to explain your position and suggest an offer of settlement. If your opponent merely rants and raves, you might try interrupting him calmly by saying he should call you back when he has regained his composure.

It is a good negotiating technique to assure your adversary you'll give serious consideration to whatever he decides is his best offer.

Put any offer that is made and accepted into writing, signed by both parties. Never settle for an oral agreement. Once a written agreement is signed, you have a binding contract which itself can be enforced in court should your adversary later try to renege on any part of his obligations.

If you are able to settle the dispute prior to trial, you should notify the court clerk that neither you nor your opponent will be appearing before the court on the day scheduled for your trial.

If you decide to accept your opponent's offer on the day of trial, both of you should appear before the judge when your case is called. Inform the court clerk or the judge that a settlement has been reached. Request the judge to enter judgment in your favor for the amount that was agreed upon.

If the defendant is prepared to pay you right there in court, the judge can dismiss your case. The advantage to both parties appearing in court and reporting the settlement to the judge is that if either of you later reneges, the matter can be either rescheduled without filing a new claim, or an automatic judgment may be granted against the party not adhering to the settlement.

Filing a Claim

Sue promptly upon realizing that your grievance cannot be resolved out of court. Most states have a two-year statute of limitations for the kinds of claims appropriate to a small-claims court, but some have an even shorter period. The statute of limitations is often longer for contract actions.

If you fail to bring suit within the statutory period, the defendant can escape an otherwise valid claim for damages. Since the periods of statutory limitations vary from state to state and differ according to the type of claim you are asserting, you should always check as to the limitation that applies to your case.

Once your claim is filed, most states require that your suit be heard between thirty and ninety days from the time papers are served. This is in stark contrast with the normal civil case, which often takes years before the parties reach court.

It is not difficult to file a claim. The telephone number of your small-claims court should be listed in the phone book. (If you get stuck, try dialing Information.) Ask where the court is located, the hours and days you can file a claim, the cost of doing so, and whether the filing fee should be in cash or by check. Ask if any documents need be produced at the hearing. You will probably be told to bring any applicable contracts, letters, canceled checks, promissory notes, leases, accident reports, as well as any estimates of damage or repair you may have in your possession. Make sure to keep copies if you give any original papers to the clerk.

You must be able to supply certain information about your opponent. The full legal name of the person or corporation that you are suing must be entered. When suing a married woman, use her full name and not the name of her husband (i.e., "Mary Smith" rather than "Mrs. John Smith"). Avoid initials.

Most states require that a business be sued under its proper legal name. (New York is more flexible, allowing a defendant to be sued under either its legal name or the name it uses to conduct business.) Finding out the correct legal name of a business might take some investigation, including a few phone calls to local and state governmental offices. Remember that the business name printed on a sign, bill, or letterhead is not necessarily the correct legal name of the entity you intend to sue. You might try phoning or visiting the municipal or county clerk's office in the area where the defendant does business, since corporations operating under an assumed name usually are required by law to file a certificate of their true identity. Likewise, if the business must be licensed (a requirement for many), it usually must apply for one under its legal name: try contacting the appropriate licensing board. Another source of information is the state and local business-tax offices (where companies must register and file their tax returns). Note also that corporations doing business in a state usually must register their legal name with a special state office, generally the secretary of state.

If the business is a sole proprietorship or partnership, you should bring suit against the names of the individuals "doing business as" the name of the company (for example, Mary Smith and Jane Jones doing business as "Ms. Prints"). Suing under the name of either the individuals alone or of the business alone is not sufficient. If the business is a corporation, however, it can be sued under the name of the corporation only—not the individuals who own or run it.

You must also determine the proper legal address of the person or company you are suing so that you can send the required notice to the defendant. The address should be as complete as possible, including the zip code.

Assemble all the relevant documents before visiting the small-claims clerk. In addition, try to prepare a brief summary of why you believe the defendant owes you money. Has there been a breach of contract? Negligence? Defective merchandise? Failure to perform a service properly? Bring with you the defendant's correct legal name and complete address. And don't forget the money to pay the filing fee.

Small-claims clerks are supposed to be helpful. Most are. Either you or the clerk will fill out a form which includes the type of suit being filed, the proper legal names of all the parties and their full addresses, the amount of money claimed, and a brief explanation of why you think the defendant owes you something.

After you sign and date the form and pay the filing fee, the clerk will give you a receipt. This should include the name of the case, a docket number, and the date of the scheduled court appearance. Be sure to keep this document, since you may have to present it or refer to it when you appear in court.

You shouldn't be offended if the clerk suggests that you don't have a valid claim or points out some weakness in your case. She knows how the system works and is simply attempting to be helpful by keeping you from wasting your time. On the other hand, clerks sometimes underestimate the strength of a claimant's case. Note that although small-claims court clerks may be helpful, they cannot be sued if they err in giving you information. If you want to double-check a clerk's advice, ask him for the book in which the law is contained.

It doesn't cost much to sue in a small-claims court. Filing fees generally range from two to ten dollars, plus the cost of serving notice upon the person against whom a claim is brought. If the court finds in your favor, it may order the defendant to pay these costs as part of the damage award.

The court itself notifies your opponent. After you file your claim, a notice will be sent by the clerk to the defendant telling him that he is being sued, the amount of damage being claimed, and the date and place of the trial. Notice is usually sent by one of three methods: (1) registered mail with return receipt (the most common method); (2) personal service by a sheriff, marshal, or other authorized person (which can cost as much as $20); or (3) first-class mail. Registered mail with return receipt is preferred over first-class mail because it gives proof (the receipt) that the defendant has been notified. Even if he refuses to pick up his registered mail at the post office, the process is still considered by most courts to be sufficient service—so that if she doesn't appear in court, the judge will hear your case and can enter a judgment in your favor.

Beware of "sovereign immunity." This legal doctrine protects the state or federal government from being sued. It is usually necessary to consult with an attorney before suing either a federal or state agency.

On the other hand, your local government is often subject to the same kinds of claims as are individuals and corporations. An exception is a negligence action, for which a notice-of-claim form—which should be available from the government agency you wish to sue—must be filed first, often within a short time frame.

If you don't file the notice, you can't file a lawsuit. The usual time period in which the claim notice must be filed is from sixty to ninety days from the event which led to your suit, but it can be as little as three days in some jurisdictions to a hundred and twenty in others.

The purpose of such notice is to allow the municipal body to investigate the validity of your claim before a lawsuit is begun. The notice of claim states your name, address, the time and place of the event in question, and the damages you have suffered. It must usually be sworn to before a notary public.

The claim notice can be personally served upon a designated agent for the governmental body, or sent by registered or certified mail.

If you are filing a claim against a town, you may generally serve the town clerk; if against a city, the city clerk; if against the local school district, you usually have a choice of serving any member of the school board or the secretary of the board.

Don't be shy about asking questions; governments today are so used to being sued they are no longer insulted by such inquiries.

You do not have to wait for the bureaucracy to act on your claim. Even if the public official has assured you that your claim will be paid, the statute of limitations may begin to run from the moment the event which is the focus of the suit actually occurred. Unless there is a mandatory waiting period, once you have filed the required notice of claim you can proceed directly to the small-claims court. Bring proof with you that you have already forwarded a notice of claim to the local governmental body. (Have the person receiving it sign on your copy.) Then file your claim with the small-claims clerk just as you would as if it were an ordinary case.

If you are injured by someone's employee, sue both. If the person who causes your injury did so while acting as an employee of someone else, you should sue both the employee and his employer. Under the legal doctrine of *respondeat superior* (Latin for "let the master answer"), an employer is ordinarily liable for legal wrongs committed by his employees within the scope of their employment. But you should sue the employee as well, in case the judge finds that the employee was not acting within the scope of his employment when the injury occurred. Of course, you will be allowed only one recovery of damages.

There are different ways to determine how much to sue for. The law has developed several methods by which damages can be measured, depending on the facts involved. In a breach-of-contract case, for example, you are entitled to be "made whole again"— that is, to be put in as good a position as you would have occupied if the defendant had performed his obligations rather than breaching his contract with you. The person suing must be prepared to show that he made reasonable efforts to keep his losses at a minimum (such as trying to re-rent an apartment that has been vacated).

In cases involving property damages resulting from the intentional or negligent acts of another, the general measure of damages is the fair market value of your property just before the accident, or the amount of money it would take to restore it to the condition it was in just before the incident occurred—whichever sum is lower.

The measure of damages in a personal injury case (when you are hurt as a result of either the intentional or the negligent acts of another) is less black and white. Assuming you can prove that the person being sued is legally responsible for your injuries, you may claim damages for the following: present and future medical bills and lost wages; pain and suffering; mental distress; and, in a defamation case, the injury to your reputation. But putting a dollar value on the latter items is subjective, and if you were severely hurt, your recovery is likely to be far in excess of the small-claims limit.

Finally, in some consumer-protection cases you may be allowed by law to collect statutory penalties—amounts over and above your true losses. This is the only time a plaintiff might expect to wind up in a better position than had he not been injured.

The general rule is that you cannot recover punitive damages—those designed to "teach a lesson" to the guilty party—in a small-claims action. There are, of course, exceptions to this rule.

Separation Agreements

You can use a small-claims action to enforce a domestic separation agreement. The key to bringing an action in a small-claims court in order to enforce a separation agreement is to make certain that the overdue amount does not exceed the jurisdictional limits for that court. Therefore you might consider a small-claims action even when your spouse is only a few weeks late in making the agreed-upon payments.

Note that a small-claims court can enforce the terms of an agreement or a contract, but not an order of a higher court. Thus if there was no separation agreement—that is, if the terms of a divorce decree were dictated by a judge at trial—they may be enforced only by the court that awarded the decree. (See Chapter 6 for information about court-awarded decrees.)

It's a good idea to copy the appropriate section of the agreement, highlighting the clause specifying payment, and bring it to court. Also bring a copy of the entire original agreement in case the judge wishes to examine the signatures. In addition, prepare a list of payments made and their dates (typed, if possible), together with an indication of the payments missed.

Try to handle the matter as a simple breach-of-contract case, avoiding all discussion of the misbehavior and character flaws of your spouse that you may think led to the breakup of the marriage or the nonpayment of money due. The small-claims judge is likely to be grateful to any party taking "the high road" in a domestic-relations matter.

Preparing for Your Day in Court

Know your case and organize the evidence. By the time you have talked with the small-claims clerk and filled out a claim form, you should already have a good idea of the facts you'll be expected to prove to persuade the judge to rule in your favor. It is wise to scrutinize even the most meritorious case for fatal flaws—such as a signed release allowing the defendant to act as she did—before going through the effort to initiate a small-claims suit.

The next step is to organize the relevant documents and request any important witnesses to come to court on the day of your trial. Remember that the judge will likely be influenced less by the number of witnesses than those who actually observed or know something relevant to your case. In some jurisdictions you can present statements of witnesses without asking them to appear personally in court. Check with the clerk to see if a statement would be satisfactory. Certain written statements, such as those concerning repair estimates, are usually permitted although courts have different rules regarding repair estimates and their accompanying affidavits.

Most often, testimony from an absent witness (known as "hearsay") is not accepted, because she cannot be cross-examined by the other party.

If you want a particular witness in court but that person will not appear voluntarily, you may ask the clerk to issue a subpoena—a court order requiring a witness to appear at the time a case is heard. You may have to arrange to have the subpoena properly served and pay certain mileage costs and a witness fee to the person you subpoena. Perhaps the most important question to ask yourself before requesting the issuance of a subpoena, however, is whether the testimony of a witness who has been dragged into the courtroom against his or her will is really going to be helpful to your case.

If you need papers or records in the possession of your opponent, you may ask the clerk to issue a *subpoena duces tecum*. This document will require that the person who has custody of the papers deliver them to the court before you present your case.

Be patient. The waiting period between filing and trial can vary from two weeks to four months. And once the actual trial date comes, you will almost certainly have to wait for your hearing to take place until other cases have been cleared.

If you believe that physical or demonstrative evidence will simplify or clarify your claim, prepare appropriate charts or diagrams. In cases involving defective merchandise or similar physical evidence, bring the articles into the courtroom whenever possible. Photographs can also be helpful—although pictures that need an extensive explanation, however, are often worthless.

Familiarize yourself with the courtroom procedures. You might want to visit a small-claims court before your trial date to get an idea of how "rough justice" is meted out in the "people's court."

What to Do and Say in Court

Look forward to informality. It is a good idea to arrive early. Dress in something neat, presentable, and comfortable. In addition to the court stenographer, clerk, and various attendants, expect to see many other people waiting to have their cases heard. The stenographer records everything that is said on the record. A number of courts now use tape machines instead of stenographers. The clerk is there to assist you and the judge in handling the evidence and making the proper entries into court files. Attendants serve as ushers and sergeants-at-arms.

When the judge enters, the clerk or bailiff will say something like, "All rise!" Everyone stands until the judge is seated.

The docket of cases is then called to determine which parties are present. Listen carefully for your name to be called. When the clerk announces your case, walk up to the bench together with your witnesses, if any. The clerk will swear you in by administering an oath (or demand that you affirm to tell the truth), and the trial will begin.

Your opponent may not appear. If your opponent fails to appear after having been properly served, the judge may ask you to establish a *prima facie* case. This means that you have to give the judge enough evidence proving your case that he or she will be justified in granting an award. If damages are legally recoverable, you may be awarded a default judgment. The judgment should also include the court costs you have paid. Once you are granted a default judgment, contact the clerk for advice on how to collect. Some attorneys specialize in collection cases.

If the reason your opponent failed to appear was that he was never served a summons, you will have to come back on another court date after he is properly served. Many debtors are experts at avoiding service. Make arrangements with the clerk for another attempt at serving notice.

The claimant speaks first. If the defendant is present, you will be asked by the judge to present your claim. Try to be calm, brief, and courteous. Outline to the court how your case arose and why you believe your opponent owes you a specific sum of money. If there was a settlement letter, offer it into evidence—along with the original of any other documents or physical evidence you have prepared. If you have any estimates, bills, letters, or other documents for the court to view, make sure to have copies available for yourself and your opponent.

You may ask your witnesses, if any, to testify on your behalf. If the judge asks any questions, answer them as directly as possible, addressing him as "Your Honor." Try to anticipate your opponent's case. For example, even if a defendant would otherwise be held legally responsible for your loss, he may avoid liability if he can show that the statute of limitations has run out on your claim (that is, you've waited too long to assert your grievance), or that you signed a release or waiver allowing him to act as he did.

Allow your opponent to speak without interruption. Generally, the time for asking questions is *after* your opponent has completed his presentation. The best idea is to look to the judge for direction in this matter, since each court conducts the hearing differently.

The importance of being polite to both the judge and your opponent cannot be overemphasized. Failing to be courteous harms your case by distracting the judge and impairing your effectiveness and credibility. It is also important to avoid trying to act like a lawyer during a small-claims court proceeding; using legalese will probably backfire. Finally, don't overextend your welcome: expect your presentation to be completed in less than fifteen minutes. If you are still talking and the judge asks you to wrap up, do so quickly for maximum effectiveness.

The hearing will not last long. Usually a small-claims hearing does not take longer than twenty minutes. After the judge has heard both sides, he may render a decision immediately and attempt to work out a payment schedule. Or she may decide to reserve judgment—to think about the facts or to research the law. If this happens, you will generally be notified of the result within a few days.

Collecting Judgments

The defendant may not pay immediately. After you receive word of the judgment, you should contact the losing party—preferably by mail—and ask for payment within ten days. This should not be the defendant's first notification, since he was informed of the decision by the court at the same time you were. If he chooses to pay the sum of the judgment directly to the court, the clerk will accept a check and place it in the court account; you will be paid once the check has cleared. If the defendant pays the judgment directly to you, you should advise the clerk of that fact. You should also inform any other place where you have filed a judgment that the amount has been paid in full. This is called "filing a satisfaction." Your failure to do so may unjustifiably affect the defendant's credit record. In some states, failure to file a satisfaction upon demand is a violation of the law.

If your adversary does not voluntarily pay the amount awarded, you must pursue a specific course of action. You will have to avail yourself of the local remedies associated with your status as a *judgment creditor*. You may have to do some detective work to find out the nature and location of the defendant's assets before returning to the small-claims court to obtain a court order known as a *writ of execution*. If possible, discover where the defendant works, banks, runs a business, or owns real estate or personal property. Note that if your judgment is against the defendant alone, any property owned by both a defendant and his spouse as tenants by the entirety is generally "judgment-proof." Practically speaking, any jointly owned property is difficult to seize. Sheriffs most often go after wages and bank accounts, although even the latter are hard to get at if jointly titled.

Once you ascertain the defendant's assets, return to the small-claims court. The clerk will send you to the enforcement officer who deals with civil awards and court orders—usually called a "sheriff," "marshal," or "constable." Tell him what you've discovered about the defendant's assets. The officer will obtain from the clerk a document called an execution of judgment, and attempt to notify the respondent that he must pay the judgment. If the payment is still not forthcoming, the officer may seize assets, tie up bank accounts, attach personal property, or garnish the wages of the respondent. Generally up to ten percent of the gross wages earned is subject to garnishment. If the respondent is self-employed, the court may issue an installment-payment order for a certain amount to be paid each week to the court officer.

If the respondent has real property such as land, a home, or a building, you should file the judgment in the county clerk's office or with the property registrar where it is located. The judgment will then serve as a lien against the real property—that is, the property cannot be sold or otherwise transferred until the judgment is paid in full. If a judgment is not paid promptly, interest from the date of the award to the time of payment is added.

Collection procedures differ from state to state. Some states are more helpful than others in small-claims matters. New Yorkers, for example, are given some special legal ammunition for collecting judgments from slow-paying businesses. If a business has not paid a judgment within thirty-five days after being notified by the court, the plaintiff will be entitled to sue the business all over again—but this time the amount of damages will be for the amount of the original unpaid judgment plus reasonable attorney's fees plus a statutory penalty of $100. New York law also provides for treble damage awards (three times actual damages) against businesses that have not paid three small-claims court judgments.

If all else fails, contact a collection attorney. Some lawyers specialize in collecting bad debts, and have refined their techniques to the point that they can be considerably more productive than a layperson—even after their fees have been deducted.

CHAPTER FIFTEEN

Traffic Violations

Back to thy punishment, false fugitive,
And to thy speed add wings.
—Milton, *Paradise Lost*

For most Americans, contesting a ticket in traffic court is not only their first contact with the judicial system but frequently the most frustrating as well. Nevertheless, time-consuming and troublesome as it may be, thousands of people across the country appear every day to contest traffic tickets. Only a fraction are represented by lawyers; the rest fend for themselves—usually with similar results.

If you get a ticket and decide it's worth the time, money, and frustration to fight it, you should understand that, with or without a lawyer, very few people win when it's their word against the police officer's. If you've been "caught by radar," your chances of success are even less. Therefore it's probably a good idea to save a lawyer's fee by representing yourself—unless the offense is one for which a serious punishment is involved (such as jail or loss of your driver's license), or there is an injury to someone else or serious damage to property.

Whatever you do, there are a number of steps to take that will make your life much easier later on.

At the Time of the Incident

Cooperate as fully as possible when you're stopped by a traffic officer. Remain seated in the car unless the officer instructs you to get out. The law dictates that you show him your driver's license and registration. Common sense says that you should show him courtesy. If he's annoyed by your attitude, he's more likely to look for additional violations (such as equipment failures). If you remain pleasant, there's always a chance he'll give you a break.

Once the officer starts writing your name, however, you can be certain you'll get either a warning or a ticket. Answer any identification questions politely. Hand your driver's license alone to the officer; giving him the whole wallet is a gesture traditionally associated with offering a bribe. Ask if you can look in the glove compartment for your registration—lunging for the glove compartment could be an alarming gesture. Ask the officer why you were stopped, and listen carefully to the answer. If what he says at the time of the violation differs from his story at trial, it will weaken his case in court. If he says you were caught by radar, ask how long before your alleged violation his unit had been calibrated. Finally—unless you really were rushing your pregnant wife to the hospital to have a baby—fight the impulse to play "true confessions." An admission of guilt is almost certain to be written down in the officer's notes, and can be used against you in court.

Sign the citation even if you don't think you're guilty. Signing a citation is not an admission of guilt—only a promise to appear in court at the time and date specified. On the other hand, if you refuse to sign the citation, the officer may feel he has no choice but to arrest and escort you to jail until a judge can hear the case.

Gather the facts. Make notes of what happened: when and where you were when stopped, your driving speed, the weather, traffic conditions, etc. This data will be useful should you decide to plead not guilty and stand trial. You may want to draw a diagram of the scene and take photographs. Finally, if there is a space on the citation where you can request the presence of the officer at the time of trial, check it off. You may want to cross-examine him. Moreover, if he fails to appear, the case will probably be dismissed.

Do the same things if you get a traffic ticket while out of state. After you sign the citation, you must choose between having to travel out of state again in order to defend yourself in court or simply paying the bail when you receive the ticket and then forfeiting it by not showing up in court. The latter choice has the same effect as if you had pleaded guilty and paid a fine.

In some tourist-oriented cities, the general policy is to avoid giving tickets to out-of-state motorists on the grounds that forcing them to appear on a later date would be unfair. In other areas the officer may ask a tourist to follow him to the nearest judge so that the case can be heard immediately. You may have to post bond to ensure your return; a failure to appear could result in an automatic plea of guilty and a forfeiture of your bond as the fine.

An officer can sometimes confiscate your license. If any part of the license has been altered, if it has somebody else's name or picture, or if you have more than one, it may be taken away from you. Sometimes, if the trial is scheduled for a distant court, the officer will take your license to ensure that you will appear to reclaim it— much the same as an appearance bond. Likewise, at the scene of an accident, an officer will often take the licenses of drivers, passengers, and witnesses to make sure that they all stay around until he has finished his report and recorded their statements.

Tickets and Warnings

There is a difference between a warning and a ticket. A warning is often titled "Notice of Vehicle Code Violation" or "Traffic Warning" and can be given for parking, defective equipment, or moving violations. Parking and moving warnings usually require no corrective action on your part. Equipment warnings, on the other hand, must be heeded; violations have to be corrected and certified within a given period of time, usually fifteen days. Equipment warnings often have a provision for mailing in an attached form after the violation has been corrected. Be sure to do so, or you may get a ticket for failing to correct the violation in time. If there is nothing else suspicious and you look like an honest citizen, many officers will let you off with a warning. Even if the officer does give you a citation for not having a license or registration card, most courts will dismiss the case if you can present a license or registration in court that was valid at the time of your violation.

A ticket or citation is actually a summons to appear in court on a specific date and time. Unless you plead guilty by paying the fine, you must appear in court or face the possibility of being arrested for failure to obey a summons.

"Moving violations" involving the use of alcohol are the most serious. Moving violations cover a variety of offenses, such as exceeding the posted maximum speed limit, violating rights-of-way, failing to obey a stoplight or stop sign, or performing various types of illegal turns.

A person violates the basic speed law by driving too fast in areas where no limits are posted. If weather or road conditions make a slower speed than that posted advisable—such as driving at thirty miles per hour in a heavy rain while traveling through a zone posted at forty-five—a motorist can also be stopped and ticketed.

A driver who exceeds the speed limit actually posted on a roadway has committed a *prima facie* speeding violation—that is, he is *presumed* to have been driving at an unreasonable and improper speed, and in all likelihood will be found guilty. But if a person is charged with violating the state's *maximum* speed limit, the circumstances will have no bearing whatsoever—unless he can prove the charging officer was in error.

Violations involving rights-of-way occur when a person fails to yield to emergency vehicles, to cars already in an intersection, to horses in an equestrian crossing, or to pedestrians in a crosswalk. One is also required to yield the right-of-way to other vehicles when making a left turn, when making a right turn on a red signal (where permitted by state law), when approaching a yield sign, when turning onto a public road from a driveway or other private road, and when entering traffic from an alley. Generally, any time your actions on a highway interfere with another vehicle's use of that highway, and you cause them to brake, swerve, or otherwise avoid your vehicle.

Parking violations are the most common. A parking violation occurs any time a vehicle is parked in an illegal place or manner, or at an illegal time according to posted signs. The ticket is issued to the owner of the vehicle, and is written, filed, processed, and recorded by reference to your license plate rather than to your driver's license.

Most states hold the registered owner of the vehicle responsible if it was illegally parked, regardless of who was driving. The only way to establish someone else's responsibility is to prove that the vehicle was stolen, or that it had been loaned, rented, leased, or sold to someone else at the time of the violation.

Nowadays there is an increased concentration on illegal parking in handicapped spaces.

You may automatically get a ticket if you're involved in an accident. An accident citation is a ticket written by a traffic officer and issued to a driver who caused an accident, or to any driver involved in one. It is not based on the officer's actual observation of the accident, but upon his assessment of the evidence collected at the scene: statements from witnesses and drivers, skid marks, and the like. The ticket may be presented at the time of the accident, or it may be mailed to you a few days later.

Attorneys

Accident citations usually require a lawyer's attention. Defending oneself against an accident citation is very important. A guilty verdict will often be admitted into evidence in a civil suit arising from the accident, and a great deal of money could be involved. This is one time when you should seriously consider having an attorney for a traffic-court offense. At the very least you should notify your automobile insurance company.

You should also hire an attorney if you are charged with a serious moving offense—such as automobile manslaughter, driving under a suspended license, or recklessness caused by alcohol. Traffic courts are increasingly harsh on those convicted of alcohol-related offenses. These are jailable offenses, and you might have the right to be represented by a public defender if you cannot afford to hire a lawyer. Make sure, however, that the attorney you choose is familiar with traffic-court matters. Like doctors, attorneys are specialists. Unless he has effective expertise in traffic court or "driving under the influence" cases, you probably won't be getting your money's worth.

Young drivers should also consider attorneys. In many metropolitan areas today, a young driver who is penalized three points in traffic court can expect his annual insurance premium to increase by $500. A driving-while-intoxicated conviction can mean additional thousands of dollars in premiums.

If you don't understand the violation, have it explained to you. Obviously, you must understand the nature of the charges against you before determining how to prepare a defense. If you are uncertain about the ticket, try phoning the agency which issued the citation. The knowledge and solicitude of the person who takes your call will vary greatly; if you aren't satisfied with the response, his agency's public information officer may be more helpful (see Appendix V). Try breaking down the charge against you into separate elements. Unless you believe that the state can prove beyond a reasonable doubt that each of these elements was present at the time of the alleged violation, you should plead not guilty. (See page 158.)

Arraignment and Pleas

Read the dockets first. Find and read the court dockets to determine the courtroom where your case will be heard. Traffic-court dockets are usually computer printouts containing your name and citation number, and are posted prominently. When you enter the appropriate courtroom, notify the clerk or bailiff that you are present, then have a seat until your case is called. When that happens you will have the opportunity to make your plea to a judge. (This is formally known as an *arraignment*.) The judge will call your name, read off the charge against you, and ask how you plead.

Know the kinds of pleas that are available. The usual choice of pleas is from among the following: guilty, guilty with an explanation, not guilty, and *nolo contendere* (or no contest). If you plead not guilty, a trial will ensue.

When in doubt, plead not guilty. If you have any doubts as to your guilt, by all means plead not guilty. The worst that can happen is that the judge will find you guilty and probably assess the same penalty as if you had admitted your guilt or not appeared in court. Many attorneys advise that if you take the time and trouble to go to court in the first place, a not-guilty plea will accomplish the same purpose as a guilty with an explanation plea—a reduced fine or fewer points on your record. Conversely, a bare plea of guilty is usually a waste of time—in most cases you could have done the same by mail.

A final, more expensive option is to appear by proxy—that is, to have an attorney appear at the arraignment and enter a plea on your behalf.

Don't fail to appear at the arraignment or neglect to send in bail. You must appear—unless you are prepared for a lot of trouble such as having your license renewal held up and even the possibility of imprisonment. If you can't appear in person at the specified time or arraignment, you can usually plead not guilty by mail—or by appearing in court prior to the hearing date.

"Guilty with an explanation" means guilty. For purposes of your record, the two pleas are the same. If you plead guilty with an explanation, you are hoping that the court will suspend or reduce the amount of the fine or the number of points.

Your explanation should be concise, to the point, and offered in a respectful manner. Don't deny that you committed the violation after making this plea, because the judge will probably either tell you to plead not guilty or become irritated and cut you off short and sentence you. Simply outline the factors you believe should mitigate your punishment: good prior driving record, weather conditions, light traffic, etc. Try to maintain an attitude of polite contrition. Avoid groveling.

Nolo contendere affords small protection. As far as your driving record is concerned, a plea of _nolo contendere_ is also the same as a guilty plea. However, in a subsequent civil suit against you resulting from an accident in which you received a citation, the plea of _nolo contendere_ cannot generally be used against you as an admission of guilt.

If you plead not guilty, the judge can't look at your record before the trial. It is improper for the judge to consider your past record in deciding guilt or innocence. The theory is that you are being tried for this one incident, and not for a propensity to commit a certain type of offense; admitting as evidence your prior similar convictions is considered prejudicial. But the judge can (and often does) refer to past records when passing sentence. Always tell the truth. Some states allow for "probation before judgment" and permit the defendant to claim no conviction even though there technically was one. Most courts nowadays have computerized retrieval systems. After hearing the evidence, the judge will sometimes simply ask you about your driving record, and sometimes he will look it up. Good drivers may be put on probation, without even a fine. Repeat offenders may be fined the maximum allowed by law or have their licenses suspended or revoked.

You have a constitutional right to a speedy trial. Following arraignment, if you have pleaded not guilty, you should be tried right away. On the other hand, if you need more time to consider the charges against you, to prepare a defense, or to hire an attorney, you can ask for a postponement (sometimes called a "continuance"). The prosecutor may also request a continuance, but unless you too have asked for one (thereby waiving your right to a quick trial), the prosecutor cannot be guaranteed a postponement beyond the period within which you are guaranteed a speedy trial—generally a month to a month and a half after the arraignment. Prosecutors are not generally granted continuances when the officer involved does not appear for the trial; instead, the judge may dismiss the case. This is particularly true in states where the officer serves as the prosecutor.

Quite often a continuance can be to your strategic advantage. By extending the period of time between your violation and the actual trial, you increase the chances of the officer's not being available, his memory of the incident fading, and the evidence being lost or misplaced. The prosecutor generally needs the police officer's personal testimony in order to present his case.

Do not agree to a trial by deposition. A trial by deposition is one in which the evidence against you is an officer's out-of-court statement of the facts—generally his written investigative report. Do not agree to such a trial, because you cannot cross-examine (question) a piece of paper. As the defendant, you have a constitutional right to be confronted by your accuser.

Trial

Prepare well. As noted earlier, preparation of a defense should really begin the moment you are stopped by the officer. Avoid making any statements which you wouldn't want to hear again at the trial. Obtain names of witnesses. Draw a diagram of the scene. Take photographs if you feel they'll be useful. As soon as possible, write down everything you remember: what the officer said to you; when and where you were at the time; the speed of your car and the others around you; the weather, lighting, and traffic conditions. You can subpoena witnesses or physical evidence not in your possession if you believe such evidence is necessary to your case. Finally, prepare your own testimony—as well as questions you may want to ask the police officer.

Don't rely on the officer's diagram and photographs. Chances are he won't have any. If he does, there is no legal reason you can't use his evidence—but there are better reasons for relying upon your own. If your diagram conflicts with the officer's, and your diagram is found to be correct, the officer's credibility will be damaged.

If your case centers upon your visual perception of the area, photographs can be important to your defense. For example, photographs showing a stop sign blocked by a tree, or the sun setting directly behind a traffic light, could vividly illustrate your testimony that you never saw the light at all, let alone that it was red.

Most traffic-court cases are finished in a few minutes. Depending on the jurisdiction, you are usually scheduled to appear in the courtroom in either the morning or the afternoon. Expect to spend the greater part of a half day in traffic court: your case will probably be one of many, and it may be hours before your name is called. Generally, all violations written by a particular traffic officer are scheduled together. This may be convenient for the officer, but not for you. You can make the best of it by using this opportunity to observe how the judge handles similar cases—to which defenses he's sympathetic, how he treats speeders, and the effects of a good driving record on his decision.

Divide the violation charge into manageable parts. Make sure the prosecution produces evidence that each of the elements needed for conviction was present at the time of your alleged violation. If only one element is missing, you technically have not committed the violation and should be found not guilty. For example, if the date on the officer's report conflicts with that on the ticket, you should be acquitted.

It is more likely, however, that the evidence supporting one of the elements in the state's will be weak rather than nonexistent. In that case you should emphasize this weakness by way of cross-examination or with your own contradictory evidence. The important thing to remember is that the state has the burden of proving you were guilty beyond a reasonable doubt. You don't have to prove you are innocent in order to win.

Be calm when being cross-examined. If you or any witness testifies in court, you must give the opposing side the opportunity of cross-examination. The best advice is to think before you speak, hold your temper, and refrain from arguing. Do your best to answer the questions; try not to take it personally if the state's attitude is that you are obviously lying or contradicting yourself.

Don't talk until the judge tells you to, and ask questions that are relevant. The state's (prosecution's) argument is presented first. All of your questions should be oriented toward the goal of establishing a reasonable doubt about the officer's observation. Since in most traffic cases the state's case against you is made up primarily of the testimony of the police officer, if you can prove that the officer was mistaken at the time of the offense—or that the equipment he used could have been malfunctioning, or that his story at the time of the trial is different from what he told you at the time of the offense—then you have created sufficient doubt about your guilt and the judge should dismiss the case.

During cross-examination you might ask the police officer about his location at the time he first observed your vehicle; what he was doing at the time; the conditions (weather and traffic) under which he observed you; his observation and memory of the location of the offense; and his precise recollection of your alleged violation. Listen carefully for any discrepancies, inaccuracies, or contradictions in his answers. Take notes if you can. If the officer testifies that he clocked your vehicle with his speedometer, make him prove that the instrument was a calibrated speedometer; ask when it was tested, who did the work, and what their qualifications were for the job.

Above all, maintain a polite and respectful demeanor. Your best bet for winning is proving that this very human traffic officer made a simple mistake in your case. Being openly suspicious and resentful toward the officer will only make him a more sympathetic witness.

Understand, though, that most courts nurture the myth that the officer is a neutral witness with no ax to grind. Moreover, most judges—whether they admit it or not—tend to presume the validity of the state's case over yours.

Ask to see the officer's notes. Since the officer is probably basing his testimony almost entirely on his notes, you might ask to see them. If the favorable information outweighs the unfavorable, ask the judge to enter the notes into evidence. If the officer testifies to anything during the trial that is not written on the citation or in his notes, you should challenge that portion of his testimony: point out that he has written many tickets in addition to yours, that there is a good chance he could have been mistaken about the facts, and that your memory of the event and your own notes are at least as good as his recollection.

Make your argument after the state rests its case. After the prosecution has presented its evidence, you have cross-examined the opposing witnesses, and the state has rested its case, make your argument. If you can make a reasonable assertion that the state did not establish all the elements of its charge against you beyond a reasonable doubt, ask the judge to dismiss the case against you. If he grants your motion, the case ends in your favor.

Your testimony and closing argument should be concise, well organized, and prepared in advance. An outline of the points you want to cover is often helpful. Try not to read, since you shouldn't lose the chance to have direct eye contact with the judge.

Radar Cases

Winning a radar case is difficult. In many states your chances range from slim to none. A recent study in Maryland concluded that the overwhelming majority (up to ninety-six percent) of those charged with a speeding violation that had been detected by radar were found guilty. However, some jurisdictions—Florida in particular—have thrown out thousands of radar cases on the grounds of equipment unreliability. You might try asking a lawyer friend about the chances of winning a radar case in your state. If he indicates the judges have open minds—which, though a constitutional requirement, is unlikely in radar cases—by all means try to fight the alleged violation.

Although many court observers feel that the chances of winning a radar case are minimal—because most judges continue to be swayed by the "objective" proof of guilt provided by machinery—if you really want to fight a radar-generated speeding ticket, you should check with the engineering department of your city or county to see if a traffic engineering survey is required, and if so whether one exists. Likewise, if your state, county, or local laws require that radar warning signals be posted, make sure that the signs were posted correctly in compliance with the law.

Even in radar cases, the state must supply valid evidence. The prosecution, through its witness the police officer, has to establish the time, place, and location of the offense, and show that you were the driver of the offending vehicle. The officer must demonstrate that the state laws regarding speed limits and radar signs were complied with, and that your speed was "unreasonable" or in excess of the maximum limit. He must also give his qualifications in radar operation, and testify that the unit used had been tested for accuracy and was operating correctly. Finally, he must be able to identify your vehicle and testify that it was clearly in view, by itself, and nearest the radar unit when the reading was obtained. Keep in mind that radar is only a tool used to verify the officer's visual observation—which itself must be stated. All these elements have to be established by the state beyond a reasonable doubt.

Sentences

The judge usually decides and delivers the verdict immediately after the case has been heard. If he finds you not guilty, the citation will not appear on your permanent driving record, and you are entitled to a full refund of any bond that you may have posted to ensure your appearance at trial.

If you are found guilty, you will usually be sentenced in the same breath. But if you can speak before the judge renders a sentence, ask if you can argue in *mitigation*. This is a term lawyers use when they hope the judge will be lenient after considering extenuating circumstances. Factors that might be mentioned in mitigation include a good prior driving record; weather and/or road conditions; low volume of traffic; and the unlikelihood that you will commit another violation in the future.

Various kinds of sentences are meted out in traffic court. Depending on the severity of your crimes and your past record, the sentences imposed in traffic cases range from a fine to a jail term, from points on your record to the loss of your driver's license. As noted earlier, courts today are particularly harsh on those convicted of alcohol-related offenses.

The judge may impose a sentence and then suspend all or part of it, provided that you meet various conditions he specifies. A typical proviso is that you not be convicted of a similar violation for a certain period of time, such as one year. If you violate this condition, you will be liable for the full amount of the suspended sentence plus whatever may result from the second offense. Occasionally the judge will either suspend the sentence or even dismiss the case if you agree to attend a traffic violator's school. But a suspended sentence will appear on your record like any other sentence.

Appeals

It is seldom feasible to appeal a traffic conviction. Appeals are costly and time-consuming. Generally, you'll need the services—at least the advice—of an experienced attorney. Even if you choose to proceed without one, you'll have to pay a filing fee and wait a fair amount of time before your appeal is heard.

Moreover, judges don't take kindly to frivolous appeals. You should be certain in your own mind that there was a serious miscarriage of justice at the lower court trial—that there was a *legal* error of some kind, not just that the judge chose to believe the officer rather than you.

Of course, if you have lost your license and driving is vital to your work, an appeal may be your only recourse.

CHAPTER SIXTEEN

Personal Rights and Liberties

Congress shall make no law respecting an establishment of religion, or prohibiting the free exercise thereof; or abridging the freedom of speech, or of the press; or the right of the people peaceably to assemble, and to petition the Government for a redress of grievances.

—*First Amendment to the United States Constitution*

The makers of our Constitution . . . conferred, as against the Government, the right to be let alone—the most comprehensive of rights and the right most valued by civilized men.

—Justice Louis D. Brandeis *(Olmstead* v. *U.S.)*

The terms *civil liberties* and *civil rights* are often used interchangeably, but strictly speaking they mean different things. Civil liberties traditionally refer to those freedoms enumerated in the First Amendment. Civil rights most often mean the concepts of equal opportunity and equal protection of the law. Both can involve protecting your privacy or gaining access to information which concerns you. Either way, representing yourself in these matters is often more a necessity than a choice. That is why it is important to know exactly what your rights and liberties are.

Civil Liberties

In terms of their ability to think, say, and do what they want, Americans today enjoy the greatest degree of civil liberty in the history of mankind. Many countries have constitutions which guarantee the rights we have come to take for granted, but none protects those freedoms in practice to the extent we do.

The Constitution is a noble document, whose first ten amendments afford every citizen a broad variety of rights and liberties. The most commonly known and cited of the Bill of Rights are the four freedoms guaranteed by the First Amendment—of religion, speech, press, and assembly—and those guaranteeing fair criminal proceedings.

The First Amendment protects you from actions of the government, not private parties. Lawyers call this "state action"—when the government, through its laws, regulations, or orders, violates an individual's constitutional rights. In a state action the government may be directly involved (for example, in funding a school or other agency) or indirectly involved (for example, in approving or authorizing the alleged infringement).

With few exceptions, you can practice your religion as you please. The exceptions are generally when the state can prove a "compelling interest" to limit free exercise—as, for example, if the religious practice involves use of illegal drugs. Another example: the government may restrict one's practice of religion by refusing to grant state unemployment benefits to an employee who was fired for not working on his or her sabbath day.

The freedom of speech is virtually absolute. In other words, with but a few narrowly defined exceptions, you can say whatever you want whenever you want to.

The exceptions are relatively easy to understand. They involve:

- matters of national security (you cannot divulge classified information)
- defamation (you cannot damage another person's reputation by telling an untruth about him)
- "fighting words" (you cannot invoke the First Amendment to justify language spoken in a nose-to-nose confrontation that is likely to provoke a physical response)
- obscenity (the state can prosecute if you offend "contemporary community standards" of decency)

- restrictions on free expression which the government can demonstrate are necessary to protect a "compelling state interest" (and even then they must be neutrally applied, or merely limit the time, place, or manner of the speech)

Freedom of the press extends to private publications. This freedom is similar to that of speech, with the same exceptions. Libel is written defamation and is usually brought as a civil action.

The freedom of assembly has likewise been liberally construed by the courts. The only illegal organizations are those whose stated purpose is to overthrow the government by force or violence, and who actively pursue the means to do so.

Free speech, freedom of the press, and freedom of assembly benefit from the "prior restraints" doctrine. A law which restrains speech or assembly before it occurs is deemed more constitutionally defective than a law that prescribes subsequent punishment for such speech or assembly. The underlying principle—deemed as fundamental in American society—is to allow virtually absolute freedom of expression in a "marketplace of ideas," whose relative importance can be judged by everyone. If the government wants to enforce a prior restraint, it has the burden of showing a "compelling interest." Examples of prior restraints are permit requirements for parades and court injunctions.

Few lawyers specialize in the protection of civil liberties. Pursuing rights under the First Amendment is most often an endeavor carried on by private citizens on their own time and at their own expense. The lawyers who do practice in this area are generally volunteers doing pro bono work for the American Civil Liberties Union or one of its local affiliates (see below).

If you have a problem related to your rights under the First Amendment, contact the American Civil Liberties Union. Most states and large cities have either a chapter or an affiliate; if yours doesn't, call the national offices in New York ([212] 944-9800). The ACLU is not a government agency, and limited resources preclude its acceptance of many meritorious cases that are brought to it. Those it pursues are generally chosen because they have special legal significance or educational value, or are deemed to be particularly egregious violations of an individual's or group's liberty.

The ACLU also offers a variety of useful publications. Available from the ACLU's national headquarters are a number of helpful pamphlets, policy reports, briefing papers, and handbooks—as well as a Bill of Rights bibliography. For a free list of publications, call (212) 944-9800; fax (212) 869-9065; or write to the American Civil Liberties Union, 132 West 43rd Street, New York, NY 10036.

There are other ways to address a First Amendment problem. Take a close look at your situation—the specific facts may suggest potential alternatives. For example, if you feel you are subject to discrimination by your employer (a private party) because of your religious beliefs, you might get relief under a Title VII claim. (See Chapter 11.)

The Individual Rights Foundation, a division of the Center for the Study of Popular Culture, represents parties whose First Amendment rights are in question. It publishes *The Defender,* and can be reached by mail (P.O. Box 67398, Los Angeles, CA 90067), fax (310-843-0137), or Compu-Serve (74201-3561). In addition, some large organizations located in the Washington, D.C., area might be of assistance: People for the American Way ([202] 467-4999); the American Jewish Congress ([202] 332-4001); Americans United for Separation of Church and State ([301] 589-3707); and the Reporters' Committee for Freedom of the Press ([202] 466-6312). Closer to home, you might also try contacting a law school in your area, local human-rights commissions, or citizen-action coalitions.

Civil Rights

Complaints about discrimination or equal opportunity should first be addressed to the government. Most states have "human rights commissions" or branch offices of the federal Equal Employment Commission. Discrimination because of your race, religion, color, gender, or age is prohibited by various federal laws. Some jurisdictions also have statutes prohibiting discrimination on the basis of appearance or sexual orientation. If you feel you are the victim of such discrimination, try calling one of the government agencies noted above.

If you are a government employee, first try contacting your agency's personnel office. Grievance procedures for government employees are carefully delineated, including those for pursuing complaints about alleged violations of one's civil liberties. Some are handled internally, others by administrative law judges.

For all criminal proceedings, it's best to have a lawyer. Criminal procedure can be highly technical, and there's no substitute for a good lawyer who knows the ropes. Your physical freedom is at stake, and you rarely have much to gain by representing yourself. Besides, in all matters when imprisonment is a possibility, you are entitled to a lawyer even if you can't afford to pay for one.

Prisoner complaints can be filed under the Civil Rights Act. Section 1983 of the Civil Rights Act (in volume 42 of the *United States Code*) enables prisoners or their representatives to file specific complaints against prison authorities or others. To begin an action the original and a copy of the complaint must be filed for each defendant named. It must be legibly handwritten or typed.

Each complaint must be accompanied by the filing fee of $120. In addition, the United States marshal requires payment of the cost of serving the complaint on each of the defendants. If the prisoner is unable to pay the filing fee and service costs, he may petition the court to proceed *"in forma pauperis."*

The Right to Privacy

Today, no matter who you are or what you do, the federal government is almost certain to have information about you or about some subject that interests you. This presents you with two separate problems: how do you get the information you want, and how do you prevent the government from disseminating private information about you to others who have no legitimate interest in it?

On the information-gathering side, the problem is made more difficult because of bureaucratic inertia, a tendency on the part of government officials to treat government files as their own, and a desire by officials at all levels of government to want to hide information that may be embarrassing to them.

Sometimes government secrecy is in the public interest. Surely no one would suggest that the invasion plan for the Battle of Normandy should have been released to the *New York Times* before D-day, or that the leader of an organized-crime ring should have access to all the FBI files on him. Similarly, there are often good reasons for one federal agency to ask another agency for information about you—such as when you apply for a job.

Who's to decide whether disclosure or secrecy is in the public interest? Not, says Congress, the bureaucracy itself.

Fortunately, the government has sought to protect American citizens from unwarranted intrusion into their private affairs, as well as from the wrongful withholding of information that is rightfully theirs. Under both the Freedom of Information Act (FOIA) of 1966 and the Privacy Act of 1974, the extent to which federal information can be disseminated has been strictly defined.

Through the Freedom of Information Act, private citizens can review personal data gathered about them by the Federal Bureau of Investigation, the Central Intelligence Agency, or other government bureaucracies. Taxpayers have gained access to material as diverse as Justice Department files concerning corporate mergers, records of the Commodity Futures Trading Commission pertaining to the Chicago Board of Trade's application to trade future contracts in gold coins, and internal policy memoranda of the Social Security Administration suggesting guidelines for deciding disability claims.

On the other hand, the Privacy Act has served to stem the flow of information about citizens from one agency to another, or to persons not entitled to have access to it.

Because the government's store of information is so enormous and the right of access not absolute, acquiring government records is often an exercise in the arts of communication, persuasion, and, on occasion, compromise. Many of the sensitive disclosures related above succeeded only after the seekers had brought suit and obtained a court order.

The Privacy and Information acts overlap. Whereas the Freedom of Information Act enables you to obtain federal agency records, the Privacy Act protects against unwarranted disclosures about your private life. It also provides a separate means of obtaining records about yourself which is in addition to, and in some instances broader than, your rights under the FOIA. Also, the Privacy Act provides a means to have erroneous information in your files corrected.

The Privacy Act extends to any records that pertain to you individually, such as your tax or personnel file. Such personal records maintained by the federal government cannot be released to anyone "except pursuant to a written request by, or with the prior written consent of, the individual to whom the record pertains." And they can be sent to another agency only if that agency uses them for certain authorized purposes.

Conversely, the Privacy Act provides that an agency must permit any individual, on his request, to gain access to and copy any part of her personal records. Copying costs—but not search costs—can be charged to the person making the request. Citizens also have the right to demand that their records be amended if they are not accurate, timely, relevant, or complete.

As with the FOIA, Congress saw fit to provide for certain exceptions to the Privacy Act. For example, the Central Intelligence Agency (or any other bureau whose principal function is criminal-law enforcement) can deny access to personal records—but cannot exempt itself from the requirement of prior written consent.

In addition, any federal agency can exempt certain records from access, as follows:

- those already under the FOIA's national security exemption
- investigative material compiled for civil or criminal law-enforcement purposes
- records maintained in connection with protective services accorded the president and other officials
- records required by statute to be purely statistical in nature and use
- material compiled solely for the purpose of determining suitability for federal civilian employment, promotion, military

service, federal contracts, or access to classified information (but only to the extent that disclosure would reveal the identity of a confidential source)
- test data used solely for appointment or promotion in the civil or armed services (the disclosure of which would impair objectivity or fairness)

Finally, federal agencies are not required to provide access to information compiled in reasonable anticipation of a civil action or proceeding.

Request under the Privacy Act should be made in writing. The more specific and clear the request, the faster the response. Although a request need not always be in writing, a written demand is best for expediting the process. The request must be lodged with the agency in control of the records, and must conform to its regulations (which appear in the *Code of Federal Regulations* or can be obtained from the agency itself). Fee schedules are also listed in the agency's regulations.

Mention both the FOIA and the Privacy Act. In asserting your right of access to the records, refer to both laws as your legal authority. Many agencies will process a request under whichever statute provides greater access; if the records are exempt under the Privacy Act, they might still be available under the FOIA. If the agency you have approached does not subscribe to this policy—and some don't—it will let you know. You must limit your demands, at least initially, to what's available under the companion statute.

Identify yourself and the records you seek. To protect your records from unauthorized release, you must identify yourself to the satisfaction of the agency. At minimum you should be prepared to offer your full name (including any other names used during the period when the records were compiled), your address, and a notarized signature. If you want to inspect the documents in person, identification cards may be necessary.

The Privacy Act requires that each agency publish in the *Federal Register* a list of its records systems which contain information pertaining to individuals. These lists have been compiled in a document entitled *Protecting Your Right to Privacy: Digest of Systems of Records,* available in libraries or from the Superintendent of Documents, U.S. Government Printing Office, Washington, D.C. 20402. Your request will be easier for the agency to process if you indicate to which particular records system you want access.

Know the time limits. There is no statutory time limit within which the agency must respond under the Privacy Act. The Office of Management and Budget, which is authorized to create guidelines for implementation of the act, has determined that an agency "should" respond within ten working days, and provide access (if no exemption is asserted) within thirty working days. OMB guidelines provide for additional time to comply if the agency advises the requester there is "good cause" for delay.

Administrative appeal is not a matter of right. The Privacy Act does not *require* that there be an administrative appeal in the event you are dissatisfied with the agency's response (or lack of one). Whether there is an intra-agency appeal process depends on the agency involved. But if your demands are not met, the Privacy Act also provides for the right to sue.

The right to amend personal records is yours. If you discover upon reviewing your records that they are not accurate, timely, relevant, or complete, you have the right to request that they be amended. The agency must acknowledge such a request within ten working days, and must determine its merits "promptly." If the request is denied, you have the right to appeal to the head of the agency or the appeals officer he has appointed. The agency's decision on appeal must be made within thirty working days, unless the agency has "good cause" for delay.

The Freedom of Information

The FOIA is broadly applied. Though it has been amended twice since its enactment in 1966, the FOIA has remained essentially unchanged in its basic application to records held by any federal agency—which means any executive or military department, any government or government-controlled corporation, any establishment in the executive branch (including the Executive Office of the president), or any independent regulatory agency. It does not apply to Congress, the president and his closest advisers, the judiciary, or state agencies—although many states have their own FOIA modeled after the federal law.

"Records" encompass many different kinds of data. Although the FOIA does not define *records,* it is clear that the term is a broad one—encompassing all documents, photographs, computer tapes, and data recorded electronically. Government records are divided into three categories. The first must automatically be published in the *Federal Register* whether requested by a citizen or not. These include an agency's rules of procedure, its substantive regulations, information describing its organization, and other matters basic to the public's understanding of how it functions. The second category need not be published but must be available for public inspection and copying: final opinions and orders rendered by the agency in deciding cases, policy statements and interpretations not published in the *Federal Register,* and certain agency staff manuals. The third category covers almost all other records—which must be furnished upon request—and it engenders the most litigation. These records, if properly requested and *not statutorily exempt from disclosure,* must be made "promptly available" to the individual requesting them.

Nine kinds of records are exempt from disclosure. With a few exceptions (such as when another statute forbids disclosure), an agency may choose to waive an exemption and release the documents sought. The exemptions are for matters related to:

1. *national security* (information deemed confidential—according to criteria established by an executive order signed by the president—"in the interest of national security or foreign policy")
2. *agency personnel practices* (information relating "solely to the internal personnel rules and practices of an agency")

3. *a special statute* (information specifically exempted from disclosure by a statute other than the Privacy Act, provided that the statute either requires the matters be withheld from the public in such a manner as to leave no discretion, or that it establishes particular criteria for withholding)

4. *trade secrets* (designed to protect free enterprise by shielding from disclosure certain kinds of commercial information submitted to the government by businesses, if its release would harm their competitive position in the marketplace)

5. *inter- and intra-agency memoranda* (designed to permit agency personnel to exchange advice and ideas with one another without the stifling threat of publicity; its criteria are not noted for their clarity)

6. *personnel files* (medical and similar files the disclosure of which would constitute a clearly unwarranted invasion of personal privacy)

7. *law-enforcement and investigatory records* (exempt if disclosure would interfere with law-enforcement proceedings, deprive an individual of a right to fair trial or impartial adjudication, constitute an unwarranted invasion of personal privacy, disclose the identity of a confidential source, disclose investigative technicalities and procedures, or endanger the life or physical safety of law-enforcement personnel)

8. *financial institution data* (data "contained in or related to examination, operating, or condition reports prepared by, on behalf of, or for the use of an agency responsible for the regulation or supervision of financial institutions"—that is, about banks)

9. *oil and gas wells* (geological and geophysical information, including maps, concerning wells)

Exemptions are not always clear-cut. Even a cursory review of these exemptions makes plain that their application to a particular FOIA request is not always clear. Hence the litigation. The simplest advice is that since the exemptions are sometimes vague and never obligatory unless made so by some other statute, they should not deter you from making an FOIA request. The agency will let you know if it wishes to claim an exemption.

When making an FOIA request, you have three preliminary concerns. These statutory provisions must be kept in mind when requesting records under the Freedom of Information Act:

1. the request must "reasonably describe" the records sought
2. it must conform to the rules and procedures of the agency involved
3. the agency may charge a fee to cover the cost of copying the records and for time spent searching for them. (However, if release of the records "can be considered as primarily benefitting the general public," the agency must release them free of charge. Nor can it charge for time spent reviewing documents for possible exemptions.)

Find out where the records are kept. An agency has no obligation to track down and release records over which it has no control. Therefore, before spending the time and money on a request, the information seeker should be reasonably certain which agency has the material she wants. Your request will be denied if it is found that the records are not in that agency's possession. Note that many government agencies have more than one branch, and some requests will not be forwarded even to another office unless you ask. Moreover, if the request is forwarded, time has been lost.

If you are uncertain which agency or branch has the information you seek, taking the following steps might be helpful in tracking it down. First, call the agencies you think are the likely custodians of the data. Most of them have public information (or FOIA) departments, which should be able to tell you if the records you want are of the type usually kept, or if a branch office or another agency should have them. You might try consulting the *United States Government Manual*. Revised yearly, this handbook lists all federal government agencies and describes their respective functions. (It is available in libraries or from the Superintendent of Documents, U.S. Government Printing Office, Washington, D.C. 20402, for about $15.) You should understand that regional offices usually maintain an agency's working files—those with facts pertaining to specific operations. If the information you seek is general or policy-making in nature, the national headquarters of the agency is more likely to have it. Similarly, if the files are old (compiled and closed several years ago), they might be stored at the National Archives or at its regional records centers. Almost every state has a regional Federal Information Center.

Try to assess the agency's reputation. You may find that more than one agency possesses the records you want. If that's the case, further investigation would be to your advantage: which agency has the better reputation for cooperation? Is one subject to an exemption—for example, a statute prohibiting it from releasing the records—while the other is not? Another preliminary but important consideration is whether there is any possibility that the target agency will lose custody of the records in the near future. If your FOIA request was received after such a transfer has taken place, you're out of luck: the agency cannot honor it even if the records sought are not exempt from disclosure. But if the records were transferred *after* your request was received, your request is still legally enforceable.

Determine the agency's FOIA rules and procedures. Once you know exactly what material you are looking for and which agency is likely to have it, you must conform your FOIA request to the rules of that agency. Such rules are first published in the *Federal Register* (which appears daily), then compiled and updated in the *Code of Federal Regulations*. Typically, they include a schedule of fees, a list of items which must be included in the request in order to locate the documents, notification if the request must be in writing, and other pertinent procedural requirements. The *Code of Federal Regulations* is composed of fifty sections (called "titles"), many of which contain more than one volume. If you plan to deal with an agency on a regular basis, you may wish to purchase the title pertaining to that agency from the Superintendent of Documents. They cost from $7 to $10 per volume. If you do not wish to buy a CFR title, you can obtain the rules from the agency itself or consult the *Code* in a library which carries it.

Put the request in writing. Asking for information by letter ensures that there will be a written record in the event misunderstandings arise. Also, many people express themselves with more clarity on paper, and that is important if you want your request to be processed efficiently.

Include a precise description of the records you seek. A description will be legally sufficient if it is clear enough to enable a professional employee of the agency, familiar with the subject area, to locate the records "with a reasonable amount of effort." As a practical matter, simple and precise requests get the quickest and least expensive agency response. Large-scale requests (for example, "all records concerning the pesticide DDT") will obviously take up more time and effort for both of which you will pay unless the agency has agreed to waive fees. You might fare better if you break down such large demands into a series of smaller, more specific requests. It is also a good idea to make direct, personal contact with agency personnel before sending the letter to ascertain how it can best be worded in order to expedite the search.

Determine if the materials you seek have been previously released under the FOIA. If so, the agency should have no difficulty finding the records, as long as you can provide the name of the person or organization to whom they were disclosed and/or the date. In many agencies, each release is given an identifying number; if you can supply it, so much the better. Note in your letter that because of the prior release you do not expect to pay additional search fees.

State the reason you want to have the records. The FOIA does not require this, but explaining your need for the documents might persuade the agency to waive fees if there is a chance that disclosure could be considered as "primarily benefitting the general public." A legal exemption might also be bypassed if the explanation demonstrates that the benefit to the public resulting from disclosure outweighs that which might result from strict application of the exemption. Finally, if your need for the material is immediate, an explanation of the urgency might prompt a quicker response.

Decide how much expense you are willing to incur. Fees should be discussed in advance. Some agencies, in fact, require a portion of the fees to be paid in advance. If you do not want to spend above a specific amount, indicate your limit in the request letter. If the agency estimates that the search and copying costs will exceed your ceiling, you might be able to reduce costs by narrowing your request, or by asking to review the material in person once it is found to save on copying charges for useless documents. Some agencies have reading rooms specifically for such a purpose.

Specify the authority on which you are relying. Indicate in your request that it is pursuant to the Freedom of Information Act and that you are cognizant of your rights under that law—including the following rights: to see nonexempt portions of exempt files if such portions can be segregated from the rest of the file; to be given a response within the statutory time limits; and to appeal an adverse decision.

Your request letter should be enclosed in an envelope addressed to the agency from which data are sought, with this notation on the front: "Attention: Freedom of Information/Privacy Act Unit."

The statutory time limits: by when must the agency respond? From the time it receives your request, the agency has ten working days (not counting weekends or legal holidays) either to comply with your request or claim an exemption. The agency can extend this period up to ten more days if it can demonstrate "unusual circumstances." Such an extension, however, must likewise be claimed in a written notification to you.

If a time period has expired and the agency has not responded, you can either appeal to its chief officer, institute a legal action in federal court, or wait a bit longer. Displaying patience is often the best strategy: at such an early stage in the process you need not view the agency as an adversary. You can determine the cause of the delay by keeping open the lines of communication; a call or letter can also help to establish a tentative decision date, or clarify the request if a misunderstanding has occurred.

The agency may tell you it has been forced to delay in order to satisfy the demands of another statute—especially when the information requested has been submitted to the government by a third party such as a private corporation. Some statutes or rules require notice to the third party before data are released.

If the agency says the records are unavailable, destroyed, or not in existence, do not give up. Such responses need not necessarily end the inquiry. Call again or send another letter. If the records have been sent someplace else, ask where and when. If the agency says they don't exist, state reasons you might have indicating the contrary. It is always possible, given the size of the bureaucracy, that other agency personnel are more familiar with the type of material requested than the individual who processed your initial request. Ask about the nature and scope of the search. Make the agency convince you that it has made a genuine effort to locate the records sought. If you're told the files were destroyed, ask when that happened—note that it is illegal to destroy records once they have been requested.

In short, if you believe that the agency might be mistaken or evasive, don't give up. Remember that public servants are your employees. Treat them fairly—and expect good service.

When the agency responds by denying all or part of your request, consider an appeal. If some or all of the requested materials are withheld, you still have the right to appeal to the head of the agency, or to whomever he has appointed to handle FOIA appeals. The letter of denial from the agency is important. It should confirm that you have such a right of appeal, indicate when and to whom it should be addressed—and provide details as to which materials are being withheld and exemptions claimed, as well as the names and titles of the persons responsible for the decision to withhold the records. The denial letter might also state what fees you owe if any, and why they were not waived if so requested.

Your appeal should also be by letter. Make sure that it is sent within the time limit set by the agency's regulations (usually thirty days), that it is addressed to the correct official, that it states clearly the agency decision which you'd like to challenge (including the dates of request and denial, the records sought, and any other relevant information), and that it gives reasons you think the denial was wrong.

Just as with the initial request letter, you should also declare that you are making an appeal pursuant to your rights under the Freedom of Information Act, that you expect a reply within the statutory time limit (twenty working days from the date the appeal is received), and that you have a right to a definitive list of both documents retrieved and those withheld (under specified exemptions). If you feel you have been charged excessive fees, you can appeal the fee assessment using the same procedures as for an appeal of a denial.

Even at the appellate stage, informal lines of communication should be maintained. Personal contact can move the process along to your greater satisfaction, as well as promote a spirit of compromise. Agency personnel are supposed to be at your service, but they should be treated as civilly as you would have them treat you.

If the appeal fails, consider going to court. If the agency refuses to change an initial adverse decision, or fails to respond within the twenty-day time limit, you have the right to take the matter to court. This should be a last resort, however. Before rushing into litigation, consider two final alternatives:

- Write to the Freedom of Information Clearinghouse (P.O. Box 19367, Washington, D.C. 20036), which sometimes can give advice or assistance not otherwise available. It also has an excellent booklet on the FOIA that is available for the asking
- Ask your congressman or senator for assistance (See Chapter 17.)

If you decide to sue, you are not required to have an attorney— but you should probably hire one to help. Lawyers are not cheap, but if you go to court and win, the government must pay your lawyer's reasonable fees.

CHAPTER SEVENTEEN

Getting the Most Out of Washington

> I'm surprised that a government organization
> could do it that quickly.
> —Jimmy Carter
> *(when told it took twenty years
> to build the Great Pyramid)*

Perhaps the most revealing aspect of what's right with America is that no other people on earth are as addicted to self-scrutiny, self-criticism, and self-realization. Practically everyone voices a grievance or joins a fight for rights: minorities for equal opportunity, women for pay and status, consumer advocates for fair play in the marketplace. Peace demonstrators and environmentalists are as purely American as flag-waving patriots. All cite the dictum "It's still a free country!"—and are quick to invoke the freedoms of religion, speech, press, and assembly, or the guarantees of privacy and due process. Our threshold of resignation to existing problems, whether personal or public, is exceedingly low: we may say you can't fight city hall, but we refuse to stop trying.

But the image many Americans have of the federal government—one that may not be far from accurate—is that of a big, bungling, boondoggling bureaucracy. When forced to deal with its maze of departments, divisions, agencies, and offices, citizens frequently come away feeling confused, frustrated, and inadequate. There are some three million federal employees, whose essential humanity is often camouflaged by steadfast adherence to regulations and covered by an avalanche of paperwork. Public servants are often rightly perceived as little more than pencil-pushing automatons, caught forever in a colossal entanglement of red tape. The best of them are regarded as diligent drones, the worst as pompous and over-paid parasites.

The barriers that exist between the 250 million Americans who aren't in Washington and those few who are frequently seem like iron curtains. This is especially true for individuals (as opposed to interest groups) who need or want something done by "the feds." It is not unusual even for skilled attorneys to encounter stupefying obstacles when dealing with government bureaucracies—some of which seem to be in direct competition with one another. Trying to reach a bureaucrat by telephone can be a time-consuming ordeal: he is likely to be "in a meeting," "on a long-distance call," "at a conference," "out to lunch," "out of town," "out of the office," or, ultimately, "no longer with us." Diligent and conscientious public servants, on the other hand, are frequently shunted aside and neutralized by their own agencies.

Congress itself, maintain many critics, is too obese, arthritic, parochial, and unresponsive or overresponsive. Visitors to the House and Senate galleries often want to know, "Where is everybody? Why aren't the others here to listen to what he is saying?"

In fact, members of the House and Senate spend only a small portion of their time in the two chambers. Most of their days are consumed in committee hearings or briefings, legislative lunches or organized dinners. A considerable amount of time is devoted to meeting with constituents.

There is even less understanding about one of the most important functions filled by elected public officials—that of ombudsmen, problem-solvers for individuals who have been ignored, trampled upon, or otherwise shabbily treated by the government. It's called "case work," and it covers a wide variety of dilemmas: your Social Security check has been stopped or stolen and you have no other means of support; an agency writes and says that you are no longer disabled and your compensation has been terminated; an IRS agent, without advance notice, snaps a lock on the front door of your business; your visa has expired and cannot be extended, so you must leave the country.

The cases of individual hardship inflicted by government practice or neglect are legion and, it seems, never ending. While the workload and dedication of individual representatives and senators may vary, it is fair to say that most congressional offices devote a good portion of their resources to resolving conflicts between their constituents and the government. Yet many people are unaware that the service is even available, much less that it often provides relief.

The easiest and best way to get what you want out of Washington is to know someone with both power and information. Perhaps even more fundamental is to recognize that such resources are not limited to the landed gentry or useful only to established interest groups. The fact is that most Americans have at least several agent/advocates in Washington who are virtually ideal problem-solvers. They work long hours, pursue difficult situations to reasonable resolutions—and do not charge for their services.

Most important, they are skilled at penetrating the red tape of bureaucracy. Indeed, this chapter could conceivably begin and end with one thought: in an almost endless variety of circumstances, *getting the most out of Washington means calling or writing your congressman or senator.* This is frequently the first, foremost, and last action necessary.

A surprising number of Americans don't realize that it's unnecessary to have a special relationship with their elected representatives—either by party affiliation or past campaign support, or through family or friends—in order to get things done on their behalf.

Most calls or letters will receive at least some response, usually quick and courteous. It is unlikely that the senator or congressman himself will handle the problem, but someone from his usually well-trained staff of caseworkers probably will. Even mass mailings of postcards advocating a particular position will often be answered if there are return addresses. In fact, the only correspondence that is unlikely to be answered is hate mail.

Not only do letter writers get a response, they receive the personal attention of a variety of aides. First, the assistant assigned to the issues covered in the letter (for example, military matters) writes a response, which is usually reviewed by the chief legislative assistant, who in turn shows it to the chief administrative assistant. The senator or congressman himself often gives final approval.

Writing is generally a more effective approach than phoning. In some cases, written inquiries are a legal necessity: the Privacy Act of 1974 prohibits federal agencies from releasing information about an individual without his authorization in writing.

Letters are most helpful when they reflect a balanced and realistic grasp of a particular issue—when they thoughtfully present the way things are and offer a feasible solution or another option. Be sure to include copies of all relevant documents, including correspondence with the agency in question.

All of this should be as complete, clear, concise, and chronological as possible. If your letter describes a problem you are having with the federal government, it is important to provide all the relevant background details—your name, address, phone numbers (day and evening), and Social Security number. Then give a full explanation of the problem—developing it in chronological order if possible—including the agencies with which contact has already been made, the names and titles of those government employees to whom questions were presented, their responses to date, and exactly what corrective action you seek.

If you call instead of writing, organize your thoughts before picking up the telephone. You might take advantage of the service offered by an elected official's local (district) offices. They are equipped to deliver messages directly to the Washington headquarters—and in many cases can save you the cost of a long-distance telephone call.

In calling a congressional office with a problem or opinion, it is equally important to supply all pertinent information. Make notes if necessary. If you are seeking a copy of a bill or want to know its status in the House or Senate, be as specific as possible; provide both a description of the bill and its number if you know it.

On occasion real political clout may be needed. Except for giving final approval, senators and representatives themselves ordinarily become involved in constituent problems only when their staffs are unable to handle them. When that happens, high-level calls may be placed directly: a cabinet officer will generally not talk to a staff member—nor will another senator or a White House official.

Some congressional offices are better than others. With over four hundred representatives and a hundred senators in Washington, the quality of service from office to office is likely to differ. In gross terms, however, the great majority of legitimate problems submitted by constituents are solved—sooner or later—to their satisfaction.

At the state level the quality of service to constituents differs even more. Depending on the state in which you live, agency responsiveness to taxpayer requests varies widely. But the same strategic philosophy and assumptions maintain: government exists to serve the people, and government agencies are supposed to be helpful.

Thus, citizens with problems handled by state agencies should seek to solve them using the same techniques outlined above.

The Social Security Administration has varied functions. Several of the government-provided insurance programs—old age, survivors and disability insurance; supplemental security income; and aid to families with dependent children—are administered by the Social Security Administration (SSA).

Of the many government agencies, the SSA is probably the quickest to respond to inquiries from citizens. With a simple phone call the SSA will promptly send you a pamphlet addressing the question you have. The SSA will also calculate an estimate of your retirement benefits—free of charge. This calculation will show your "work record" (the agency's term for your history of paying Social Security taxes). Since mistakes can be made, many people ask for a calculation of benefits every three years (because there is a three-year statute of limitations on SSA mistakes).

Telephone service centers answer your questions by phone. Although the SSA's main headquarters is located in Baltimore, it has over a thousand district and branch offices in operation nationwide. For further information, contact: Social Security Administration, 6401 Security Boulevard, Baltimore, MD 21235. Phone: (410) 965-7700 or 1-800-772-1213.

The Veterans Administration is responsible for most of the benefits offered to veterans. In addition to health-care services provided through hundreds of VA hospitals, clinics, and nursing homes scattered across the country, the agency provides compensation and pension benefits (including disability, death benefits, and a burial allowance). The VA also provides education and rehabilitation assistance, loan guaranties on home mortgages, and life insurance.

Veterans, their dependents and beneficiaries, or their representatives can obtain information, advice, and assistance in applying for VA benefits. Contact: Veterans Affairs Department, 810 Vermont Avenue, N.W., Washington, DC 20420. Phone: (202) 535-8165.

Getting the most out of the Internal Revenue Service (or giving the least tax allowed by law to it) requires perseverance. The Internal Revenue Service is charged with the task of assuring the maximum voluntary compliance with the tax laws. The IRS has a multitude of "publications" available to the taxpayer that attempt to explain a particular tax form or forms. These publications are available free of charge, and the IRS can answer particular questions as well: call 1-800-829-1040.

The IRS has ten regional field offices located at the addresses listed below. Inquiries should be addressed to the Internal Revenue service center at the following locations (no street address is necessary):

1. Service center:　Andover
　　　　　　　　　Andover, MA 05501

　 States served:　CT, MA, NH, NY (all other counties), RI, and VT

2. Service center:　Brookhaven
　　　　　　　　　Holtsville, NY 00501

	States served:	NJ and NY (NYC and counties of Nassau, Rockland, Suffolk, and Westchester)
3.	Service center:	Philadelphia Philadelphia, PA 19255
	States served:	DC, DE, MD, PA, VA, and U.S. territories and foreign countries
4.	Service center:	Memphis Memphis, TN 37501
	States served:	AL, AR, LA, MS, NC, and TN
5.	Service center:	Atlanta Atlanta, GA 39901
	States served:	FL, GA, and SC
6.	Service center:	Cincinnati Cincinnati, OH 45999
	States served:	IN, KY, MI, OH, and WV
7.	Service center:	Kansas City Kansas City, MO 64999
	States served:	IA, IL, MN, MO, and WI
8.	Service center:	Austin Austin, TX 73301
	States served:	KS, NM, OK, and TX
9.	Service center:	Ogden Ogden, UT 84201

States served: AK, AZ, CA (counties of Alpine, Amador, Butte, Claveras, Colusa, Contra Costa, Del Norte, El Dorado, Glenn, Humboldt, Lake, Lassen, Martin, Mendocino, Modoc, Napa, Nevada, Place, Plumas, Sacramento, San Joaquin, Shasta, Sierra, Siskiyou, Solano, Sonoma, Sytter, Tehma, Trinity, Yolo, and Yuba) CO, ID, MT, ND, NE, NV, OR, SD, UT, WA, and WY

10. Service center: Fresno
                       Fresno, CA 93888

States served: CA (all other counties) and HI

These regions are further divided into fifty-eight district offices. Your district office is the one closest to you. It is there that auditing, deficiency assessment, and reviewing of protest letters is done. Also, the district offices take delinquent tax returns, collect delinquent taxes, investigate civil and criminal violations of IRS laws (except for those relating to alcohol, tobacco, and firearms) and determine pension-plan qualifications. For more information, contact any district office or write the Internal Revenue Service at 1111 Constitution Avenue, N.W., Washington, DC 20224. (The toll-free phone number is 1-800-829-1040.)

CHAPTER EIGHTEEN

Hiring a Lawyer

For a crust of bread he can be hired
either to keep silence or to speak.
—Cato,
Noctes Atticae

There is no right way to hire a lawyer, any more than there's only one way to engage a painter or find a doctor. A great many people pick lawyers by word of mouth—that is, they go to an attorney who's been recommended by a friend or relative, or who has a good reputation in the community.

And indeed, recommendations of friends and relatives can be helpful. But there are other techniques by which you can make yourself a wise shopper for a good lawyer. The following suggestions (some of which have been excerpted and adapted with permission from *Finding and Hiring a Lawyer,* published by the Citizens' Advisory Committee of the District of Columbia Bar) should prove helpful.

If you're new in a community, you might want to contact a lawyer referral service. Some lawyer referral services are better than others. Practically every bar association maintains such a service, but the best ones seek to match people with particular legal problems and attorneys qualified to handle them. Ignore those which handle you strictly on a first-come, first-serve basis. Services vary from one bar association to another. Most require a simple contact either by telephone or in writing. Listings can usually be found in the classified telephone directory under "Lawyer Referral Service."

The stated goals of referral services sound noble—but the proof is in the pudding. The stated philosophy and purpose of one typical service are "to supply needed general or legal information to persons who do not know if they have a legal problem or who do not know a lawyer to consult; to locate qualified lawyers who have listed themselves in various kinds of legal practices; to remove financial barriers to legal services for poorer people; to monitor costs, services, and client satisfaction; to filter out those cases not needing legal services and provide information about other available social services; and to coordinate activities with other legal service organizations."

All of this sounds very high-minded and public-spirited, but you'd be wise to screen prospective counsel carefully.

Legal Aid is still available if you qualify. Despite cutbacks in federal funding, most communities still have some form of legal aid service available to low-income people. The functions performed may be limited, however, and the income ceilings may also have been raised. Because services and criteria vary so widely, it's best to contact your local legal aid agency—generally listed in the telephone book under "Legal Aid."

Many public-interest organizations provide legal services. Often they are in specialized areas of the law. Some of them can refer you to lawyers who are the most experienced and qualified in their fields.

Clinical programs of law schools can be helpful. Many law schools nowadays have specialized clinical programs (as, for example, in juvenile law or housing or consumer protection). Check with the universities in your area to determine what clinics are available.

Prepaid legal services are similar to health-insurance plans. In the past, prepaid legal service plans usually have been available only to groups such as labor unions, credit unions, and cooperatives. More recently, prepaid legal service plans have become available to individual consumers. Some of these plans are excellent. Others promised too much for too low a payment and have gone out of business. If you find a prepaid plan that interests you, inquire carefully about it through the National Resource Center for Consumers of Legal Services by calling (202) 842-3503 or writing to National Resource Center, 1444 I Street, N.W., Washington, DC 20005.

Many lawyers now advertise. Although advertising by lawyers is still frowned upon by the established bar, in searching for lawyers you should not ignore those who tout their services through the media. If your problem is routine, this may be a good method of finding a lawyer who will provide a service for a fixed fee.

Legal clinics, which work on a volume basis, using standardized forms with the assistance of trained non-lawyers called paralegals, are likely to advertise frequently. They are often able to handle routine legal problems at lower costs. Some of them give free initial consultations.

Before you make an appointment, call the offices of the lawyers on your list. Find out the name of the person with whom you are speaking. Describe your problem and ask questions like these:

- "Do you have experience with this kind of problem?"
- "Do you charge for an initial interview?" If so, "How much?"
- [if you believe your problem is routine] "Do you have a standard fee for this kind of problem? What does that standard fee cover?"
- [if your problem is more complicated or the lawyer does not have a standard fee] "Do you charge by the hour, and if so, what is your hourly fee?"
- "Do you provide a written agreement describing fees and the services provided for the fees?"

Keep a list of the information and think about the answers you receive from the lawyers. Then call back to make an appointment with the attorney whose answers satisfied you the most. Don't be embarrassed: you are entitled to ask these questions and receive answers to them before you hire a lawyer.

Plan to go to the first interview with an open mind. You do not have to decide to employ the lawyer you are interviewing until you have had time to think about the interview. Do not be rushed into signing a retainer agreement.

A lawyer works for you. He or she should be genuinely interested in your problem and in giving you the best possible advice. The lawyer may not be able to accomplish everything you wish because of the facts or the law that applies in your case. Many times a good lawyer will advise you to avoid court action. A lawyer should be able to explain, in terms you can understand, what he or she hopes to accomplish for you and how he or she plans to do it. Keep this in mind as you reflect on your impressions of your contacts with the lawyer and his or her staff.

Be organized in presenting your concerns. Lawyers spend years in law school and in law practice learning, among other things, how to approach a problem in a logical, well-organized manner. Most lawyers respond better to clients who are well organized in interviews and phone conversations.

Remember also, a lawyer's time is his or her income. Be punctual for your interview and try to be unemotional in explaining your problem. When you go to the meeting, it is important to bring these items with you:

- a written summary or detailed notes outlining your problem
- the names, addresses, and phone numbers of all parties and witnesses and their lawyers and insurance companies, if you know them
- all documents which you have received from lawyers or a court or which may otherwise be important, for example: receipts, contracts, medical bills, repair estimates, checks, etc.

(Some lawyers will ask you to deliver written materials in advance of your first interview in order to review them.)

Confirm the cost of the interview. If you first spoke with someone else about the appointment, confirm the cost of the interview with the lawyer. Many charge for the initial interview at their usual hourly rate. In other cases a reduced initial consultation fee may pay for only a short time with the lawyer. Make sure you understand the cost if the interview is going to take more time.

Check carefully the lawyer's experience. Not all lawyers are expert in every subject. If your case is going to involve a trial or administrative hearing, be sure the lawyer is experienced with these proceedings. Whomever you decide to hire, you should feel confident in her.

The hourly fee of an experienced lawyer is usually higher than that of an inexperienced one, but if the former is more efficient, in the long run the total cost may be less and the results better. On the other hand, a young lawyer may be more interested in and enthusiastic about your case, even if it is routine, and thus could be more effective. The bottom line is to avoid the lawyer with a high hourly fee who is not experienced with the type of problem you have.

If you are working with a law firm, ask who will actually be working on your case, and you should talk directly with that person. If someone other than a partner is going to be doing the work, you should know about it. The cost of a non-partner (usually called an associate, or a paralegal if the person is not a lawyer) should be less.

If your situation involves a common legal problem, like a divorce or employment-discrimination case, you can simply ask: "What percentage of your practice is devoted to this kind of problem?"

Make the decision to hire a lawyer based on relevant factors. You should consider the following factors before hiring a lawyer:

- Personality—Do you get along well with and trust the person?
- Experience—Has the lawyer had enough experience with your type of problem?

- Could you communicate effectively with the lawyer? Was he or she clear and easy to understand?
- Are fees reasonable in comparison with other lawyers' charges?
- Did your lawyer give clear explanations of how she or he will let you know about progress in your case?

Trust your common sense and feelings as you look for a lawyer, interview lawyers on the phone, and, finally, deal with your lawyer as a client. Asking your lawyer straightforwardly about anything you do not understand should help keep your relationship on a sound working basis.

You can take an active role in the case. Explain to the lawyer what you would like your role to be. People experienced in dealing with lawyers often put in a substantial amount of time assisting them in gathering evidence, lining up witnesses, and (after receiving the lawyers' advice) making final decisions about their cases. More active clients generally receive better legal service.

If this is what you want to do, make it clear at the first meeting. Tell your lawyer that you want a copy of all documents received or written in your case at the lawyer's out-of-pocket cost, or to have these documents made available to you at his or her office. Say also that you want to be informed about all developments in the case, and to be consulted before decisions are made in the case. In important matters, you would like to make the decisions yourself.

If you are satisfied with the interview so far, tell the lawyer everything about your problem, including facts which may be unfavorable to you. There are strict rules prohibiting lawyers from repeating to anyone what you say to them unless you confess ongoing or planned criminal activity. Remember, your lawyer can give you a realistic explanation of what can be accomplished only if you are completely honest.

If you are uncertain about your case, you can ask the lawyer to explain both the positive and the negative aspects.

Determine a timetable for your case. Ask if a timetable can be established. Find out what the lawyer will be doing, and when and how you will be back in touch with each other. Most cases have a legal time limit (the *statute of limitations*) before which they must be filed or you will lose all your rights.

Regarding a timetable, you should ask the following questions:

- "Can you give me a list of events that are likely to occur in my case, and a timetable for them?"
- "Will you give me your best estimate of how long this case will take to complete?"
- "What will you do next?"
- "Is there a statute of limitations on the case? When does it expire?"
- "When will we talk again?"

Discuss fees and payments. Disagreements about fees are a common source of dissatisfaction between lawyers and clients. It is important to your lawyer's comfort—and your confidence in him or her—to establish a fully understood fee arrangement. Even if your lawyer is a friend, or says he or she is taking the case on a reduced-fee basis, it is to the advantage of both of you to be clear about payments.

Fee arrangements vary from lawyer to lawyer, reflecting a few basic approaches. Only some of the details on fees and payments listed below will apply to your case.

Put the fee arrangement in writing. A contract setting forth the lawyer's charges—as well as what services you expect to be performed for that payment—is important. Presently, most agreements provide only for the fee to be paid by the client. Consumers Union publishes a model form that can give you an idea of the kind of information that can be provided by a written agreement.

Clients are entitled to itemized bills showing the work done and disbursements made. At the interview, ask the lawyer to bill you on a regular basis as his or her time charges mount so that you will never be surprised by the total size of the bill you receive. You can ask that the lawyer not exceed a specified amount of time or money spent on your case without first obtaining your permission.

Some fees are standard, but expenses are not. Many attorneys and legal clinics offer fixed or standard fees for routine legal problems, such as drafting a simple will, probating an estate, handling an uncontested divorce with no property or custody issues, or executing an uncomplicated real estate settlement. To see who offers standard fees for their services, you can check advertisements in the newspapers or listings in a local lawyers' register or directory.

If your problem is uncomplicated, ask the lawyer to let you have an estimate of the total cost of the case as soon as possible.

Some expenses are not covered in the fee. Lawyers usually expect to be reimbursed for expenses that they incur in connection with the client's case. These may include travel costs, meals away from home, long-distance telephone calls, and postage and copying costs. Be sure to discuss any expenses for which you may be charged that are not included in the fee, and an estimate of how much they may be. Then you can plan realistically to meet this financial obligation.

More complicated cases are billed by the hour. Fees can vary from $20 to well over $200 for each hour of the attorney's time. Lawyers usually bill for all the time they spend on a case, including that spent talking with a client on the telephone, at the courthouse waiting to appear in court, and elsewhere. Many charge in units as small as one-tenth of an hour—that is, the client is billed for every six minutes the lawyer spends on the case.

Lawyers cannot always estimate how many hours a case will take. If you agree to an hourly arrangement, your written agreement should include a provision requiring that the lawyer not exceed a specified amount of time or money without obtaining your permission. Insist that the lawyer keep you advised every month (or more often if necessary) of the number of hours that he or she is spending on your case. You are also entitled to a more detailed written explanation of how those hours were spent.

Some lawyers work "on retainer." This is essentially a payment in advance, usually representing a number of hours of the attorney's time at his or her usual hourly rate. Should the number of hours exceed the amount covered by the retainer, the lawyer will bill you for the additional charges. If that's the arrangement, you and your lawyer should also agree beforehand that a refund will be made if the attorney does not spend as much time as has been anticipated by the retainer.

Occasionally, the retainer is for a flat fee. This covers the entire cost of the lawyer's services, regardless of the amount of time the lawyer spends. You may be unable to get a refund from your advance payment even if the lawyer does very little work, but you will not owe more if the lawyer underestimates the time it will take.

You should also determine if the fee paid for the initial consultation will be included in the retainer or flat fee. In any event, be sure to get a receipt for fees paid in cash or by money order.

Contingency fees are common in personal-injury cases. Some lawyers will agree to accept as their entire fee a percentage of the money you receive only in the event you win the case. If there is no recovery, the client usually pays the lawyer only for expenses incurred in the case, like court fees.

Contingency fee contracts are like others, except that if you don't get something in writing, your lawyer will probably tell you that his interpretation is the customary one. Invariably it is the client who is expected to pay the costs of the lawsuit and other items such as medical expenses. But there is no harm in trying to make other arrangements, such as a contingency fee in which the lawyer is paid one-fourth to one-half of the recovery. For example, if your medical costs, lost salary, and case-related expenses have been high, you might suggest allowing you to pay them off first, and then assign a higher percentage of the remaining recovery to the lawyer. In many states, such agreements must be in writing, but even in those that don't have this requirement, you should insist on it.

If your lawyer proposes to settle the case, determine precisely how much you will end up with. After paying the lawyer's fee, court costs, and other expenses, you may decide that you are ending up with too little and your lawyer too much and decide not to settle. Remember that it is always *your* decision as to whether the settlement offer is a reasonable one.

Be specific about billing too. For example, specify if you want to be billed monthly or whenever your lawyer has spent a certain number of hours on your case. This should be included in your written fee agreement.

Here is a checklist of questions related to fees and payments:

- "Can you give me an estimate of how much this legal matter will cost?"
- "Can we have a written fee agreement that sets forth not only my obligation to pay but also exactly what you will do for me?"
- "How often will I be billed? Will you agree to let me know when a specific dollar amount of your time has been spent on my case so that I can authorize further payments?"
- "Can you estimate how much court costs, witness and deposition fees, and any other costs will be, aside from your fees? Can I pay by personal check?"
- "When will I have to pay?" (Explain to the lawyer the payment schedule which is best for you.)

A client has the right to discharge an attorney at any time. Once you are in court, however, a judge may not permit this change except for a very good reason. Likewise, an attorney has the right to resign from representation of a client, but once in court the judge's permission is needed.

Before changing lawyers, remember that:

- Other lawyers may be more reluctant to take your case if they know you have already discharged someone else, especially if your first lawyer has a good reputation.
- You probably owe the lawyer for services already rendered. A new lawyer may have to repeat and charge you again for the work already done.
- Your attorney may be unwilling to return legal paper he or she has unless the fee has been paid in full or your written

fee agreement specifies that the attorney must do this if he or she stops representing you.

- In a case where the court appoints the lawyer, for example in a criminal case where you cannot afford to pay for a lawyer, a judge must approve a change of lawyers.

If you have a dispute with your lawyer over a fee, contact your local bar association. Ask if it has a fee arbitration program. Many bar associations maintain such a service, which is usually fair, fast—and much less expensive than going to court.

Glossary

Following are brief definitions of legal terms used in this book. For more comprehensive explanations of these terms, consult either of the two leading law dictionaries—*Black's* (West Publishing Company, fifth edition, 1979) or *Ballentine's* Lawyers' Cooperative, third edition, 1969)—or the multivolume series of judicial interpretations called *Words and Phrases* (West, updated annually).

Adjudication The process by which a court resolves a dispute. It implies that the claims of the parties in a case have been considered and decided upon, by judge and/or jury.

Adoption A procedure that establishes a parent-child relationship between persons not related by blood, and which terminates the rights and duties of the natural birth parents.

Affidavit A statement under oath, usually required to be signed and sworn to before a notary public.

Agency A fiduciary relationship between two persons or entities created by express or implied contract, whereby one (the agent) acts on behalf of the other (the principal) and is subject to the other's control. The relationships may consist of master and servant or employer and independent contractor.

Alimony Money that one spouse pays to the other for financial support during a separation or after a legal divorce; generally expires upon remarriage of receiving spouse.

Annulment A judicial determination that a legal genuine marriage never took place.

Antenuptial agreement A premarital contract signed by a prospective husband and wife regarding such subjects as property and inheritance rights, division of household responsibilities, and payment of expenses.

Arrears Overdue and unpaid money (for example, rent or mortgage payments).

Assets Real and personal property belonging to a person, association, corporation, or estate that is subject to the payment of that person's or entity's debts.

Assignment The transfer to another person of one's entire interests, rights, and obligations in real or personal property, services, etc.

Assumable mortgages Mortgage loans which may be transferred from seller to buyer, where the buyer continues to make payments at the interest rate (presumably lower) which prevailed at the time of the original mortgage.

Attachment A process by which a creditor, having obtained a judgment, can take possession of a debtor's property to sell it to pay the judgment.

Attestation Formalities associated with the act of witnessing a written legal document (such as a will or contract) at the request of the person signing the document.

Balloon mortgage A mortgage agreement under which only the interest is due during the term (usually short), with the entire principal due at the end of the term.

Bankruptcy The discharging of debts through an action in the federal courts, where all your nonexempt property is turned over to a trustee who tries to pay creditors as fully as possible; see *debt adjustment*.

Bankruptcy trustee The person appointed by a court to administer property for someone who is in a bankruptcy proceeding, to make sure that creditors receive what they are supposed to under the law.

Bona fide occupational qualification (BFOQ) A qualification which is considered to be necessary to perform a specific job.

Breach Breaking or violating a law, right, obligation, engagement, or duty, by commission or omission; when a party to a contract fails to carry out his contractual promise.

Capacity The legal competency of a person to enter into a contract (e.g., whether one is of age and of sound mind).

Cause of action The facts which give a party the right to sustain action and the right to seek a judicial remedy for relief against another.

Child support Money a noncustodial parent pays toward maintenance of the children raised by the custodial parent; to be distinguished from alimony.

Closed-end credit account A credit account in which the balance must be paid before one is allowed to make additional purchases.

Codicil An amendment adding to, deleting from, or modifying the terms of a will.

Cohabitation agreement A contract signed by two unmarried persons who are living together which outlines their mutual expectations regarding support and the division of property, household responsibilities, and expenses.

Collateral Property promised to a lender as security; that is, property which passes to the lender if there is a failure to pay a loan.

Collusion An agreement between two or more persons to accomplish a fraudulent or deceitful purpose.

Commission Money paid to an agent; in real estate, a percentage of the selling price of the house, paid by the seller to the real estate agent who found the buyer.

Common property Property held by two or more persons in common with each other; in marriage in a common-law system, each spouse owns whatever he or she earns; to be distinguished from community property.

Community property A legal concept regarding property ownership in marriage, that all property acquired by either spouse during marriage is owned by both of them no matter whose name is on the legal title; currently in operation in the states of Arizona, California, Idaho, Louisiana, Nevada, New Mexico, Texas, and Washington; to be distinguished from common property.

Condominium A dwelling unit and a specified common area, generally part of a larger building or high-rise, which is owned (not rented) by the dweller.

Consideration The money, services, or property, or anything of value which one party gives up or gains as a result of a contract.

Constructive eviction A "legal fiction" that relieves a tenant of her obligations under a lease, allowing the tenant to abandon the premises because conditions within the control of the landlord make the property unsuitable for occupancy.

Contempt Willful disregard or disobedience of public authority.

Contract An agreement whereby certain promises or acts are exchanged, and the parties are legally obligated to perform their part of the bargain.

Convey To transfer or deliver property or title by deed, instrument under seal, or bill of sale.

Cooperative housing An apartment building or group of dwellings owned by a corporation, in which the lessees have shares of stock entitling them to live in a specific apartment or building.

Corporation An artificial entity with the legal power to do anything an individual or partnership can do, but which allows its owners (stockholders) to shield themselves from liability for debts and losses.

Covenant A promise; often a clause or condition in a contract.

Cross-examination Part of trial when one side asks questions of the opponent (or of a witness testifying for the opponent).

Custody Usually the right to raise a minor child, and the duty to be responsible for such child.

Damages A pecuniary compensation that may be recovered in court by a person who has suffered loss or injury through the unlawful act or omission of another, or through a breach of contract.

Debt adjustment A method under the bankruptcy laws by which a debtor can retain all or most of his assets while paying current creditors over a period of time out of income.

Decedent A deceased person, usually the author of a will.

Decree A court order, either interlocutory (temporary) or final.

Deed The document used to transfer title to real or personal property from a seller to a buyer.

Deed of trust Similar to a mortgage, except that usually a third party (not the lender or borrower) keeps legal title to the property until either a default occurs (in which case the lender may sell the property to repay the loan) or the borrower pays off his obligation.

Defamation Injuring another's reputation through the unprivileged publication of false statements; see *libel* and *slander*.

Default Failure to pay an amount due, in either a mortgage or some other loan, whereby the lender gains certain rights to property (either by agreement of the parties or through court decree).

Defendant The person sued by a plaintiff.

Discrimination In employment, favoring or disfavoring certain types of people.

Domicile A person's legal (permanent) home, although it need not be lived in (for example, a college student living in a dorm may have his domicile elsewhere).

Down payment An outright cash payment made before money is borrowed.

Easements Rights that other people have in real estate allowing them to do certain things on a specific parcel of land, usually to cross over it to get to their property.

Emancipation Surrender of care, custody, and earnings of a minor child. Renunciation of parental duties.

Encumbrance A legal right to or interest in property, which right or interest is owned by someone else—such as a tax lien, easement, zoning ordinance, or restrictive covenant; generally, encumbrances are "clouds on title" and diminish a property's value.

Equitable distribution A legal concept that allows a judge in a divorce proceeding to distribute property according to what he feels is fair rather than according to who holds legal title.

Escrow agreement A document under which one or more parties designate a certain party (the escrow agent) to hold money (e.g., rental fees) until certain other events occur, such as the fulfillment of other obligations.

Estate The total property, whether real or personal, owned by a decedent before the distribution of that property according to the terms of a will, or, in the absence of a will, by the laws of inheritance in the state of domicile of the decedent.

Eviction A legal action initiated by a landlord demanding that a tenant move out before expiration of a lease.

Exclusive right to sell A type of real estate listing agreement in which only one agent is permitted to sell a piece of property.

Executor/executrix A male/female appointed by a testator/testatrix to carry out directions and requests in his or her will and distribute property according to his or her testamentary provisions after his or her death.

Exemption Property that a debtor does not have to relinquish by virtue of bankruptcy proceedings.

"Fault" divorce A divorce based on grounds such as adultery, cruelty, or desertion, in which one of the parties is blamed for causing the divorce.

Foreclosure The process by which a bank (or other lender) can sell the property of a borrower who is in default in order to pay off the money owed.

Fraud A false representation of a fact for the purpose of inducing another to act in reliance upon it and surrender a legal right.

Freedom of Information Act A federal or state law that requires government agencies to disclose their records, with certain exceptions.

Garnishment A process by which a creditor may have a debtor's wages paid directly to him; must follow a court judgment obtained by creditor, and is generally limited to a modest percent of wages (typically 10 percent).

Gift A voluntary transfer of real or personal property to another, made without conditions or consideration.

Grant A transfer of real or personal property by deed or writing.

Grievance procedure The terms of a particular employment contract that must be followed, if an employee has a complaint, before he can go to court.

Guardian A person legally given the power and duty to take care of someone who by age or disability is considered incapable of administering his own affairs.

Harassment Conduct directed at a specific person that causes emotional distress to that person and serves no legitimate purpose.

Hearsay Testimony given by a witness who relates what others have told him or her or what he or she has heard, instead of personal knowledge; often offered as evidence of the truth of matters, but excluded on grounds of fairness.

Holographic will A will that is handwritten, dated, and signed by the testator, without witnesses or other formalities normally required by law.

Illusory Deceptive.

Implied warranty of habitability An implied-by-law guarantee by landlord to tenant that the leased premises meet a reasonable standard.

Incidental damages Damages that occur as an indirect result of a product's deficiency of breach of a contract.

Indemnify To restore the victim of a loss by payment, repair, or replacement, or to give security for an anticipated loss.

Informed consent The understanding that a doctor must obtain from a patient before treatment that the patient is fully aware of the possible risks and benefits of the medical procedure to be performed.

Injunction A court order that forbids a party from doing an act (or restrains a party from doing an act which he has already committed) if the act if unjust, inequitable, and injurious to the plaintiff.

Intestate succession The statutory method of distributing the estate of a person who dies without a will.

Joint tenancy A form of joint ownership whereby property automatically transfers to the survivor (or survivors) upon the death of the other party.

Joint venture A form of business whereby two or more persons agree to act together to complete a single business transaction (rather than establish and operate a continuous business).

Judgment A court decision that one person is entitled to certain rights, either to specific property or in more general terms.

Judgment creditor A person who has obtained a judgment against his debtor but has not yet been paid.

Judgment debtor A person against whom a judgment has been recovered and has not paid; includes the judgment debtor's successors in interest.

Jurisdiction The power or authority of a court to decide a particular case.

Landlord One who rents premises to another (the tenant).

Lease Contract between landlord and tenant, outlining the rights and obligations of each regarding the rented property.

Letters testamentary A legal document giving the estate's personal representative permission to transact matters on behalf of the estate.

Libel Spoken defamation.

Lien A legal method of enforcing a debt, whereby the property under lien cannot be sold or transferred before the creditor enforcing the lien has been paid.

Limited partnership A partnership in which some of the parties are liable only for a fixed amount of money, and are generally limited as well in their share of the profits.

Listing agreement An agreement between a seller of property and a real estate agent, setting forth the contractual arrangement between them for advertising, showing, and selling the property.

Litigant An active party to a lawsuit (i.e., a plaintiff or defendant).

Magistrate A public civil officer with legislative, executive, or judicial power, or an inferior judicial officer, such as a justice of the peace.

Malpractice Unreasonable lack of skill in professional or fiduciary duties, or failure to perform professional obligations.

Minor A person below the specific age of majority set by state law, who is afforded various protections by the law (such as not being liable for certain contracts); generally the age of majority is anywhere from eighteen to twenty-one years old, depending on the state (and, in some cases, depending on the circumstances).

Mitigate To minimize, reduce, or alleviate a penalty or punishment imposed by law.

Modification Changing a contract after it has been signed.

Mortgage/mortgagor/mortgagee An agreement (the mortgage) between a buyer (the mortgagor) and a moneylender (the mortgagee), where the mortgagor borrows money to buy property—which in turn is used as collateral on the loan.

Necessaries Articles indispensable for the sustenance of human life (i.e., food, drink, clothing, medical care, and suitable housing).

Negligence A legal word used to describe a defendant's failure to act as a reasonable and prudent person under the circumstances, which failure directly causes injury to a plaintiff.

"No-fault" divorce A divorce in which neither party is blamed for causing the difficulty leading to the divorce.

Notice Knowledge of facts which apprise a person of a proceeding in which his or her interests are involved.

Nuisance Activity that annoys and disturbs one in possession of his or her property, producing such discomfort that damage is presumed. Smoke, odors, noise, or vibration are examples.

Oath Attestation of the truth of a statement that renders wilfully asserted untrue statements perjurious.

Option An agreement which gives the optionee the right to accept an offer for a limited time.

Partition Division of real or personal property between co-owners, which severs unity of possession and creates individual ownership of the interests of each.

Partnership A form of doing business in which two or more persons voluntarily agree to share both profits and losses from the operation of a business.

Pecuniary Relating to money; financial.

Perjury A false statement knowingly and intentionally made in a court proceeding where the person is under oath to swear or affirm the truth of statements made.

Personal property Assets other than real estate, including household goods, stocks, cars, etc.

Personal representative One appointed to handle the probate of the will or (when no will exists) to oversee the distribution of an estate according to intestate succession; often known as an executor.

Petition A formal document filed in a court of law outlining the pertinent facts of a situation and requesting the judge to give certain relief.

Petitioner One who initiates a court action.

Plaintiff The person who files a complaint against a defendant in a lawsuit.

Points In real estate, a percentage of the loan that a buyer must sometimes pay to a lender in order to obtain a mortgage; sometimes known as document-processing fees or discount points.

Power of attorney A written legal paper in which one appoints someone else as his agent to whom he gives either a general or limited authority to act in his behalf.

Prima facie A fact presumed to be true unless disproven by contradictory evidence.

Privity Actual knowledge or means of knowledge of things likely to contribute to a loss.

Pro forma Statements or conclusions based upon assumed facts, or an appealable decision that was rendered only to facilitate further proceedings.

Probate The process by which a will is proved to the proper authorities (usually a probate court) to be valid.

Publication The act of giving some type of notice to the public—usually through a newspaper ad—of a petitioner's request for legal action (such as a change of name).

Quiet enjoyment A covenant, often in leases and conveyances, that protects the tenant's right to freedom from disturbance.

Real estate agent A middleman, generally representing the seller, who sells property and receives a commission based on the selling price.

Real property Land, including buildings and any interest in them (such as a lease or condominium ownership).

Reciprocity Relationship between two commercial or political entities, where each gives the customers or citizens of the other certain privileges and assumes certain responsibilities.

Residence requirements State laws that prohibit persons from bringing certain suit (such as divorce) until one of the parties has lived in the state for a specified minimum period of time.

Respondeat superior A legal doctrine which holds one person (often an employer) legally responsible for wrongs committed by another (typically an employee) when the agent is acting on behalf of the other person.

Respondent The defendant in a lawsuit.

Restrictive covenant In real estate, an agreement binding subsequent owners of property to do or refrain from doing certain things (for example, building a wall that shades another's house).

Retainer Agreement between attorney and client which sets forth the nature of services to be performed, costs, and expenses.

Revolving credit account An open-ended credit account in which a monthly payment must be made on the balance but other items may still be bought on the account, up to a certain limit.

Satisfaction Paying a party that which is due, or what has been awarded by a court judgment.

Secured debt A debt whose payment is guaranteed by some other property (collateral) in the event of a default.

Security deposit Money required by a landlord to be paid by a tenant at the beginning of a lease and to be returned to the tenant at the end if the premises are undamaged and no back rent is due.

Separate maintenance A "legal separation" arrangement whereby married parties live apart, free from harassment or control of each other, although they are not legally divorced.

Separation agreement A contract signed by husband and wife in contemplation of a separation or divorce, regarding such subjects as division of property, support, and custody of children.

Service of process The act of notifying all involved parties of legal proceedings about to take place.

Settlement In real estate, when a buyer and seller make final the sales process; the date when the buyer makes the remainder of his payment and the seller signs the deed of title.

Settlement sheet A paper which sets out the costs (taxes, stamps, etc.) to be paid by the seller and the buyer and the amount paid to each of them and to others (such as the real estate broker, title company, attorney, etc.).

Slander Written defamation.

Sole proprietorship A form of business in which the owner acts alone and is personally responsible for all debts and losses incurred by the business.

Statute of limitations A law which prohibits a claimant from bringing a lawsuit after a specified number of years have passed from the date of the claimed injury.

Sublease The renting of an unexpired lease by an original tenant to a third party; it neither terminates the original tenant's obligation to pay rent to the landlord nor creates a direct landlord-tenant relationship between the landlord and the third-party tenant.

Subpoena A court order requiring a witness to appear at the time the case is heard, and/or requiring that certain records be brought forth.

Tenancy at sufferance A type of informal tenancy when there is no valid written lease and either landlord or tenant can end their relationship at any time without notice.

Tenancy at will A written rental agreement which continues until either the landlord or the tenant gives proper notice to the other of an intention to end the lease.

Tenancy by the entirety A form of joint ownership allowed only to married couples; similar to a joint tenancy except that neither spouse can sell his or her share without permission of the other, and the tenancy can be terminated only by death, divorce, or mutual agreement.

Tenancy for years A long-term written lease which provides that the tenancy expires on a specific date in the future, without the need for either landlord or tenant to act or give notice.

Tenant A person who rents premises from another (the landlord).

Testator/testatrix Male/female who makes a will.

Title insurance An insurance policy that protects either the owner or lender or both against any legal defects in the title to a house (such as unreleased mortgages or liens on the property that the buyer or seller did not know about).

Tort A civil wrong; a violation of a duty imposed by law upon a person or property.

Trespass Unlawful interference with the property or rights of another.

Trust A legal arrangement whereby ownership of certain property or funds is given to a trustee, who must act for the benefit of another person (the beneficiary) as directed by the document creating the trust.

Unconscionable Fundamentally unfair, such as a clause in a contract so one-sided that it oppresses one party, violates reasonable expectations, or involves a gross disparity in price.

Undue influence Improper or wrongful pressure that overpowers the will of a person so that he is induced to do or forbear an act which he does subject to the will of a dominating party.

Unilateral One-sided; related to only one of two or more things.

Unsecured debt A debt whose payment is not backed up by specific property in the event of a default.

Usury The charging of an unlawfully high rate of interest when lending money.

Venue The particular county or city in which a court with jurisdiction may hear and decide a case.

Verification A signed statement in which a petitioner swears the facts contained in his petition are true, and that if necessary the petitioner is prepared to testify to them under oath or to prove them through documentation.

Void Incapable of being enforced by law, such as an ineffective instrument or transaction which has no force and cannot be corrected.

Waiver Intentional or voluntary relinquishment of a known legal right, or conduct which warrants an inference of relinquishment.

Ward A person, usually a child or incompetent, placed by the court under the care and supervision of a guardian.

Warranty A promise that the manufacturer or seller of an item makes about his product; may be either express (stated in writing or verbally) or implied (found to exist automatically, by virtue of the type of product involved).

Will A legal document in which a person states what she wishes to happen to his property upon his death.

Yield Stock dividends or bond interest paid, expressed as a percentage of the current price.

Zoning Division of a city or town by regulation into districts where land usage and architectural designs are limited.

APPENDIX I

Getting the Most Out of Washington

Primary Federal Departments
(Addresses and Phone Numbers)

NOTE: All area codes are (202), for Washington, DC, unless otherwise indicated.

Agriculture

Headquarters
14th St. & Independence Ave.,
    S.W. 20250
Locator: 720-8732
Information: 720-2798

Extension Service
14th St. & Independence Ave.,
    S.W. 20250
Locator: 720-8732
Information: 720-2798

Food and Nutrition Service
3101 Park Center Drive
Alexandria, VA 22302
Locator: (703) 305-3348
Information: (703) 305-2286

Food Safety & Inspection Service
14th St. & Independence Ave.,
    S.W. 20250
Locator: 720-7943
Information: 720-7943

Forest Service
14th St. & Independence Ave.,
    S.W. (mailing address:
    P.O. Box 96090,
Washington, DC 20090)

**Rural Electrification
    Administration**
14th St. & Independence Ave.,
    S.W. 20250
Locator: 720-8732
Information: 720-1260 (press);
    720-1255 (public)

Commerce

Headquarters
Main Commerce Building
14th St. & Constitution Ave.,
    N.W. 20230
Locator: 377-2000
Information: 377-4901 (press);
    377-3263 (public)

Census Bureau
Suitland & Silver Hill Rds.,
    Suitland, MD (mailing
    address: Washington,
    DC 20233)

Locator: (301) 763-7662
Information: (301) 763-4040

Patent and Trademark Office
2121 Crystal Drive
Arlington, VA
    (mailing address:
    Washington, DC 20231)
Locator: (703) 557-3158
Information: (703) 305-8341
    (press); (703) 557-4636
    (public)

Defense

Headquarters
The Pentagon, Washington,
    DC 20301
Switchboard: (703) 545-6700
Information: (703) 695-0192
    (defense news); (703) 697-5131
    (armed forces news); (703)
    697-5737 (public affairs)

Air Force Department
The Pentagon, Washington,
    DC 20330

Locator: (703) 695-4803
Information: (703) 695-5554

Army Department
The Pentagon, Washington,
    DC 20310
Locator: (703) 545-6700
Information: (703) 697-7589
    (press); (703) 614-0741
    (public)

Navy Department
The Pentagon, Washington,
  DC 20350
Locator: (703) 614-9221
Information: (703) 697-5342
  (press); (703) 695-0965
  (public)

Marine Corps Information:
  (703) 614-1492 (press);
  (703) 614-8010 (public)

Education

Headquarters
400 Maryland Ave., S.W. 20202
Locator: 708-5366
Information: 401-1576

Energy

Department of Energy
1000 Independence Ave.,
  S.W. 20585
Locator: 586-5000
Information: 586-5806 (press);
  586-5575 (public)

**Federal Energy Regulatory
  Commission**
825 N. Capital St., N.E. 20426
Locator: 208-0200
Information: 208-1088 (press);
  208-1371 (public)

Health and Human Services

**Department of Health and
  Human Services**
200 Independence Ave.,
  S.W. 20201
Locator: 619-0257
Information: 245-6343 (press);
  245-6867 (public)

**Alcohol, Drug Abuse, and
  Mental Health Administration**
5600 Fishers Lane, Rockville,
  MD 20857
Locator: (301) 403-2403

Information: (301) 443-8956
  (press); (301) 443-3783
  (public)

Food and Drug Administration
5600 Fishers Lane, Rockville,
  MD 20857
Locator: (301) 443-1544
Information: (301) 443-3285
  (press, Rockville); 245-1144
  (press, Washington);
  (301) 443-3170 (consumer
  affairs)

National Institutes of Health
9000 Rockville Pike, Bethesda,
    MD 20892
Locator: (301) 496-5787
Information: (301) 496-5787

Public Health Services
200 Independence Ave.,
    S.W. 20201
Locator: (301) 443-2403
Information: 245-6867

Social Security Administration
6401 Security Blvd., Baltimore,
    MD 21235
(Washington office:
    200 Independence Ave.,
    S.W. 20201)
Locator: (410) 965-5882 in
    Baltimore
Information: (410) 965-7700 in
    Baltimore

Housing and Urban Development

**Department of Housing and
    Urban Development**
HUD Bldg.
451 7th St., S.W. 20410
Locator: 708-0980 (press);
    708-1420 (public)

**Fair Housing and Equal
    Opportunity**
451 7th St., S.W. 20410
Locator: 708-1422
Information: 708-0980

Interior

Department of the Interior
Main Interior Bldg.
1849 C St., N.W. 20240
Locator: 208-3100
Information: 208-3171

Bureau of Indian Affairs
1849 C St., N.W. 20240
Locator: 208-3100
Information: 208-7315 (press);
    208-3711 (public)

Bureau of Mines
810 7th St., N.W. 20241

Locator: 208-3100
Information: 501-9649

National Park Service
1849 C St., N.W. (mailing
    address: P.O. Box 37127,
    Washington, DC 20013)
Locator: 208-3100
Information: 208-7394 (press);
    208-4747 (public)

U.S. Fish and Wildlife Service
1849 C St., N.W. 20240
Locator: 208-3100
Information: 208-5634

Justice

Department of Justice
Main Justice Bldg.
10th St. & Constitution Ave.,
    N.W. 20530
Locator: 514-2000
Information: 514-2007

Antitrust Division
10th St. & Constitution Ave.,
    N.W. 20530
Locator: 514-2000

Bureau of Prisons
320 1st St., N.W. 20534
Locator: 307-3082

Civil Division
10th St. & Constitution Ave.,
    N.W. 20530
Locator: 514-2000
Information: 514-2007

Civil Rights Division
10th St. & Constitution Ave.,
    N.W. 20530
Locator: 514-2000
Information: 514-2007

Criminal Division
10th St. & Constitution Ave.,
    N.W. 20530
Locator: 514-2000

**Drug Enforcement
    Administration**
700 Army Navy Dr.
    Arlington, VA (mailing
    address: Washington,
    DC 20537)
Locator: 307-1000
Information: 307-7977

**Environmental & Natural
    Resources Division**
10th St. & Constitution Ave.,
    N.W. 20530
Locator: 514-2000
Information: 514-2007

**Federal Bureau of
    Investigation**
10th St. & Pennsylvania Ave.,
    N.W. 20535
Locator: 324-3000
Information: 324-3691

**Foreign Claims Settlement
    Commission of the United
    States**
601 D St., N.W. 20579
Locator: 653-6155

**Immigration & Naturalization
    Service**
425 Eye St., N.W. 20536
Locator: 514-4330
Information: 514-2648 (press);
    514-4330 (public)

Tax Division
10th St. & Constitution Ave.,
    N.W. 20530
Locator: 514-2000
Information: 514-2007

U.S. Marshal's Service
600 Army Navy Dr., Arlington,
    VA 22202

Locator: 514-2000
Information: 307-9065

U.S. Parole Commission
5550 Friendship Blvd.
    Chevy Chase, MD 20815
Locator: (301) 492-5990

Labor

Department of Labor
200 Constitution Ave.,
    N.W. 20210
Locator: 523-4000
Information: 523-7316

Bureau of Labor Statistics
441 G St., N.W. 20212
Locator: 523-4000
Information: 523-1913 (press);
    523-1221 (public)

**Mine Safety & Health
    Administration**
4015 Wilson Blvd., Arlington,
    VA 22203

Locator: 523-4000
Information: (703) 235-1452

**Occupational Safety & Health
    Administration**
200 Constitution Ave.,
    N.W. 20210
Locator: 523-4000
Information: 523-8151

**Pension & Welfare Benefits
    Administration**
200 Constitution Ave.,
    N.W. 20210
Locator: 523-4000
Information: 523-8921

State

Department of State
Main State Building
2201 C St., N.W. 20520
Locator: 647-3686
Information: 647-2492 (press);
    647-6575 (public)

Bureau of Consular Affairs
2201 C St., N.W. 20520
Locator: 647-3686
Information: 647-1488
    (passports); 647-5225
    (assistance to U.S. citizens
    overseas)

Foreign Service
2201 C St., N.W. 20520
Locator: 647-3686

Office of Protocol
2201 C St., N.W. 20520
Locator: 647-3686

Transportation

Department of Transportation
400 7th St., S.W. 20590
Locator: 366-4000
Information: 366-5580

Maritime Administration
400 7th St., S.W. 20590
Locator: 366-4000
Information: 366-5807

**Federal Highway
   Administration**
400 7th St., S.W. 20590
Locator: 366-4000
Information: 366-0660

**National Highway Traffic
   Safety Administration**
400 7th St., S.W. 20590
Locator: 366-4000
Information: 366-9550

Federal Railroad Administration
400 7th St., S.W. 20590
Locator: 366-4000
Information: 366-0881

U.S. Coast Guard
2199 2nd St., S.W. 20593
Locator: 366-4000
Information: 267-1587

Federal Transit Administration
400 7th St., S.W. 20590
Locator: 366-4000
Information: 366-4043

Treasury

Department of the Treasury
Main Treasury Bldg.
15th & Pennsylvania Ave.,
   N.W. 20220
Locator: 566-2000
Information: 566-2041

**Bureau of Alcohol, Tobacco,
   and Firearms**
650 Massachusetts Ave.,
   N.W. 20226
Locator: 927-7777 (press)
Information: 927-8500

U.S. Customs Service
1301 Constitution Ave.,
    N.W. 20229
Locator: 566-2000
Information: 566-5286 (press);
    566-8195 (public)

U.S. Mint
633 3rd St., N.W. 20220
Locator: 566-2000
Information: 874-6450

Bureau of Engraving and Printing
14th and C Sts., S.W. 20228
Locator: 874-2485
Information: 874-2778

Internal Revenue Service
1111 Constitution Ave.,
    N.W. 20224
Locator: 566-5000
Taxpayer Information:
    566-4024 or (800) 829-1040
    (public)

U.S. Secret Service
1800 G St., N.W. 20223
Locator: 566-2000
Information: 435-5708

Veterans Affairs

Department of Veterans Affairs
801 Eye St., N.W.
    (mailing address:
    810 Vermont Ave.,
    N.W. 20420)
Locator: 273-5400
Information: 535-8165

Veterans Benefits Administration
801 Eye St., N.W.
    (mailing address:
    810 Vermont Ave.,
    N.W. 20420)
Locator: 273-5400
Information: 872-1151

Veterans Health Administration
801 Eye St., N.W.
    (mailing address:
    810 Vermont Ave.,
    N.W. 20420)
Locator: 273-5400

Independent Federal Agencies
(Addresses and Phone Numbers)

Central Intelligence Agency
Langley, VA (mailing address:
  Washington, DC 20505)

Commission on Civil Rights
1121 Vermont Ave.,
  N.W. 20425
Locator: 376-8364
Information: 376-8312

**Consumer Product Safety
  Commission**
5401 Westbard Ave., Bethesda,
  MD (mailing address:
  Washington, DC 20207)
Locator: (301) 504-0100
Information: (301) 504-0580

**Environmental Protection
  Agency**
401 M St., S.W. 20460
Locator: 260-2090
Information: 260-4355 (press);
  260-4454 (public)

**Equal Employment
  Opportunity Commission**
1801 L St., N.W. 20507
Locator: 663-4264
Information: 663-4900

Farm Credit Administration
1501 Farm Credit Dr., McLean,
  VA 22102

Locator: (703) 883-4000
Information: (703) 883-4056

**Federal Communications
  Commission**
1919 M St., N.W. 20554
Locator: 632-7106
Information: 632-5050 (press);
  632-7000 (public)

**Federal Deposit Insurance
  Corporation**
550 17th St., N.W. 20429
Locator: 393-8400
Information: 898-6996

Federal Election Commission
999 E St., N.W. 20463
Locator: 219-3440
Information: 219-4155 (press);
  219-3420 (public)

**Federal Mine Safety and
  Health Review Commission**
1730 K St., N.W., 20006
Information: 653-5633

**Federal Reserve System, Board
  of Governors**
20th and C Sts., N.W. 20551
Locator: 452-2266
Information: 452-3204 (press);
  452-3215 (public)

Federal Trade Commission
6th St. and Pennsylvania Ave.,
   N.W. 20580
Locator: 326-2000

General Accounting Office
441 G St., N.W. 20548
Locator: 275-5067
Information: 275-2812

**General Services
   Administration**
18th and F Sts., N.W. 20405
Locator: 501-1082
Information: 501-1231 (press);
   501-0705 (public)

Government Printing Office
732 N. Capitol St., N.W. 20401
Locator: 275-3648
Information: 512-1991
Publications orders and
   inquiries: 783-3238

**Interstate Commerce
   Commission**
12th St. and Constitution Ave.,
   N.W. 20423
Locator: 927-7119
Information: 927-5340 (press);
   927-5350 (public)

**National Aeronautics and
   Space Administration**
400 Maryland Ave., S.W. 20546
Locator: 453-1000
Information: 453-8400

**National Archives & Records
   Administration**
8th St. & Pennsylvania Ave.,
   N.W. 20408
Locator: 501-5402
Information: 501-5525 (press);
   501-5400 (public)

**National Endowment for the
   Arts**
1100 Pennsylvania Ave.,
   N.W. 20506
Information: 682-5570 (press);
   682-5400 (public)

**National Endowment for the
   Humanities**
1100 Pennsylvania Ave.,
   N.W. 20506
Information: 786-0438

**National Labor Relations
   Board**
1717 Pennsylvania Ave.,
   N.W. 20570
Information: 632-4950

**National Railroad Passenger
   Corporation (Amtrak)**
60 Massachusetts Ave.,
   N.E. 20002
Switchboard: 906-3000
Information: 906-3860 (press);
   906-2121 (consumer
   relations/complaints)

National Science Foundation
1800 G St., N.W. 20550

Locator: 357-5000
Information: 357-9498

National Transportation Safety Board
490 L'Enfant Plaza, S.W. 20594
Locator: 382-6725
Information: 382-6600

Peace Corps
1990 K St., N.W. 20526
Locator: 606-3886
Information: 606-3010 (press);
    606-3387 (public)

Securities and Exchange Commission
450 5th St., N.W. 20549
Locator: 272-3100
Information: 272-2650

Selective Service System
1023 31st St., N.W. 20435
Locator: 724-0820
Information: 724-0790

Small Business Administration
409 3rd St., S.W. 20416
Locator: 205-6600
Information: 205-6740

Smithsonian Institution
1000 Jefferson Dr., S.W. 20560
Locator: 357-2700

U.S. Information Agency
301 4th St., S.W. 20547
Locator: 619-4700
Information: 619-4355

Agency for International Development
Main State Building
2201 C St., N.W. 20523
Locator: 663-1449
Information: 647-4274

U.S. Postal Service
475 L'Enfant Plaza, S.W. 20260
Locator: 268-2020
Information: 268-2156

White House Press Office
The White House
1600 Pennsylvania Ave.,
    N.W. 20500
Information: 456-2100 (press);
    456-7150 (public)

Grounds for Divorce, by State

Just as marriage itself must conform to certain legal requirements in order to be valid, a divorce or dissolution of marriage must also follow certain rules. Because each state has its own grounds and because laws are subject to change, you should check with the divorce court's clerk before proceeding.

Residency refers to the length of time required from the time the divorce petition is filed, unless otherwise indicated. *Remarriage* refers to the period beginning with the effective date of the decree.

Laws vary from state to state and change from year to year. Consult your local library for the latest statutory revisions. A current digest of each state's laws can be found in the Martindale-Hubbell Law Digest (revised annually), available in most libraries.

Alabama

1. Abandonment for more than one year.
2. Adultery

3. Crime against nature before or after marriage
4. Cruelty or any cause justifying divorce, if plaintiff desires separation only (also known as a partial divorce)
5. Final decree of partial divorce in effect for more than two years
6. Five successive years in insane asylum after marriage, the person so confined being hopelessly and incurably insane when divorce is filed
7. Habitual drunkenness or drug addiction contracted after marriage
8. Imprisonment in penitentiary for two years under sentence of seven years or more
9. Incapacity
10. Incompatibility
11. Nonsupport of wife by husband for two years will permit wife to obtain divorce
12. Physical violence
13. Pregnancy of wife at time of marriage without husband's knowledge will permit husband to obtain divorce
14. Irretrievable breakdown of marriage

Residency: Six months
Remarriage: Sixty days

Alaska

1. Adultery
2. Conviction of a felony
3. Cruelty impairing health or endangering life or personal indignities rendering life burdensome
4. Failure to consummate at time of marriage and continuing until commencement of legal action
5. Habitual and gross drunkenness, begun after marriage and continuing for one year
6. Habitual addiction to drugs after marriage
7. Incompatibility of temperament
8. Incurable mental illness if spouse is confined to an institution for at least eighteen months prior to the filing of the divorce

9. Parties have lived apart for eighteen months without co-habitation, whether voluntary or by mutual consent
10. Willful neglect by the husband to provide necessaries of life for the wife for twelve months, when failure is because of his idleness, profligacy, or dissipation

Residency: None
Remarriage: No restriction

Arizona

Court will enter decree of dissolution of marriage if residency requirement is met, conciliation provisions either do not apply or have been met, marriage is irretrievably broken, and, to the extent it has jurisdiction, court has considered and provided for child custody and support, spousal maintenance, and property disposition

Residency: Ninety days
Remarriage: No restriction

Arkansas

1. Adultery
2. Conviction of felony or infamous crime
3. Cruel and barbarous treatment endangering life of innocent party
4. Desertion for one year without reasonable cause
5. Habitual drunkenness for one year
6. Indignities to person of innocent party
7. Insanity—continuous confinement to institution for three years or adjudicated insane more than three years before filing of suit
8. Impotency at time of marriage continuing to time of bringing action for divorce
9. Parties have lived apart for three consecutive years without cohabitation
10. Spouse by former undissolved marriage living at time of marriage
11. Willful nonsupport

Residency: Sixty days preceding commencement of action
Remarriage: No restriction

California

1. Incurable insanity, requiring proof by competent medical or psychiatric testimony
2. Irreconcilable differences that have caused irremediable breakdown of marriage

Residency: Six months
Remarriage: No restriction

Colorado

Irretrievable breakdown of marriage relationship must be proved as essential element of action

Residency: Ninety days
Remarriage: No restriction

Connecticut

1. Adultery
2. Fraudulent contract
3. Habitual intemperance
4. Incompatibility causing parties to live apart for continuous period of at least eighteen months with no reasonable prospect of reconciliation
5. Infamous crime involving a violation of conjugal duty and punishable by imprisonment for more than a year
6. Intolerable cruelty
7. Irretrievable breakdown of marriage
8. Mental illness causing legal confinement for an accumulated period of at least five years within the six-year period next preceding complaint
9. Sentence to imprisonment for life
10. Seven years' absence, unheard from
11. Willful desertion for a year

Residency: One year
Remarriage: No restriction

Delaware

1. Separation caused by incompatibility
2. Separation caused by respondent's mental illness
3. Separation caused by respondent's misconduct, including adultery, bigamy, conviction of a serious crime, physical or oral abuse, desertion, homosexuality, refusal to perform marriage obligations, contracting venereal disease, habitual alcoholism or drug abuse
4. Voluntary separation

Residency: Six months
Remarriage: No restrictions

District of Columbia

1. Parties living separately for one year
2. Parties living separately voluntarily for six months

Residency: Six months
Remarriage: No restriction

Georgia

1. Adultery
2. Conviction of offense involving moral turpitude with penalty of two years or more in penitentiary
3. Cruel treatment, consisting of willful infliction of pain, bodily or mental, upon complaining party, such as reasonably justifies apprehension of danger to life, limb, or health
4. Force, menaces, duress, or fraud in obtaining marriage
5. Habitual intoxication
6. Habitual addition to drugs
7. Impotency at time of marriage
8. Incurable mental illness for two years
9. Irretrievably broken marriage
10. Mental incapacity at time of marriage
11. Pregnancy by man other than husband at time of marriage, unknown to husband

12. Relationship between parties such that marriage is prohibited
13. Willful and continued desertion for one year

Residency: Six months
Remarriage: Judge or jury determines rights and disabilities of parties

Hawaii

1. Expiration of term in decree of separate bed and board without reconciliation
2. Living separate and apart for two years or more
3. Marriage irretrievably broken
4. Satisfaction of court that divorce would not be harsh, oppressive, or contrary to public interest

Residency: Six months
Remarriage: No restriction (if wife remarries, alimony must be modified)

Idaho

1. Adultery
2. Conviction of a felony
3. Extreme cruelty
4. Habitual intemperance
5. Irreconcilable differences determined by court to be substantial reasons to dissolve marriage
6. Living separate and apart five years
7. Willful desertion
8. Willful neglect
9. Permanent insanity, provided insane spouse has been confined in an insane asylum in any state or foreign country for at least three years prior to commencement of action

Residency: Six weeks
Remarriage: No restriction

Illinois

1. Adultery
2. Another husband or wife at time of marriage

3. Attempt on life of spouse by poisoning or other means showing malice
4. Conviction of a felony or infamous crime
5. Desertion for one year
6. Excessive use of addictive drugs for two years
7. Extreme and repeated mental or physical cruelty
8. Habitual drunkenness for two years
9. Impotency
10. Infection of spouse with venereal disease
11. Additionally, marriage may be dissolved if spouses have been separated for two years and irreconcilable differences have caused breakdown in marriage and reconciliation has failed

Residency: Ninety days
Remarriage: No restriction

Indiana

1. Conviction of infamous crime
2. Impotency at time of marriage
3. Incurable insanity for two years
4. Irretrievable breakdown of marriage

Residency: Six months and, in county filed, three months
Remarriage: Verified application. No license issued to male with dependent children from prior marriages reasonably dependent on him for support, unless person provides proof with his application he is supporting or contributing to support his children by prior marriages and complying with court support orders.

Iowa

Breakdown of marriage in that legitimate objects of matrimony have been destroyed and no reasonable likelihood that relationship can be preserved

Residency: One year
Remarriage: No restriction

Kansas

1. Incompatibility
2. Failure to perform material marital duty or obligation
3. Incompatibility by reason of mental illness or incapacity where spouse is confined for two years

Residency: Sixty days
Remarriage: Parties cannot remarry until thirty days after entry of divorce decree, unless an appeal is taken (and then not until receipt of mandate from appellate court)

Kentucky

Irretrievable breakdown of marriage is sole basis for dissolution.

Residency: One of the parties must have been maintained in the state for 180 days before the filing of the petition, must be proved by testimony of one or more witnesses

Remarriage: No restriction

Louisiana

Divorce shall be granted upon rule to show cause filed by spouse upon proof that spouses have lived separate since filing. Divorce shall be granted upon proof that:

1. Spouses have lived separate and apart for six months
2. Other spouse has committed adultery
3. Other spouse has committed felony and has been sentenced to death or imprisonment at hard labor

Residency: Six months
Remarriage: Where divorce granted for adultery, guilty party permitted to marry accomplice

Maine

1. Adultery
2. Cruel and abusive treatment
3. Extreme cruelty

4. Gross and confirmed habits of intoxication from use of intoxicating liquors or drugs
5. Impotence
6. Irreconcilable differences
7. Nonsupport
8. Utter desertion continued for three consecutive years

Residency: Parties must have been married here or cohabited here after marriage, or plaintiff must have resided here when cause of action occurred, or plaintiff must reside here in good faith for six months before action is begun, or defendant must be resident of the state
Remarriage: No restriction

Maryland

1. Adultery
2. Desertion for at least twelve consecutive months prior to filing suit without reasonable expectation of reconciliation
3. Voluntary separation without cohabitation for twelve consecutive months prior to filing suit and with no reasonable expectation of reconciliation
4. Conviction of felony or misdemeanor and sentence of at least three years or indeterminate sentence in penal institution, twelve months of which have been served
5. Uninterrupted separation, without cohabitation, for two years prior to filing suit
6. Permanent and incurable insanity, provided insane spouse has been confined in institution for at least three years

Residency: One of the parties must have resided in the state for at least one year before filing for divorce, where grounds arose outside of state; where ground for divorce is insanity, one party must have resided in state for two years
Remarriage: No prohibition

Massachusetts

1. Adultery
2. Cruel and abusive treatment

3. Gross and confirmed habits of intoxication caused by voluntary, excessive use of liquor or drugs
4. Gross and cruel failure to support
5. Impotency
6. Irretrievable breakdown of marriage
7. Sentence to confinement for life or five years in penal or reformatory institution
8. Utter desertion for one year

Residency: Plaintiff must live in commonwealth for one year, and cause must have occurred within commonwealth

Remarriage: Allowed after divorce judgment becomes absolute (i.e., after six months); if spouse remarried after seven years of mate's absence, not guilty of polygamy

Michigan

Breakdown of marriage relationship to extent that objects of matrimony have been destroyed and there remains no reasonable likelihood that marriage can be preserved.

Residency: Plaintiff must have lived in state a hundred and eighty days unless marriage was solemnized in state and plaintiff lived in state from marriage to bringing suit.

One spouse must have resided in county ten days before bringing suit.

If not voluntary appearance, defendant must live in state when divorce filed or when cause arose, unless brought in by publication or personally served with process within state or personally served with order for appearance and publication anywhere.

When cause happened outside Michigan, one party must live in state for one year.

Remarriage: No restriction

Minnesota

Irretrievable breakdown of marriage—defenses abolished

Residency: One party must live in state one hundred eighty days
Remarriage: No provisions

Mississippi

1. Adultery, unless collusion or condonation
2. Consanguinity within prohibited degrees
3. Habitual cruel and inhuman treatment
4. Habitual excessive use of drugs
5. Incurable insanity, if insane party has been under treatment and confined to institution for three years
6. Insanity or idiocy at time of marriage, unknown to complaining party
7. Irreconcilable differences if not contested and if provisions are made for custody after sixty days
8. Pregnancy by other than husband
9. Prior marriage undissolved
10. Natural impotency
11. Sentence to penitentiary, unless pardoned
12. Desertion for one year
13. Habitual drunkenness

Residency: One party must live in state for six months unless residence acquired to secure divorce
Remarriage: In case of adultery, court may prohibit remarriage; such prohibition may be removed by court after one year, for good cause shown

Missouri

Irreconcilably broken marriage with no reasonable likelihood it can be preserved

Residency: Ninety days
Remarriage: No restrictions

Montana

Irretrievable breakdown of marriage supported by:

1. Not having lived together for one hundred eighty days
2. Serious marital discord adversely affecting one of the parties

Residency: Ninety days
Remarriage: No restriction except during appeal challenging finding that marriage was irretrievably broken

Nebraska

Marriage irretrievably broken
Residency: One party for one year with bona fide intent of making state his home, or married in state and one party has stayed there since marriage.
Remarriage: No restriction

Nevada

1. Incompatibility
2. Insanity for two years
3. No cohabitation for one year

Residency: Six weeks
Remarriage: No restriction

New Hampshire

1. Abandonment and refusal to cohabit for two years
2. Adultery
3. Disappearance for two years
4. Desertion for two years
5. Extreme cruelty
6. Habitual drunkenness for two years
7. Impotency
8. Imprisonent for more than one year
9. Irreconcilable differences leading to irretrievable breakdown of marriage
10. Joining any religious sect or society forbidding cohabitation of husband and wife and six months' refusal to cohabit
11. Treatment such as to seriously injure health or seriously endanger reason

Residency: One year; jurisdiction only when cause of divorce arose while plaintiff was living in state
Remarriage: No restriction

New Jersey

1. Adultery
2. Deviate sexual conduct voluntarily performed by defendant without consent of plaintiff
3. Desertion for one year or more
4. Extreme cruelty for three months before filing
5. Imprisonment for eighteen months, provided that, if imprisonment ended before filing, couple did not resume cohabitation
6. Institutionalization for mental illness for two years or more after marriage
7. Separation for eighteen consecutive months, if no reasonable prospect of reconciliation
8. Voluntarily induced addiction or habituation to narcotic drug or habitual drunkenness for twelve months after marriage

Residency: Either party bona fide resident of state and has stayed such, except that no divorce can be commenced on grounds other than adultery unless one of the parties has lived in state for one year
Remarriage: No restriction

New Mexico

1. Abandonment
2. Adultery
3. Cruel or inhuman treatment
4. Incompatibility

Residency: Six months
Remarriage: No restrictions

New York

1. Abandonment for one year
2. Adultery
3. Cruel or inhuman treatment

4. Imprisonment of defendant for three years after marriage
5. Living apart for one year

Residency: Parties married in state and lived there for one year; parties lived in state as husband and wife for one year; cause occurred in state and either party lived there for one year; cause occurred in state and both parties lived there when action commenced; either party lived in state two years before action commenced
Remarriage: No restriction

North Carolina

Absolute divorce

1. Continuous separation for one year
2. Separation for three or more years without cohabitation by reason of incurable insanity of one spouse

Divorce from bed and board

1. Abandonment
2. Maliciously turning out of doors
3. Cruel and barbarous treatment endangering life
4. Indignities to person rendering life unbearable
5. Excessive use of alcohol or drugs
6. Adultery

Residency: One of the parties to a divorce action based upon one year's separation must be resident of state for six months prior to filing of the divorce action
Remarriage: No restrictions

North Dakota

1. Adultery
2. Conviction of a felony
3. Extreme cruelty
4. Habitual intemperance for one year
5. Insanity with five years' confinement in an institution
6. Irreconcilable differences

7. Willful desertion for one year
8. Willful neglect for one year

Residency: Six months
Remarriage: Must be specifically permitted by court

Ohio

1. Adultery
2. Extreme cruelty
3. Fraudulent contract
4. Gross neglect of duty
5. Habitual drunkenness
6. Imprisonment in penitentiary
7. Impotency
8. Lived apart for one year
9. Incompatibility, unless either party denies
10. Other spouse living at time of marriage
11. Procurement of divorce outside of state by spouse
12. Willful absence for one year

Residency: Six months for plaintiff
Remarriage: No restriction

Oklahoma

1. Abandonment for one year
2. Adultery
3. Extreme cruelty
4. Fraudulent contract
5. Gross neglect of duty
6. Habitual drunkenness
7. Impotency
8. Imprisonment for felony at time action was filed
9. Insanity for five years
10. Pregnancy of wife at time of marriage by one other than husband
11. Procurement of divorce by spouse in other state
12. Incompatibility

Residency: Six months in good faith, thirty days in county of residence; five years of grounds of insanity
Remarriage: Six months after divorce decree

Oregon

Circumstances justifying annulment or irreconcilable differences between parties that have cause irremediable breakdown of marriage.

Residency: None if married in state, otherwise six months
Remarriage: Provisions ambiguous—check with attorney

Pennsylvania

1. Adultery
2. Conviction of certain crimes resulting in two or more years' sentence
3. Cruel and barbarous treatment
4. Desertion for two years
5. Existing prior marriage
6. Indignities suffered rendering condition intolerable and life burdensome
7. Bigamy; eighteen months' confinement in mental institution without prospect of discharge; irretrievably broken marriage
8. Insanity or serious mental disorder

Residency: Six months
Remarriage: Either may remarry, but defendant guilty of adultery may not marry other party to adultery during life of plaintiff

Puerto Rico

1. Abandonment for over one year
2. Absolute incurable impotency occurring after marriage
3. Adultery
4. Attempt to corrupt son or prostitute daughter and commerce in such corruption or prostitution
5. Conviction of a felony that may involve loss of civil rights

6. Cruel treatment or grave injury
7. Habitual drunkenness or excessive use of drugs
8. Incurable insanity if it seriously prevents spouses living together spiritually
9. Proposal of husband to prostitute wife
10. Separation for two years

Residency: One year, unless ground arose in Puerto Rico or while one spouse lived there
Remarriage: Not prohibited, but if woman remarries within 301 days of divorce, she must provide certification as to whether or not she is pregnant, for purposes of establishing paternity

Rhode Island

1. Adultery
2. Any other gross misbehavior or wickedness repugnant to and in violation of marriage covenant
3. Continued drunkenness
4. Extreme cruelty
5. Habitual, excessive intemperate use of narcotics
6. Impotency
7. Irreconcilable differences
8. Marriage originally void or voidable by law
9. Neglect or refusal for one year of husband to provide for subsistence of wife if he is of sufficient ability
10. Party deemed to be, or treated as if, civilly dead, for crime committed
11. Separation for three years
12. Willful desertion for five years

Residency: One year for either party; or in case of divorce from bed, board, and future cohabitation (not just from bond of marriage), and must have resided in state for such time as court deems sufficient
Remarriage: No restriction

South Carolina

1. Adultery
2. Continuous separation for one year

3. Desertion for one year
4. Habitual drunkenness caused by alcohol or narcotics
5. Physical cruelty

Residency: One year; if both parties are residents, three months
Remarriage: No restriction

South Dakota

1. Adultery
2. Extreme cruelty
3. Willful desertion
4. Willful neglect
5. Irreconcilable differences
6. Habitual intemperance
7. Conviction of felony
8. Incurable, chronic mania or dementia of either spouse five years or more while under confinement by order of court or appropriate agency

Residency: One party must live in state; sixty days mandatory "cooling off" period following institution of suit
Remarriage: No restriction

Tennessee

1. Adultery
2. Attempts on life of other by means showing malice
3. Bigamy
4. Conviction of an infamous crime
5. Conviction of a felony
6. Desertion for one year without reasonable cause
7. Habitual drunkenness or drug abuse
8. Impotence
9. Irreconcilable differences
10. Refusal of wife or husband to move to Tennessee for two years after parties have lived separately, not cohabited, and have no minor children

11. Wife pregnant at time of marriage with another man's child without knowledge of husband

Residency: No requirements if plaintiff lived in state when acts were committed; if one or other lived in state six months before filing, complaint can be filed on acts committed elsewhere
Remarriage: No restriction

Texas

1. Abandonment for one year
2. Adultery
3. Cruel treatment that makes living together insupportable
4. Discord or conflict of personalities that destroys legitimate ends of marriage and prevents reasonable expectation of reconciliation
5. Felony conviction and imprisonment if twelve months after final judgment (and not if pardoned or convicted on spouse's testimony)
6. Living apart for three years
7. Mental illness with three-year hospitalization without hope for permanent recovery

Residency: Six months in state, ninety days in county
Remarriage: No restriction after thirty days

Utah

1. Adultery
2. Desertion for one year
3. Felony conviction
4. Habitual drunkenness
5. Impotency at time of marriage
6. Permanent insanity
7. Physical or mental cruelty
8. Separation for three years
9. Willful neglect to provide common necessities of life
10. Irreconcilable differences

Residency: Three months in state and county
Remarriage: Prohibited during appeal or period allowed for appeal

Vermont

1. Adultery
2. Failure to provide suitable maintenance if able to do so
3. Insanity commitment for five years
4. Intolerable severity
5. Prison confinement for at least three years
6. Separation for six months with resumption of marital relations not reasonably probable
7. Willful desertion or absence for seven years

Residency: Six months; two years for insanity
Remarriage: No restriction

Virginia

1. Adultery
2. Cruelty, after one-year separation for it
3. Desertion for one year
4. Felony conviction for one year
5. Separation for one year without cohabitation
6. Sodomy or buggery outside marriage

Numbers 1 and 6 not valid if parties voluntarily cohabited after knowledge of such act; if it happened five years earlier; or if it was committed by procurement or connivance of party alleging it

Residency: Six months
Remarriage: Allowed after appeals

Virgin Islands

Breakdown of marriage relationship without likelihood that marriage can be preserved

Residency: Six weeks
Remarriage: No restriction

Washington

1. Marriage irretrievably broken
2. Marriage invalid—grounds for invalidity:
   a. Consanguinity
   b. Mental incapacity
   c. Lack of capacity to consent; or consent obtained by force, duress, or fraud
   d. Lack of parental or court approval
   e. Nonvoluntary cohabitation after attaining age of consent after cessation of force or duress or discovery or fraud
   f. Prior undissolved marriage

Residency: No specific duration
Remarriage: No restriction, except during appeal of finding that marriage is irretrievably broken

West Virginia

1. Abandonment for six months
2. Adultery
3. Child abuse or neglect
4. Cruel and unreasonable treatment or fear of bodily hurt
5. Drug addiction
6. Felony conviction
7. Habitual drunkenness
8. Insanity
9. Irreconcilable differences (sixty-day waiting period required)
10. Separation for one year

Residency: One year
Remarriage: No restriction

Wisconsin

Irretrievably broken marriage if:

1. Both parties so state
2. One party so states, and one-year separation

3. One party so states and judge finds no possibility of reconciliation
4. One party so states and, after judge finds marriage not irretrievably broken, either party states under oath that it is irretrievably broken

Residency: Six months in state, thirty days in county
Remarriage: Six months' waiting period

Wyoming

1. Insanity confinement for two years
2. Irreconcilable differences

Residency: Plaintiff must reside in state for sixty days
Remarriage: No restriction

Sample Forms

Two-Party Contract

Agreement made this _____ day of _____, 19__, between [name of first party], of [address], City of _____, State of _____, referred to as [contractual status of party], and [name of second party], of [address], City of _____, State of _____, referred to as [contractual status of party].

RECITALS

It is the intent of the parties that ...

AGREEMENT

The parties to this agreement, in consideration of the above recitals and the following mutual covenants and stipulations, agree as follows:

SECTION ONE
[Title of Section]

SECTION TWO
[Title of Section]

SECTION THREE
[Title of Section]

SECTION FOUR
[Instrument as Entire Agreement]

This instrument contains the entire agreement between the parties, and no statements, promises, or inducements made by either party or agent of either party that are not contained in this written contract shall be valid or binding.

SECTION FIVE
[Effect of Agreement]

This agreement shall inure to the benefit and be binding on the parties, and heirs, executors, administrators, assignees, and successors of the parties.

In witness whereof, the parties have executed this agreement at [place of execution] the day and year first above written.

[Signatures]

Three-Party Contract

Agreement made this _____ of _____, 19___, between [name of first party] of [address], City of _____, State of _____, referred to as [lessor or secured party or seller or as the case may be], and [name of second party], of [address], City of _____, State of _____, referred to as [lessee or party], of [address], City of _____, State of _____, referred to as [third party beneficiary or guarantor or surety or as the case may be].

The parties to this agreement, in consideration of the mutual covenants and stipulations set out, agree as follows:

SECTION ONE
[Title of Section]

SECTION TWO
[Title of Section]

SECTION THREE
[Title of Section]

SECTION FOUR
[Instrument as Entire Agreement]

This instrument contains the entire agreement between the parties, and no statements, promises, or inducements made by either party or agent of either party that are not contained in this written contract shall be valid or binding; this contract may not be enlarged, modified, or altered except in writing signed by all the parties and endorsed on this agreement.

SECTION FIVE
[Effect of Agreement]

This agreement shall inure to the benefit of and be binding upon the heirs, executors, administrators, assignees, and successors of the respective parties.

In witness whereof, the parties have executed this agreement at _____ [place of execution] the day and year first above written.

[Signatures]

(Optional Provisions)

Witness—General form

In witness whereof, the parties have executed this agreement at [place of execution] the day and year first above written.

[Signatures]

Fingerprint As Signature

In witness whereof [name of party], who cannot sign [his or her] name, has executed this agreement by affixing such person's thumb mark in the presence of the undersigned witnesses at [place of execution] the day and year first above written.

[thumb mark]

[Signature of witness]
[Signature of witness]

From the Office of:

SINGLE FAMILY DWELLING LEASE
(with tax escalator clause)

Date: _____ 19___

In consideration of the mutual promises, obligations and agreements herein set forth, the parties hereto agree as follows:

1.
PARTIES

_____   _____   _____
(Name)   (Address)   (Telephone No.)

hereinafter called "Landlord", hereby leases to

_____   _____   _____
(Name)   (Address)   (Telephone No.)

hereinafter called "Tenant", and Tenant hereby hires from Landlord, the Leased Premises described in Paragraph 2.

2.
LEASED
PREMISES

The Leased Premises consist of the land and the buildings thereon now known as and numbered

_____ , Massachusetts _____
(Street)

_____   _____
(City or Town)   (Zip Code)

3.
TERM

This Lease shall be for a term of _____ years, beginning on _____ ,19 _____ and ending on
_____ , 19 _____ .

4.
RENT

Tenant agrees to pay rent to Landlord at the rate of _____ the real ($) per month on the _____ day of each and every month in advance so long as this Lease is in force and effect. All rent shall be paid to Landlord by check mailed to the address of Landlord set forth above, or as otherwise directed in writing by Landlord.

5.
REAL
ESTATE
TAXES
(Fill in
Applicable
fiscal tax
periods)

If in any real estate fiscal tax year starting with the real estate fiscal tax year beginning July 1, 19____, the real estate taxes on the Leased Premises (which specifically includes both the land and the building), are in excess of the amount of such taxes for the real estate fiscal tax year beginning July 1, 19____ then Tenant agrees to pay to Landlord, as additional rent, when billed by Landlord, One Hundred per cent (100%) of such excess that may occur in each year of the Term of this Lease, apportioned for any fraction of a tax year in which the Term of this Lease begins or ends. In accordance with Massachusetts law, it is expressly understood and agreed that Tenant shall be obligated to pay only that proportion of such increased tax as the unit leased by him bears to the whole of the real estate so taxed [i.e., 100%], and that if Landlord obtains an abatement of the real estate tax levied on the whole of the real estate of which the unit leased by Tenant is a part [i.e., the Leased Premises], a proportionate share of such abatement, less reasonable attorney's fees, if any, shall be refunded to Tenant.

6.
CLEANLINESS

Tenant shall keep the Leased Premises in a clean condition. Tenant shall be responsible for the proper storage and the final collection or ultimate disposal of all garbage and rubbish, all in accordance with the regular municipal collection system. Tenant shall not permit the Leased Premises to be overloaded, damaged, stripped or defaced, nor suffer any waste, and shall obtain the written consent of Landlord before erecting any sign on the Leased Premises. The toilets and pipes shall not be used for any purpose other than those for which they were constructed.

7.
PETS

No dogs, birds or other animals or pets shall be kept in or upon the Leased Premises without Landlord's prior written consent obtained in each instance.

8.
GROUNDS

Tenant shall be responsible for normal grounds maintenance during the Term of this lease. Without limiting the generality of the foregoing language, Tenant shall promptly remove snow and ice from the driveway, walks and steps of the Leased Premises, and shall keep the lawn and all shrubbery neatly trimmed, healthy and of good appearance.

COPYRIGHT © 1978
GREATER BOSTON REAL ESTATE BOARD

9.
INSURANCE

Tenant understands and agrees that it shall be his own obligation to insure his personal property.

10.
COMPLIANCE
WITH LAWS

Tenant shall not make or permit any use of the Leased Premises which will be unlawful, improper, or contrary to any applicable law or municipal ordinance (including without limitation all zoning, building or sanitary statutes, codes, rules, regulations, or ordinances), or which will make voidable or increase the cost of any insurance maintained on the Leased Premises by Landlord.

11.
ADDITIONS
OR
ALTERATIONS

Tenant shall not make any additions or alterations to the Leased Premises without Landlord's prior written consent obtained in each instance. Any alterations or additions made by Tenant at his expense may be removed by Tenant at or prior to the termination of this Lease, provided that Tenant is not in default under this Lease, and provided further that Tenant repair any resulting injury to the Leased Premises and restore the Leased Premises to their former condition.

12.
SUBLETTING,
NUMBER OF
OCCUPANTS

Tenant shall not assign or sublet any part or the whole of the Leased Premises, nor shall he permit the Leased Premises to be occupied for a period longer than a temporary visit by any one *except the individuals specifically named in the first paragraph of this Lease,* their spouses, and any children born to them during the Term of this Lease, or any extension or renewal thereof, without first obtaining on each occasion the consent in writing of Landlord. Notwithstanding any such consent, Tenant shall remain unconditionally and principally liable to Landlord for the payment of all rent and for the full performance of the covenants and conditions of this Lease.

13.
UTILITIES

Tenant shall promptly pay all bills for water, sewer, fuel, heat, electricity, gas, telephone and other utilities furnished to the Leased Premises during the Term of this Lease, and shall keep the Leased Premises adequately heated during the normal heating season. Upon request of Landlord, Tenant shall promptly deliver adequate proof of the payment of utility bills to Landlord. Landlord and Tenant understand and acknowledge that the following utility equipment has been rented or purchased on credit by Landlord: _____

_____

and Tenant agrees to pay the sum of $_____ per month directly to _____ for use of such equipment during the Term of this Lease and if Tenant shall fail to pay such sums as set forth herein, then Landlord may pay such sums for the account of Tenant and Tenant shall reimburse Landlord therefor upon demand, as additional rent.

14.
ENTRY

Tenant shall permit Landlord to enter the Leased Premises prior to the termination of this Lease to inspect the same, to make repairs thereto (although nothing contained in this Paragraph shall be construed to require Landlord to make any such repairs), or to show the same to prospective tenants, purchasers, or mortgagees. Landlord shall also be entitled to enter the Leased Premises if they appear to have been abandoned by Tenant or otherwise, as permitted by Law. Any person entitled to enter the Leased Premises in accordance with this Paragraph may do so through his duly-authorized representative. Wherever possible, Tenant shall be informed in advance of any proposed entry hereunder. At any time within three (3) months before the expiration of the Term of this Lease, Landlord may affix to any suitable part of the Leased Premises a notice for letting or selling the same and keep such notice so affixed without hindrance or molestation.

**15.
KEYS AND
LOCKS**

Locks shall not be changed, altered, or replaced nor shall new locks be added by Tenant without the written permission of Landlord. Any locks so permitted to be installed shall become the property of Landlord and shall not be removed by Tenant. Tenant shall promptly give a duplicate key to any such changed, altered, replaced or new lock to Landlord, and upon termination of this Lease, Tenant shall deliver all keys to the Leased Premises to Landlord.

**16.
REPAIRS**

Subject to applicable law, Tenant shall keep and maintain the Leased Premises and all equipment and fixtures thereon or used therewith repaired, whole and of the same kind, quality and description and in such good repair, order and condition as the same are at the beginning of the Term of this Lease or may be put in thereafter, reasonable and ordinary wear and tear and damage by fire and other unavoidable casualty only excepted. If Tenant fails within a reasonable time to make such repairs, or makes them improperly, then and in any such event or events, Landlord may (but shall not be obligated to) make such repairs and Tenant shall reimburse Landlord for the reasonable cost of such repairs in full, as additional rent, upon demand.

**17.
LOSS OR
DAMAGE**

Tenant shall indemnify Landlord against all liabilities, damages and other expenses, including reasonable attorneys' fees, which may be imposed upon, incurred by, or asserted against Landlord by reason of (a) any failure on the part of Tenant to perform or comply with any covenant required to be performed or complied with by Tenant under this Lease, or (b) any injury to person or loss of or damage to property sustained or occurring on the Leased Premises on account of or based upon the act, omission, fault, negligence or misconduct of any person whomsoever other than Landlord.

**18.
EMINENT
DOMAIN**

If the Leased Premises or any part thereof, shall be taken for any purpose by exercise of the power of eminent domain or condemnation or shall receive any direct or consequential damage for which Landlord or Tenant shall be entitled to compensation by reason of anything lawfully done in pursuance of any public authority, then this Lease shall terminate at the option of Landlord or Tenant: and such option may be exercised in case of any such taking, notwithstanding that the entire interest of Landlord may have been divested by such taking. If this Lease is not so terminated, then in case of any such taking of the Leased Premises rendering the same or any part thereof unfit for use and occupancy, a just and proportionate abatement of rent shall be made. Any termination of this Lease pursuant to this Paragraph shall be effective as of the date on which Tenant is required by the taking authority to vacate the Leased Premises or any part thereof, provided however that Landlord shall have the option to make such termination effective upon, or at any time following, the date on which said taking becomes legally effective.

**19.
FIRE,
OTHER
CASUALTY**

Should a substantial portion of the Leased Premises be substantially damaged by fire or other casualty, Landlord may elect to terminate this Lease. When such fire, casualty, or taking renders the Leased Premises or any part thereof unfit for use and occupancy, a just and proportionate abatement of rent shall be made, and Tenant may elect to terminate this Lease if Landlord fails to give written notice within thirty (30) days after said fire or other casualty of his intention to restore Leased Premises, or if Landlord fails to restore the Leased Premises to a condition substantially suitable for use and occupancy within ninety (90) days after said fire or other casualty, provided however that nothing contained in this Paragraph shall be construed to require Landlord to make such restoration.

**20.
DEFAULT**

If Tenant shall fail to comply with any lawful Term, condition, covenant, obligation, or agreement expressed herein or implied hereunder, or if a petition in bankruptcy has been filed by or against Tenant or if Tenant shall be adjudicated bankrupt or insolvent according to law or if any assignment of Tenant's property shall be made for the benefit of creditors, or if the Leased Premises appear to be abandoned, then, and in any of the said cases and notwithstanding any license or waiver of any prior breach of any of the said terms, conditions, covenants, obligations, or agreements, the Landlord without necessity or requirement of making any entry may (subject to the Tenant's rights under applicable law) terminate this Lease by:

1. a seven (7) day written notice to Tenant to vacate the Leased Premises in case of any breach except only for non-payment of rent, or

2. a fourteen (14) day written notice to Tenant to vacate the Leased Premises upon the neglect or refusal of Tenant to pay the rent as herein provided.

Any termination under this section shall be without prejudice to any remedies which might otherwise be used for arrears of rent or preceding breach of any of the said terms, conditions, covenants, obligations or agreements.

**21.
COVENANTS
IN EVENT
OF
TERMINATION**

Tenant covenants that in case of any termination of this Lease, by reason of the default of Tenant, then:

A. Tenant will forthwith pay to Landlord as damages hereunder a sum equal to the amount by which the rent and other payments called for hereunder for the remainder of the Term or any extension or renewal thereof exceed the fair rental value of said Leased Premises for the remainder of the Term or any extension or renewal thereof; and

B. Tenant covenants that he will furthermore indemnify Landlord from and against any loss and damage sustained by reason of any termination caused by the default of, or the breach by, Tenant. Landlord's damages hereunder shall include, but shall not be limited to, any loss of rents, accrued but unpaid prior to termination; reasonable broker's commission for the re-letting of the Leased Premises; advertising costs; the reasonable cost incurred in cleaning and repainting the Leased Premises in order to re-let the same and moving and storage charges incurred by Landlord in moving Tenant's belongings pursuant to eviction proceedings.

C. At the option of Landlord, however, Landlord's cause of action under this Section shall accrue when a new tenancy or lease Term first commences subsequent to a termination under this Lease, in which event Landlord's damages shall be limited to any and all damages sustained by him prior to said new tenancy or lease date.

Landlord shall also be entitled to any and all other remedies provided by law. All rights and remedies are to be cumulative and not exclusive.

22.
SURRENDER

Upon the termination of this Lease, Tenant shall deliver up the Leased Premises in as good order and condition as the same were in at the commencement of the Term, reasonable and ordinary wear and tear and damage by fire and other unavoidable casualty only excepted. Neither the vacating of the Leased Premises by Tenant, nor the delivery of keys to Landlord shall be deemed a surrender or an acceptance of surrender of the Leased Premises, unless so stipulated in writing by Landlord.

23.
ATTACHED
FORMS

The forms, if any, attached hereto are incorporated herein by reference.

24.
NOTICES

Notice from one party to the other shall be deemed to have been properly given if mailed by registered or certified mail, postage prepaid, return receipt requested, to the other party (a) in the case of Landlord, at the address set forth in the first paragraph in this agreement or any other address of which Tenant has been notified, and (b) in the case of Tenant, at the Leased Premises, or if said notice is delivered or left in or on any part thereof, provided that there is actual or presumptive evidence that the other party or someone on his behalf received said notice. *Notwithstanding the foregoing, notice by either party to the other shall be deemed adequate if given in any other manner provided or recognized by law.*

25.
LIABILITY

In the event that Landlord is a trustee or partner, no such trustee or partner nor any beneficiary nor any shareholder of said trust nor any partner of such partnership shall be personally liable to anyone under any term, condition, obligation or agreement expressed herein or implied hereunder or for any claim of damage or cause at law or in equity arising out of the occupancy of the Leased Premises, the use or maintenance of said building or its approaches and equipment.

26.
DEFINITIONS

The words "Landlord" and "Tenant" as used herein shall include their respective heirs, legatees, devisees, executors, administrators, successors, personal representatives and assigns; and the words "he", "his", and "him", where applicable shall apply to Landlord or Tenant regardless of sex, number, corporate entity, trust or other body. If more than one party signs as Landlord or Tenant hereunder, the conditions and agreements herein of Landlord or Tenant shall be joint and several obligations of each such party.

**27.
WAIVER**

The waiver of one breach of any term, condition, covenant, obligation, or agreement of this Lease shall not be considered to be a waiver of that or any other Term, condition, covenant, obligation, or agreement or of any subsequent breach thereof.

**28.
SEPARABILITY
CLAUSE**

If any provision of this Lease or portion of such provision or the application thereof to any person or circumstance is held invalid, the remainder of the Lease (or the remainder of such provision) and the application thereof to other persons or circumstances shall not be affected thereby.

**29.
ADDITIONAL
PROVISIONS**

EXECUTED as an instrument under seal in duplicate on the day and date first written above, and Tenant as an individual states under penalty of perjury that he is at least eighteen (18) years of age.

Witness _____

Witness _____

Witness _____

Witness _____

_____ Landlord

_____ Landlord

_____ Tenant

_____ Tenant

TENANT: REMEMBER TO OBTAIN A SIGNED COPY OF THIS LEASE.

GUARANTEE: In consideration of the execution of the within Lease by Landlord at the request of the undersigned and of one dollar paid to the undersigned by Landlord, the undersigned hereby, jointly and severally, guarantee to Landlord, and the heirs, successors, and assigns of Landlord, the punctual performance by Tenant and the legal representatives, successors, and assigns of Tenant of all the terms, conditions, covenants, obligations and agreements in said Lease on Tenant's or their part to be performed or observed, demand and notice of default being hereby waived. The undersigned waive all surety-ship defenses and defenses in the nature thereof and assent to any and all extensions and postponements of the time of payment and all other indulgences and forbearances which may be granted from time to time to Tenant.

WITNESS the execution hereof under seal by the undersigned the day and year first written in said Lease.

STANDARD FORM
PURCHASE AND SALE AGREEMENT

From the Office of:

This _____ day of _____ 19 ___

1. PARTIES
AND MAILING
ADDRESSES

(fill in)

hereinafter called the SELLER, agrees to SELL and

hereinafter called the BUYER or PURCHASER, agrees to BUY, upon the terms hereinafter set forth, the following described premises:

2. DESCRIPTION
(fill in and include title reference)

3. BUILDINGS,
STRUCTURES,
IMPROVEMENTS,
FIXTURES

(fill in or delete)

Included in the sale as a part of said premises are the buildings, structures, and improvements now thereon, and the fixtures belonging to the SELLER and used in connection therewith including, if any, all wall-to-wall carpeting, drapery rods, automatic garage door openers, venetian blinds, window shades, screens, screen doors, storm windows and doors, awnings, shutters, furnaces, heaters, heating equipment, stoves, ranges, oil and gas burners and fixtures appurtenant thereto, hot water heaters, plumbing and bathroom fixtures, garbage disposers, electric and other lighting fixtures, mantels, outside television antennas, fences, gates, trees, shrubs, plants, and, ONLY IF BUILT IN, refrigerators, air conditioning equipment, ventilators, dishwashers, washing machines and dryers; and

but excluding

4. TITLE DEED
(fill in)

* Include here by specific reference any restric-
tions, easements, rights and obligations in party walls not included in (b), leases, municipal and

Said premises are to be conveyed by a good and sufficient quitclaim deed running to the BUYER, or to the nominee designated by the BUYER by written notice to the SELLER at least seven _____ days before the deed is to be delivered as herein provided, and said deed shall convey a good and clear record and marketable title thereto, free from encumbrances, except

(a) Provisions of existing building and zoning laws;
(b) Existing rights and obligations in party walls which are not the subject of written agreement;
(c) Such taxes for the then current year as are not due and payable on the date of the delivery of such deed;

other liens, other encumbrances, and make provision to protect SELLER against BUYER's breach of SELLER's covenants in leases, where necessary.

(d) Any liens for municipal betterments assessed after the date of this agreement;

(e) Easements, restrictions and reservations of record, if any, so long as the same do not prohibit or materially interfere with the current use of said premises;

*(f)

5. PLANS

If said deed refers to a plan necessary to be recorded therewith the SELLER shall deliver such plan with the deed in form adequate for recording or registration.

6. REGISTERED TITLE

In addition to the foregoing, if the title to said premises is registered, said deed shall be in form sufficient to entitle the BUYER to a Certificate of Title of said premises, and the SELLER shall deliver with said deed all instruments, if any, necessary to enable the BUYER to obtain such Certificate of Title.

7. PURCHASE PRICE

(fill in); space is allowed to write out the amounts if desired

The agreed purchase price for said premises is _____ dollars, of which

$ _____ have been paid as a deposit this day and

$ _____ are to be paid at the time of delivery of the deed in cash, or by certified, cashier's, treasurer's or bank check(s).

$ _____

$ _____ TOTAL

*This form has been made available through the courtesy of the Greater Boston Real Estate Board, and is protected by the copyright laws.

8. **TIME FOR PERFORMANCE; DELIVERY OF DEED** *(fill in)*

Such deed is to be delivered at .... o'clock .... M. on the .... day of .... 19 ...... , at the .... Registry of Deeds, unless otherwise agreed upon in writing. It is agreed that time is of the essence of this agreement.

9. **POSSESSION AND CONDITION OF PREMISE.** *(attach a list of exceptions, if any)*

Full possession of said premises free of all tenants and occupants, except as herein provided, is to be delivered at the time of the delivery of the deed, said premises to be then (a) in the same condition as they now are, reasonable use and wear thereof excepted, and (b) not in violation of said building and zoning laws, and (c) in compliance with provisions of any instrument referred to in clause 4 hereof. The BUYER shall be entitled personally to inspect said premises prior to the delivery of the deed in order to determine whether the condition thereof complies with the terms of this clause.

10. **EXTENSION TO PERFECT TITLE OR MAKE PREMISES CONFORM** *(Change period of time if desired).*

If the SELLER shall be unable to give title or to make conveyance, or to deliver possession of the premises, all as herein stipulated, or if at the time of the delivery of the deed the premises do not conform with the provisions hereof, then any payments made under this agreement shall be forthwith refunded and all other obligations of the parties hereto shall cease and this agreement shall be void without recourse to the parties hereto, unless the SELLER elects to use reasonable efforts to remove any defects in title, or to deliver possession as provided herein, or to make the said premises conform to the provisions hereof, as the case may be, in which event the SELLER shall give written notice thereof to the BUYER at or before the time for performance hereunder, and thereupon the time for performance hereof shall be extended for a period of thirty .... days.

11. **FAILURE TO PERFECT TITLE OR MAKE PREMISES CONFORM, etc.**

If at the expiration of the extended time the SELLER shall have failed so to remove any defects in title, deliver possession, or make the premises conform, as the case may be, all as herein agreed, or if at any time during the period of this agreement or any extension thereof, the holder of a mortgage on said premises shall refuse to permit the insurance proceeds, if any, to be used for such purposes, then any payments made under this agreement shall be forthwith refunded and all other obligations of the parties hereto shall cease and this agreement shall be void without recourse to the parties hereto.

12. **BUYER's ELECTION TO ACCEPT TITLE**

The BUYER shall have the election, at either the original or any extended time for performance, to accept such title as the SELLER can deliver to the said premises in their then condition and to pay therefore the purchase price without deduction, in which case the SELLER shall convey such title, except that in the event of such conveyance in accord with the provisions of this clause, if the said premises shall have been damaged by fire or casualty insured against, then the SELLER shall, unless the SELLER has previously restored the premises to their former condition, either

(a) pay over or assign to the BUYER, on delivery of the deed, all amounts recovered or recoverable on account of such insurance, less any amounts reasonably expended by the SELLER for any partial restoration, or

(b) if a holder of a mortgage on said premises shall not permit the insurance proceeds or a part thereof to be used to restore the said premises to their former condition or to be so paid over or assigned, give to the BUYER a credit against the purchase price, on delivery of the deed, equal to said amounts so recovered or recoverable and retained by the holder of the said mortgage less any amounts reasonably expended by the SELLER for any partial restoration.

13. ACCEPTANCE OF DEED

The acceptance of a deed by the BUYER or his nominee as the case may be, shall be deemed to be a full performance and discharge of every agreement and obligation herein contained or expressed, except such as are, by the terms hereof, to be performed after the delivery of said deed.

14. USE OF MONEY TO CLEAR TITLE

To enable the SELLER to make conveyance as herein provided, the SELLER may, at the time of delivery of the deed, use the purchase money or any portion thereof to clear the title of any or all encumbrances or interests, provided that all instruments so procured are recorded simultaneously with the delivery of said deed.

15. INSURANCE *Insert amount (list additional types of insurance and amounts as agreed)*

Until the delivery of the deed, the SELLER shall maintain insurance on said premises as follows:

Type of Insurance	*Amount of Coverage*
(a) Fire and Extended Coverage	*$
(b)	

16. ADJUSTMENTS *(list operating expenses, if any, or attach schedule)*

Collected rents, mortgage interest, water and sewer use charges, operating expenses (if any) according to the schedule attached hereto or set forth below, and taxes for the then current fiscal year, shall be apportioned and fuel value shall be adjusted, as of the day of performance of this agreement and the net amount thereof shall be added to or deducted from, as the case may be, the purchase price payable by the BUYER at the time of delivery of the deed. Uncollected rents for the current rental period shall be apportioned if and when collected by either party.

17.	ADJUSTMENT OF UNASSESSED AND ABATED TAXES	If the amount of said taxes is not known at the time of the delivery of the deed, they shall be apportioned on the basis of the taxes assessed for the preceding fiscal year, with a reapportionment as soon as the new tax rate and valuation can be ascertained; and, if the taxes which are to be apportioned shall thereafter be reduced by abatement, the amount of such abatement, less the reasonable cost of obtaining the same, shall be apportioned between the parties, provided that neither party shall be obligated to institute or prosecute proceedings for an abatement unless herein otherwise agreed.
18.	BROKER's FEE *(fill in fee with dollar amount or percentage; also name of Brokerage firm(s))*	A Broker's fee for professional services of is due from the SELLER to

the Broker(s) herein, but if the SELLER pursuant to the terms of clause 21 hereof retains the deposits made hereunder by the BUYER, said Broker(s) shall be entitled to receive from the SELLER an amount equal to one-half the amount so retained or an amount equal to the Broker's fee for professional services according to this contract, whichever is the lesser. |
19.	BROKER(S) WARRANTY *(fill in name)*	The Broker(s) named herein warrant(s) that the Broker(s) is(are) duly licensed as such by the Commonwealth of Massachusetts.
20.	DEPOSIT *(fill in name)*	All deposits made hereunder shall be held in escrow by as escrow agent subject to the terms of this agreement and shall be duly accounted for at the time for performance of this agreement. In the event of any disagreement between the parties, the escrow agent may retain all deposits made under this agreement pending instructions mutually given by the SELLER and the BUYER.
21.	BUYER's DEFAULT; DAMAGES	If the BUYER shall fail to fulfill the BUYER's agreements herein, all deposits made hereunder by the BUYER shall be retained by the SELLER as liquidated damages unless within thirty days after the time for performance of this agreement or any extension hereof, the SELLER otherwise notifies the BUYER in writing.
22.	RELEASE BY HUSBAND OR WIFE	The SELLER's spouse hereby agrees to join in said deed and to release and convey all statutory and other rights and interests in said premises.

23. BROKER AS PARTY

The Broker(s) named herein join(s) in this agreement and become(s) a party hereto, insofar as any provisions of this agreement expressly apply to the Broker(s), and to any amendments or modifications of such provisions to which the Broker(s) agree(s) in writing.

24. LIABILITY OF TRUSTEE, SHAREHOLDER, BENEFICIARY, etc.

If the SELLER or BUYER executes this agreement in a representative or fiduciary capacity, only the principal or the estate represented shall be bound, and neither the SELLER or BUYER so executing, nor any shareholder or beneficiary of any trust, shall be personally liable for any obligation, express or implied, hereunder.

25. WARRANTIES AND REPRESENTATIONS (fill in); if none, state "none"; if any listed, indicate by whom each warranty or representation was made

The BUYER acknowledges that the BUYER has not been influenced to enter into this transaction nor has he relied upon any warranties or representations not set forth or incorporated in this agreement or previously made in writing, except for the following additional warranties and representations, if any, made by either the SELLER or the Broker(s):

26. MORTGAGE CONTINGENCY CLAUSE (omit if not provided for in Offer to Purchase)

In order to help finance the acquisition of said premises, the BUYER shall apply for a conventional bank or other institutional mortgage loan of $_____ at prevailing rates, terms and conditions. If despite the BUYER's diligent efforts a commitment for such loan cannot be obtained on or before _____, 19___ the BUYER may terminate this agreement by written notice to the SELLER and/or the Broker(s), as agent(s) for the SELLER, prior to the expiration of such time, whereupon any payments made under this agreement shall be forthwith refunded and all other obligations of the parties hereto shall cease and this agreement shall be void without recourse to the parties hereto. In no event will the BUYER be deemed to have used diligent efforts to obtain such commitment unless the BUYER submits a complete mortgage loan application conforming to the foregoing provisions on or before_____ 19___

27. CONSTRUCTION OF AGREEMENT

This instrument, executed in multiple counterparts, is to be construed as a Massachusetts contract, is to take effect as a sealed instrument, sets forth the entire contract between the parties, is binding upon and enures to the benefit of the parties hereto and their respective heirs, devisees, executors, administrators, successors and assigns, and may be cancelled, modified or amended only by a written instrument executed by both the SELLER and the BUYER. If two or more persons are named herein as BUYER their obligations hereunder shall be joint and several. The captions and marginal notes are used only as a matter of convenience and are not to be considered a part of this agreement or to be used in determining the intent of the parties to it.

28. LEAD PAINT LAW

The parties acknowledge that, under Massachusetts law, whenever a child or children under six years of age resides in any residential premises in which any paint, plaster or other accessible material contains dangerous levels of lead, the owner of said premises must remove or cover said paint, plaster or other material so as to make it inaccessible to children under six years of age.

29. SMOKE DETECTORS

The SELLER shall, at the time of the delivery of the deed, deliver a certificate from the fire department of the city or town in which said premises are located stating that said premises have been equipped with approved smoke detectors in conformity with applicable law.

30. ADDITIONAL PROVISIONS

The initialed riders, if any, attached hereto, are incorporated herein by reference.

FOR RESIDENTIAL PROPERTY CONSTRUCTED PRIOR TO 1978, BUYER MUST ALSO HAVE SIGNED LEAD PAINT "PROPERTY TRANSFER NOTIFICATION CERTIFICATION"

NOTICE: This is a legal document that creates binding obligations. If not understood, consult an attorney.

_____
SELLER (or spouse)

_____
SELLER

_____
BUYER

_____
BUYER

_____
Broker(s)

EXTENSION OF TIME FOR PERFORMANCE

Date _____

The time for the performance of the foregoing agreement is extended until _____ o'clock _____ M. on the _____ day of _____ 19____, time still being of the essence of this agreement as extended. In all other respects, this agreement is hereby ratified and confirmed.

This extension, executed in multiple counterparts, is intended to take effect as a sealed instrument.

_____
SELLER (or spouse)

_____
SELLER

_____
BUYER

_____
BUYER

_____
Broker(s)

EX PARTE   *   IN THE CIRCUIT COURT
IN THE MATTER OF
THE CHANGE OF NAME OF   *   FOR
_____

BY HER MOTHER AND
NEXT FRIEND,   *
_____   *   No.

            *   *   *   *   *

Petition for Change of Name

Now comes _____, an infant, by _____, her mother and next friend, by _____ and _____, their attorneys, and respectfully represents unto this Honorable Court as follows:

1. That the Petitioner, _____, is presently nine years of age, having been born _____, in _____, State of Maryland, as evidenced by a photocopy of her birth certificate, attached hereto.

2. That your Petitioner, _____, presently resides with her mother, _____, and her stepfather, _____ at _____.

3. That your Petitioner, _____, is desirous of changing her name to _____ as she has been known for a considerable period of time in the general community in which she lives.

4. That _____, natural father of _____, presently residing in the City of Baltimore, State of Maryland, does hereby expressly join in this Petition for change of name to evidence notice and approval for the relief requested herein, and no notice need be entered in his behalf in these proceedings.

5. That the said _____ and the said _____ were not married when the Petitioner _____ was born, nor have they ever been married.

6. That the parties hereto have discussed with the Petitioner,

_____, this request for change of name and believe it to be in her best interests.

7. The request for change of name herein is not fraudulently made, and the Petitioner, _____, currently does not have any creditors.

8. That there are not other known interested parties to these proceedings and this Petition.

WHEREFORE, your Petitioner, _____, by her mother and next friend, prays this Honorable Court to:

a. Change the name of _____ to _____;

b. That these proceedings be sealed and not opened without an Order of Court upon conclusion of same;

c. That they may have such other and further relief as the nature of their case may require.

_____
_____
_____

Affidavit

The Undersigned do hereby solemnly declare and affirm under the penalties of perjury that the contents of the aforegoing Petition are true and correct to the best of their knowledge, information and belief.

_____
_____
_____

By: _____
Baltimore, Maryland 21202
Attorneys for Petitioner

Form: Petition for a Change of Name (with publication).
    Rule BH70
Common Error: Failure to verify.

General Power of Attorney

KNOW ALL MEN BY THESE PRESENTS: That I, the under-signed, do hereby constitute and appoint _____, to be by agent(s) and attorney(s), for me, in my name, place and stead and on my behalf to act in any way in which I myself could act, if I were personally present, in the following connections:

1. To attend to all business transactions of whatsoever character or description in which I have had, now have, or may hereafter have any interest or rights of whatsoever nature, whether individually, jointly with others, as a partner, or otherwise.

2. To withdraw from any banks or other financial institutions in which I have or may hereafter have any deposits, any or all monies so deposited in my name and/or in my name jointly with others; to close any accounts in any banks or other financial institutions now or hereafter standing in my name and/or in my name jointly with others; to open accounts in banks or other financial institutions in my name or jointly with others, and to close the same and to withdraw all monies which may be deposited therein to my account; to enter any safe deposit box and to remove any contents therefrom.

3. To sell, lease for any period of time (including leases for ninety-nine years renewable forever), grant options on, borrow on, hypothecate, mortgage, subordinate, exchange and/or convey any property or investments which I now have or which I may hereafter acquire, whether real or personal and wheresoever situate, with full power to execute, seal and acknowledge all necessary instruments and documents in that connection; to take possession and to dispose of any and all properties of whatsoever nature, real or personal, and wheresoever situate.

4. To buy assets of every kind and description, whether real, personal or mixed, for cash or on credit, and to execute any and all security devices, financing statements, mortgages, deeds of trust and all other instruments in writing securing any unpaid purchase price thereof.

5. To vote stock, sign proxies, exercise rights, warrants and options pertaining to stock and securities, and to execute, amend and terminate Voting Trust Agreements.

6. To use all means and process in the law, for the full and effectual execution of the business herein described; and in my name, to make and execute releases, acquittances and discharges, and in and about the premises, to appear for and represent me before and to appeal from any adverse decision of any governor, judge, justice, officer and minister of the law whatsoever, in any court of judicature, Law Court, Equity Court, District Court, Probate or Orphans' Court, Bureau, Commission, Board and other legal Authority, and there on my behalf, to institute, answer and defend and reply unto all actions, causes, matters and things whatsoever relating to the premises; to submit any matter in dispute respecting the premises to arbitration or otherwise; to compromise and settle any and all claims by or against me.

7. To sign and swear to, in my name and on my behalf, all Federal, State and Local income and Gift Tax Returns and reports and any other Returns and reports required by any governmental agency, department or body; to appear for me and represent me before any office of the Internal Revenue Service, before the United States Treasury Department and before any State or Local Tax Department in connection with any matter involving Federal, State or local Taxes in which I am or may hereafter become a party, giving my said attorney full power whatsoever requisite and necessary to be done in the premises, including the right to appeal, regardless of how long heretofore or hereafter any such matter may arise. All communications addressed to the undersigned regarding any such tax matters may be addressed to my said attorney at any address which he may furnish.

8. To execute waivers of restrictions on assessment or collection of deficiencies in tax; to execute consents extending the statutory period for assessment or collection of taxes; to execute closing agreements in respect of any tax liability or other specific matters; and to execute protests to determinations of taxes.

9. To make and substitute and appoint for any of the purposes aforesaid, one or more agents and attorneys, and the same again in pleasure to revoke.

10. To borrow any and all sums of money, upon such terms and conditions as my attorney shall deem fit and proper, and for that purpose to execute promissory notes, bonds or other evidence of indebtedness which may be necessary in the premises and to pledge, hypothecate, deposit or mortgage all property of mine to secure the repayment by my estate of any sums so honored.

11. Generally to say, act, transact, determine, accomplish and finish all matters and things whatsoever relating to my affairs and to execute all instruments in writing that may be necessary or convenient for that purpose as fully, amply and effectually, to all intents and purposes, as I, if present, ought or might personally do, although the matter should require more special authority than is hereby conferred; and I hereby ratify and confirm all and whatsoever the said agent or attorney or his substitute shall lawfully do or cause to be done in and about the premises, by virtue of these presents.

12. The foregoing enumeration of matters and things in connections with which I am empowering my agent and attorney to act shall not be interpreted as restricting said agent and attorney to those matters and things, but it is my intention to give my agent and attorney the fullest possible powers I am capable of granting to him so that my affairs may be attended to in the same manner by my agent and attorney as if I were personally present acting in my own behalf.

13. This Power of Attorney shall not be affected by any future disability or incompetence of mine.

14. In the event that I shall become incapacitated, then I do hereby nominate, constitute and appoint _____, as successor agent and attorney, and hereby confer upon him all rights and powers originally conferred upon _____.

15. I HEREBY RATIFY and CONFIRM every act and thing which my said attorney or successor attorney or any agent appointed by them hereunder shall do or cause to be done in the premises.

IN WITNESS WHEREOF, I have hereunto set my hand and seal this   day of   , 19 .

_____ (SEAL)

ACKNOWLEDGMENT

COUNTY OF MONTGOMERY)
)   SS :
STATE OF MARYLAND   )

I HEREBY CERTIFY that on this _____ day of _____, 1984, before me, a Notary Public in and for the State and County aforesaid, personally appeared _____ and acknowledged the foregoing deed to be his act.

_____
NOTARY PUBLIC

General Power of Attorney

{Short Form}

City of _____
State of _____

I,[name of party granting power of attorney], the undersigned, of [address], [city], [state], make, constitute, and appoint [name of party being granted power of attorney], of [address], [city], [state], my true and lawful attorney-in-fact, in my name, place and stead, giving attorney-in-fact full power to do and perform all and every act that I may legally do through an attorney-in-fact, and every proper power necessary to carry out the purposes for which this power is granted, with full power of substitution, revocation, ratifying and affirming that which attorney-in-fact or a substitute shall lawfully do or cause to be done by an attorney-in-fact or a substitute lawfully designated.

[If period of power of attorney is to be limited in duration, add: This power ends at (time) on (date)].

Dated:

[Signature]

[Acknowledgment]

Revocation of Power of Attorney

{From Principal to General Public or Specific Persons}

To [customers or creditors of principal and other specific persons entitled to notice] and to whom it may concern:

Notice is given that I [name of party revoking power of attorney], the undersigned, of [address], [city], [state], have revoked that written power of attorney executed [date], by which [name of party whose power is being revoked], of [address], [city], [state], was appointed my true and lawful attorney-in-fact for the purposes and with the powers set forth in the instrument. [Where applicable, make reference to fact of recording.]

This notice constitutes revocation of all power and authority given, or intended to be given, by the power of attorney to named attorney-in-fact.

Dated:

[Signature]

[Acknowledgment]

Power of Attorney to Manage Affairs and Property of Principal

{Short Form}

City of _____
State of _____

This power of attorney is made on [date].

SECTION ONE
{Powers Granted}

I, [name and address of party granting power of attorney], appoint [name and address of party being granted power of attorney] as attorney-in-fact to act for me and in my name, in any way I could act in person, with respect to the following powers, but subject to any limitations on the specified powers described in Section Two:

A. Real property transactions.
B. Financial institution transactions.
C. Stock and bond transactions.
D. Tangible personal property transactions.
E. Safe deposit box transactions.
F. Insurance and annuity transactions.
G. Retirement plan transactions.
H. Social Security, employment, and military service benefits.
I. Tax matters.
J. Claims and litigation.
K. Commodity and option transactions.
L. Business operations.
M. Borrowing transactions.
N. Estate transactions.
O. All other property powers and transactions.
P. Making of gifts.
Q. Exercise of powers of appointment.
R. Naming or changing of beneficiaries of insurance policies.

S. Naming or changing of joint tenants of benefits.

T. Revocation or amendment of trusts.

SECTION TWO
{Limitation on Powers}

The powers granted above shall be modified or limited in the following particulars: [specific limitations to powers granted in Section One].

SECTION THREE
{Delegation of Powers}

Attorney-in-fact shall have the right, by written instrument, to delegate any or all of the granted powers that involve decision-making to any person or persons whom attorney-in-fact may select. Such delegation may be amended or revoked by attorney-in-fact or by a successor attorney-in-fact named by me who is acting under the power of attorney at the time.

SECTION FOUR
{Compensation of Attorney-in-Fact}

Attorney-in-fact shall be entitled to [reasonable compensation for services rendered as attorney-in-fact under this power of attorney or specify compensation].

SECTION FIVE
{Effective Date}

This power of attorney shall become effective on [date or event].

SECTION SIX
{Termination}

This power of attorney shall terminate on [date or event].

SECTION SEVEN
{Successor Attorneys-in-fact}

If attorney-in-fact shall die, become legally disabled, resign or refuse to act, I name the following persons, each to act alone and successively in the order named, as successor to attorney-in-fact: [name and address of nominated successor attorney-in-fact].

SECTION EIGHT
{Guardian of Person}

If a guardian of my person is to be appointed, I nominate the following person to serve as such guardian: [name and address of nominated guardian of the person].

SECTION NINE
{Guardian of Estate}

If a guardian of my property is to be appointed, I nominate the following person to serve as such guardian: [name and address of nominated guardian of the estate].

SECTION TEN
{Awareness of Import of Instrument}

I am fully informed as to all of the contents of this form and understand the full import of this grant of powers to attorney-in-fact.

Signed [Principal]

Specimen signatures.

I certify that the signatures of attorney-in-fact [and successor attorneys-in-fact] are correct.

[Attorney in fact]
[Principal]
[Successor attorney-in-fact]
[Principal]
[Successor attorney-in-fact]
[Principal]

City of _____
State of _____

The undersigned, a notary public in and for the above county and state, certifies that [name of party granting power of attorney], known to me to be the person whose name is subscribed as principal to the foregoing power of attorney, appeared before me in person and acknowledged signing and delivering the instrument as the free and voluntary act of principal, for the uses and purposes set forth, [and who certified to the correctness of the signatures of attorneys-in-fact].

Dated:

[Notarial seal]

Notary Public

My commission expires [date].
This document was prepared by: [name and address].

Power of Attorney to Manage Real Property

City of _____
State of _____

I, [name of party granting power of attorney, of [address], [city], [state], make, constitute and appoint [name of party being granted power of attorney, of [address], [city], [state], my true and lawful attorney-in-fact, in my name, place, and stead, with respect to real property [including, but not limited to, real property I may subsequently acquire or receive, including my personal residence]:

A. To lease real property.

B. To accept real property as a gift or as security for a loan.

C. To collect, sue for and receive all rents, receipts, and profits of real property.

D. To conserve, invest, and utilize any and all of such rents, profits, and receipts.

E. To eject and remove tenants or other persons from real property.

F. To recover possession of real property by all lawful means.

G. To do any act of management and conservation of real property.

H. To maintain, protect, repair, preserve, insure, build on, demolish, alter, or improve all or any part of real property.

I. To employ laborers about real property.

J. To subdivide, develop, dedicate to public use without consideration, or to dedicate easements over, real property.

K. To obtain or vacate plats and adjust boundaries of real property.

L. To adjust differences in valuation in exchange or partition of real property by giving or receiving consideration.

M. To pay, compromise, or contest tax assessments, and to apply for tax refunds in connection with real property.

N. To release or partially release resale property from a lien.

I revoke all powers of attorney previously made by me authorizing any person to do any act relative to real property generally or particular real property, or any part of such real property.

By this instrument, I ratify and affirm all acts of attorney-in-fact appointed in the instrument, or any substitute of attorney-in-fact appointed by attorney-in-fact, that is done in the matter by virtue of this appointment.

Dated:

[Signature]

[Acknowledgment]

Durable Power of Attorney

City of _____
State of _____

I, [name of party granting power of attorney], of [address], [city], [state], appoint [name of party being granted durable power of attorney], my [spouse or parent or child or brother or sister or as the case may be], of [address], [city], [state], my attorney-in-fact, in my name, place, and stead, and for my use and benefit: [insert powers, for example: to any in my behalf to do every act that I may legally do through an attorney-in-fact].

This durable power of attorney shall not be affected by any disability on my party, except as provided by the statutes of [state]. The power conferred on my attorney-in-fact by this instrument shall be exercisable from [date], notwithstanding a later disability or incapacity on my part, unless otherwise provided by the statutes of [state].

All acts done by my attorney-in-fact pursuant to the power conferred by this durable power of attorney during any period of my disability or incompetence shall have the same effect and inure to the benefit of and bind me or my heirs, devisees, and personal representatives as if I were competent and not disabled.

This durable power of attorney shall be nondelegable and shall be valid until such time as I [die or revoke this power or am judged incompetent].

Dated:

[Signature]

[Acknowledgment]

Consent for Organ and Tissue Donation by Donor

I, _____ (Name), with present home address of _____
_____ (Address), hereby authorize and direct that in
the event of my death under circumstances permitting the medical
use of my organs or tissues, that a gift be made to the _____
(Name of Regional Center) of the usable organs and tissues identified below for the purpose of transplantation and therapy.

I authorize the performance of all necessary tests and procedures,
including testing for the HIV antibody, to determine the medical
suitability of the organs and tissues for the purposes intended. [As
long as these tests do not interfere with my comfort, they may be
performed prior to my expected death.]

I agree to the release of all my medical records to the _____
_____ (Name of Regional Center). Provided strict
confidentiality will be maintained, these records may be made
available to appropriate representatives of the center prior to
my death.

Description of Gift

1. Circle "Yes" for organs and tissues to be donated.

Kidneys	Yes	No	Heart	Yes	No
Liver (plus iliac vessels)	Yes	No	Skin	Yes	No
Heart for valves	Yes	No	Eyes	Yes	No
Bone and associated					
tissues	Yes	No	Lungs	Yes	No
Pancreas	Yes	No	Other [Any]	Yes	No

2. If the organs and tissues I have donated for transplantation
    and therapy cannot be used for those purposes, I [agree]/[do
    not agree] that they be used for medical research or educa-
    tional purposes.

3. In addition to any organs and tissues noted above that may
    be used for medical research, I also consent to the gift of the

following organs and tissues for medical research or educational purposes: (Describe the gift or write "None.")

_____

Signed this _____ day of _____, 19___

Witness to Consent

First:

Name	Relationship, if any
Address	Telephone

Second:

Name	Relationship, if any
Address	Telephone

Advance Directive

PART A
APPOINTMENT OF HEALTH CARE AGENT

(Optional Form)

(Cross through this whole part of the form if you do not want to appoint a health care agent to make health care decisions for you. If you do want to appoint an agent, cross through any items in the form that you do not want to apply.)

1. I, ———————————————————————————————,
   residing at ———————————————————————————
   ——————————————————————————————————————

   appoint the following individual as my agent to make health care decisions for me:

   ——————————————————————————————————————
   ——————————————————————————————————————

   (Full Name, Address and Telephone Number of Agent)

   Optional: If this agent is unavailable or is unable or unwilling to act as my agent, then I appoint the following person to act in this capacity:

   ——————————————————————————————————————
   ——————————————————————————————————————

   (Full Name, Address and Telephone Number of Back-up Agent)

2. My agent has full power and authority to make health care decisions for me, including the power to:
A. Request, receive, and review any information, oral or written, regarding my physical or mental health, including, but not limited to, medical and hospital records, and consent to disclosure of this information;
B. Employ and discharge my health care providers;
C. Authorize my admission to or discharge from (including transfer to another facility) any hospital, hospice, nursing home, adult home, or other medical care facility; and
D. Consent to the provision, withholding, or withdrawal of health care, including, in appropriate circumstances, life-sustaining procedures.

3. The authority of my agent is subject to the following provisions and limitations:

_____

_____

4. If I am pregnant, my agent shall follow these specific instructions:

_____

_____

5. My agent's authority becomes operative (*initial only the one option that applies*):

_____   *When my attending physician and a second physician determine that I am incapable of making an informed decision regarding my health care; or*

_____   *When this document is signed.*

6. My agent is to make health care decisions for me based on the health care instructions I give in this document and on my wishes as otherwise known to my agent. If my wishes are unknown or unclear, my agent is to make health care decisions for me in accordance with my best interest, to be determined by my agent after considering the benefits, burdens, and risks that might result from a given treatment or course of treatment, or from the withholding or withdrawal of a treatment or course of treatment.

7. My agent shall not be liable for the costs of care based solely on this authorization.

By signing below, I indicate that I am emotionally and mentally competent to make this appointment of a health care agent and that I understand its purpose and effect.

_____   _____
(Date)   (Signature of Declarant)

The declarant signed or acknowledged signing this appointment of a health care agent in my presence and, based upon my personal observation, appears to be a competent individual.

_____   _____
(Witness)   (Witness)

_____   _____

_____   _____

_____   _____

(Signatures and Addresses of Two Witnesses)

Page 2 of 4

PART B
HEALTH CARE INSTRUCTIONS
(Optional Form)

*(Cross through this whole part of the form if you do not want to use it to give health care instructions. If you do want to complete this portion of the form, **initial** those statements you want to be included in the document and **cross through** those statements that do not apply.)*

If I am incapable of making an informed decision regarding my health care, I direct my health care providers to follow my instructions as set forth below. (**Initial** *all those that apply.*)

1. If my death from a terminal condition is imminent and even if life-sustaining procedures are used there is no reasonable expectation of my recovery:

   _____ *I direct that my life not be extended by life-sustaining procedures, including the administration of nutrition and hydration artificially.*

   _____ *I direct that my life not be extended by life-sustaining procedures, except that, if I am unable to take food by mouth, I wish to receive nutrition and hydration artificially.*

2. If I am in a persistent vegetative state, that is, if I am not conscious and am not aware of my environment nor able to interact with others, and there is no reasonable expectation of my recovery:

   _____ *I direct that my life not be extended by life-sustaining procedures, including the administration of nutrition and hydration artificially.*

   _____ *I direct that my life not be extended by life-sustaining procedures, except that, if I am unable to take food by mouth, I wish to receive nutrition and hydration artificially.*

3. If I have an end-stage condition, that is, a condition caused by injury, disease, or illness, as a result of which I have suffered severe and permanent deterioration indicated by incompetency and complete physical dependency and for which, to a reasonable degree of medical certainty, treatment of the irreversible condition would be medically ineffective:

   _____ *I direct that my life not be extended by life-sustaining procedures, including the administration of nutrition and hydration artificially.*

Page 3 of 4

———— *I direct that my life not be extended by life-sustaining procedures, except that, if I am unable to take food and water by mouth, I wish to receive nutrition and hydration artificially.*

4. ———— *I direct that, no matter what my condition, medication to relieve pain and suffering not be given to me if the medication would shorten my remaining life.*

5. ———— *I direct that, no matter what my condition, I be given all available medical treatment in accordance with accepted health care standards.*

6. If I am pregnant, my decision concerning life-sustaining procedures shall be modified as follows:

_____

_____

_____

7. I direct (in the following space, indicate any other instructions regarding receipt or nonreceipt of any health care):

_____

_____

_____

By signing below, I indicate that I am emotionally and mentally competent to make this Advance Directive and that I understand the purpose and effect of this document.

_____   _____
(Date)   (Signature of Declarant)

The declarant signed or acknowledged signing these health care instructions in my presence and, based upon my personal observation, appears to be a competent individual.

_____   _____
(Witness)   (Witness)

_____   _____
_____   _____
_____   _____

(Signatures and Addresses of Two Witnesses)
Page 4 of 4

Living Will

(Optional Form)

If I am not able to make an informed decision regarding my health care, I direct my health care providers to follow my instructions as set forth below. (***Initial*** *those statements you wish to be included in the document and* ***cross through*** *those statements which do not apply.*)

A. If my death from a terminal condition is imminent and even if life-sustaining procedures are used there is no reasonable expectation of my recovery:

_____ *I direct that my life not be extended by life-sustaining procedures, including the administration of nutrition and hydration artificially.*

_____ *I direct that my life not be extended by life-sustaining procedures, except that, if I am unable to take food by mouth, I wish to receive nutrition and hydration artificially.*

_____ *I direct that, even in a terminal condition, I be given all available medical treatment in accordance with accepted health care standards.*

B. If I am in a persistent vegetative state, that is, if I am not conscious and am not aware of my environment nor able to interact with others, and there is no reasonable expectation of my recovery within a medically appropriate period:

_____ *I direct that my life not be extended by life-sustaining procedures, including the administration of nutrition and hydration artificially.*

_____ *I direct that my life not be extended by life-sustaining procedures, except that, if I am unable to take in food by mouth, I wish to receive nutrition and hydration artificially.*

_____ *I direct that I be given all available medical treatment in accordance with accepted health care standards.*

C. If I am pregnant, my decision concerning life-sustaining procedures shall be modified as follows:

_____

_____

_____

Page 1 of 2

By signing below, I indicate that I am emotionally and mentally competent to make this Living Will and that I understand its purpose and effect.

_____   _____
(Date)   (Signature of Declarant)

The declarant signed or acknowledged signing this Living Will in my presence and, based upon my personal observation, the declarant appears to be a competent individual.

_____   _____
(Witness)   (Witness)

_____   _____
_____   _____
_____   _____

(Signatures and Addresses of Two Witnesses)

SIMPLE WILL

Will of William J. Smith

I, William J. Smith, also known as William John Smith, William Smith, and Will Smith, of the City of Columbus, County of Franklin, and State of Ohio, do make, publish, and declare this to be my last will, and I hereby revoke all wills and codicils heretofore made by me.

I give, devise, and bequeath all of my property of whatever kind and wherever situate, as follows:

(1) to my wife Mary A. Smith;

(2) if my wife Mary A. Smith predeceases me, to such of my children as survive me, in equal shares, provided, however, should a child of mine predecease me, survived by a child or children who survive me, such grandchild or grandchildren of mine shall take the share his or their parent would have taken had such parent survived me;

(3) if my wife Mary A. Smith and all of my children predeceases me, to such of my grandchildren as survive me, in equal shares;

(4) if my wife Mary A. Smith, all of my children, and all of my grandchildren predecease me, one-half to my parents, William M. and Anne R. Smith, or to the survivor of them, should only one of my parents survive me, and one-half to the parents of my wife, Thomas E. and Eleanor C. Rundell, or to the survivor of them, should only one of the parents of my wife survive me.

Except as hereinbefore provided, I intentionally make no provision for children of mine now living, or for any child or children born to or adopted by me hereafter.

If my wife Mary A. Smith predeceases me, and I am survived by a minor child or children, I nominate my sister Helen E. Smith to be guardian of the person and estate of such minor child or children. If my sister Helen E. Smith predeceases me, or is unable or unwilling to accept such appointment, or, having undertaken her duties, is unable or unwilling to continue to serve, then I nominate my sister Georgia R. Kendall to be the guardian of the person and estate of such minor child or children. I direct that any guardian nominated by me be exempted from the requirement of furnishing bond.

I nominate my wife Mary A. Smith to be executrix of my last will. If my wife Mary A. Smith predeceases me, or is unable or unwilling to accept such appointment, or, having undertaken her duties, is unable or unwilling to continue to serve, then I nominate my sister Georgia R. Kendall to be executrix of my last will. I direct that any executrix nominated by me be exempted from the requirement of furnishing bond.

Without the necessity of obtaining leave of any court, my executrix shall have full power (1) to sell (at public or private sale), mortgage, transfer, and convey, in such manner and on such terms (including credit) as seem advisable, any and all property in my estate; (2) to settle, adjust, compromise, or pay claims asserted in favor of or against my estate, and to agree to any rescission or modification of any contract or agreement made by me; and (3) to make distribution in kind at a valuation set by her for such purpose, such valuation to be final and conclusive to the distributee or distributees.

In witness whereof I have hereunto set my hand to this my last will, consisting of this page and the one preceding typewritten page initialled by me at the left margin thereof, in the presence of the three persons who have at my request and in my presence and in the presence of each other acted as witnesses this _____ day of _____, 19__, at Columbus, Ohio.

_____

William J. Smith

The foregoing instrument of two typewritten pages, including this page, was signed at the end by William J. Smith and by him acknowledged to be his last will before us and in our presence, and by us subscribed as attesting witnesses in his presence, at his request, and in the presence of each other on the day and year last above written. And we and each of us declare that we believe William J. Smith to be of sound mind and memory.

_____ residing at _____
_____ residing at _____
_____ residing at _____

Your Rights as a Patient

A Hospital Guide for Patients*

The following hospital patients' bill of rights was recently adopted by a California hospital—the Sharp Cabrillo Hospital in San Diego. Although its adoption by every American hospital would represent a major step forward for all but a few of them as far as the rights of patients are concerned, there are two warnings which need to be discussed.

First, Sharp Cabrillo Hospital adopted the bill of rights only in settlement of a lawsuit brought against the hospital for alleged medical malpractice. Instead of suing the hospital for damages, the family wanted to assure that patients who used the hospital in the future might benefit from the improvements implemented by the patient bill of rights. This is but another example of the deterrent effect of malpractice litigation. By looking narrowly only at

*Reprinted from Public Citizen Health Research Group "Health Letter," April 1991.

the individual patients or families who bring these lawsuits, it is easy to overlook the deterrent effect of a change in hospital policies including better communication between patients and their families and hospital staff and improvement in the prevention of risks to patients. These improvements are often adopted only after one or more tragedies prompt the hospital toward prevention.

Our second warning is that the list, even though a significant improvement over what is routinely done in many hospitals, is far from complete in terms of the rights of patients. Two of a much longer list of omissions bear mentioning here.

First, the hospital should provide access to data allowing you to compare the hospital you are going to with other hospitals. In New York and Massachusetts, laws now require every hospital to disclose, upon request, information on the percentage of deliveries done by cesarean section. Other important data would include the number of operations and the mortality rate for difficult surgical procedures such as coronary artery bypass surgery.

Second, the right to ask for different menus for hospital meals should be made explicit rather than waiting until the first unacceptable meal shows up and putting the burden on the patient to make a change. Being in the hospital and having to eat hospital meals are often difficult enough and any increase in the extent to which patients have more control is extremely important.

Sharp Cabrillo Hospital, its physicians, nurses and entire staff are committed to providing you with quality medical care as our patient. It is our policy to respect your individuality and your dignity. We support your right to know about your medical condition and your right to participate in the decisions which affect your well-being. Therefore, we have adopted the following policy concerning patient rights. Should we not meet these goals, please let us know. Your comments will be of help to us and to future patients.

1. You have the right to receive appropriate medical care regardless of your race, color, religion, national origin, or the source of payment for your care.

2. Emergency services are available at this facility. Such services will be provided on request where medically appropriate without first questioning you or any other person as to your or the other

person's ability to pay for such services. You or your legally responsible relative or guardian will be asked to sign an agreement to pay for emergency services or otherwise supply insurance or credit information after the services are rendered.

3. You have the right to considerate and respectful care. You can expect to receive reasonable responses to any reasonable requests you make for services.

4. You have the right to full consideration of privacy concerning your medical care program. Case discussion, consultation, examination and treatment are confidential and will be conducted discreetly. You have the right to know the reason for the presence of any individual.

5. You have the right to confidential treatment of all communications and records pertaining to your care and your stay in the hospital. Written permission shall be obtained, as required by law, before your medical records are made available to anyone not directly concerned with your care.

6. You have the right to seek and receive information about your medical situation, the course of your treatment and the prospects for your recovery in terms you can understand. You have the right to know the name of the physician who has primary responsibility for coordinating your care (the attending physician) and the right to talk with that physician and any others who give care to you within an appropriate response time. You have the right to know the names and professional relationship of other physicians and nonphysicians who will see you.

You have the right to receive as much information on a timely basis about any proposed treatment or procedure as you may need in order to give informed consent or to refuse this course of treatment. Except in emergencies, this information shall include a description of the procedure or treatment, the medically significant risks involved in this treatment, alternate courses of treatment or nontreatment and the risks involved in each, and the name of the person who will carry out the procedure or treatment. If you need an interpreter, one will be obtained for you.

You have the right to participate actively in decisions regarding your medical care, including the right to seek additional consultations. To the extent permitted by law, this also includes the right to refuse treatment. You have the right to reasonable continuity of care and to know in advance the time and location of appointments as well as the identity of persons providing the care. If two or more physicians on your case have a disagreement regarding your treatment, you should discuss the situation with your attending physician. You may also contact the hospital's patient representative if you wish. If you so request, the physician who is the chief of the appropriate service at the hospital may also be available to assist in resolving the matter, when warranted by the circumstances.

7. California law generally allows you, on request, to have access to information in your medical records, either by allowing you or, in certain cases, your representative to inspect or copy the records, or by allowing the hospital, if it so chooses, to prepare a summary of the records and to furnish you or your representative with the summary or a copy of the summary. A complete hospital record must include the attending physician's discharge summary, usually available within a month of your discharge from the hospital. The law sets forth the time limits within which the hospital must respond to your request. The law allows the hospital to charge you, in advance, copying costs and a reasonable charge for clerical costs associated with making the information available to you. Our policy is to notify the attending physician of any patient request for access to medical records, and we encourage the physician to discuss the requests with the patient. Please let us know if you have any questions or wish further information regarding patient records.

8. You are entitled to know whether any facilities recommended for your use are facilities in which those making the recommendations have a significant ownership or financial interest. If you are referred to any laboratories or other ancillary health services providers outside the hospital, you have a right to know whether the hospital or physicians have an ownership or financial interest in the facility.

9. You have a right to leave the hospital even against the advice of physicians. If you decide to leave the hospital against your physician's advice, the hospital will not be responsible for any harm your leaving may cause you, and you will be asked to sign a "Discharge Against Medical Advice" form.

10. You have a right to be informed of continuing health care

requirements following your discharge from the hospital. Whether you visit our facility as an inpatient or as an outpatient, you will be given instructions before your discharge from the hospital as to how you and your family can promote your recovery and ongoing health care. You have a right to have a thorough understanding of all of your instructions, and an instruction sheet will be given to you for your home reference, complete with the telephone number of the hospital should you need assistance or clarification once you are home.

11. In order to reduce financial concerns, we attempt to handle payment issues before the patient comes to the hospital. We inform patients of services available to them to assist in payment for hospital services. We screen and make referrals to agencies such as MediCaid if the patient qualifies. Please let us know if you need information concerning financial assistance. Patients have the right to examine and receive an explanation of their hospital bill regardless of source of payment.

12. If you are unhappy with your care, you have the right to express any grievances orally or in writing. If you have concerns that you need to discuss, you should notify your physician or nurse, or you may dial extension 3884 to reach our patient representative. It may be necessary to leave a message, but our patient representative will respond to your call as soon as possible. If your concern is of an urgent nature, please dial "O" for an operator and have the patient representative paged during the day.

At Sharp Cabrillo Hospital we are committed to providing you with quality patient care in a caring and cost-effective manner. We hope this information assists you in understanding what your rights are as a patient at Sharp Cabrillo Hospital, and we hope you have a satisfactory stay.

Small-Claims Courts, by State

Following is a list of small-claims courts, by state, as of 1993. Note that the amounts for which you can sue, as well as other aspects of specific small-claim systems, are routinely changed by new legislation. Check with your local clerk for the currency and accuracy of the information below.

ALABAMA

SMALL CLAIMS (DISTRICT
  COURT)
Maximum dollar amount: $1,500.
Where to file suit: Where
  defendant resides or injury
  or property damage
  occurred. Corporation
  resides where it does
  business.

ALASKA

SMALL CLAIMS (DISTRICT
  COURT)
Maximum dollar amount: $5,000.
Where to file suit: Court nearest
  defendant's residence or
  place of employment or
  district in which property
  damage or injury
  occurred.

ARIZONA

JUSTICE COURT (SMALL
  CLAIMS DIVISION)
Maximum dollar amount: $1,500.
Where to file suit: Where
  defendant resides.
  Corporation resides where it
  does business.

ARKANSAS

SMALL CLAIMS (MUNICIPAL COURT) JUSTICE OF THE PEACE

Maximum dollar amount: $3,000.
Where to file suit: Where defendant resides or injury took place. A corporation resides where it does business.

CALIFORNIA

SMALL CLAIMS DIVISION (JUSTICE OR MUNICIPAL)

Maximum dollar amount: $5,000; $1,500 for claims against surety.
Where to file suit: County where the defendant resides or injury occurred. Corporation resides where it does business.

COLORADO

SMALL CLAIMS DIVISION (COUNTY COURT)

Where to file suit: County in which the defendant resides or an injury occurred.

CONNECTICUT

SMALL CLAIMS (SUPERIOR COURT)

Maximum dollar amount: $2,000.

Where to file suit: County or judicial district where the defendant resides, does business, or where injury occurred.

DELAWARE

JUSTICE OF THE PEACE (NO SMALL CLAIMS SYSTEM)

Maximum dollar amount: $5,000.
Where to file suit: Any county within the state.

DISTRICT OF COLUMBIA

SMALL CLAIMS AND CONCILIATION BRANCH (SUPERIOR COURT)

Maximum dollar amount: $2,000.
Where to file suit: There is only one court in the District of Columbia.

FLORIDA

SUMMARY PROCEDURE (COUNTY COURT)

Maximum dollar amount: $2,500.
Where to file suit: County where the defendant resides or injury occurred. Corporation resides in its place of customary business.

GEORGIA

MAGISTRATE COURT (NO SMALL CLAIMS SYSTEM)
Maximum dollar amount: $5,000.
Where to file suit: County where the defendant resides.

HAWAII

SMALL CLAIMS DIVISION (DISTRICT COURT)
Maximum dollar amount: $2,500. No limit in landlord-tenant security deposit disputes.
Where to file suit: Judicial district where the defendant resides or where rental premises is situated.

IDAHO

SMALL CLAIMS DEPARTMENT OF MAGISTRATE'S DIVISION (DISTRICT COURT)
Maximum dollar amount: $2,000.
Where to file suit: County where the defendant resides or where the claim arose.

ILLINOIS

SMALL CLAIMS (CIRCUIT COURT)
Maximum dollar amount: $2,500.
Where to file suit: Where the defendant resides or injury occurred. A corporation resides where it is doing business.

INDIANA

SMALL CLAIMS DIVISION (CIRCUIT COURT)
Maximum dollar amount: $3,000.
Where to file suit: County in which defendant resides or is employed or injury occurred, or where obligation incurred or was to be performed by defendant.

IOWA

SMALL CLAIMS DOCKET (DISTRICT COURT)
Maximum dollar amount: $2,000.
Where to file suit: County in which defendant resides or injury occurred, or obligation incurred.

KANSAS

SMALL CLAIMS (DISTRICT COURT)
Maximum dollar amount: $1,000.
Where to file suit: County in which defendant lives or has a place of business or employment.

KENTUCKY

SMALL CLAIMS (DISTRICT
   COURT)
Maximum dollar amount: $1,500.
Where to file suit: Judicial district
   where defendant resides or
   does business.

LOUISIANA

RURAL—NO SMALL CLAIMS
   PROCEDURE (JUSTICE
   OF THE PEACE)
URBAN—(CITY COURT:
   SMALL CLAIMS DIVISION)
Maximum dollar limit: $2,000;
   $1,500 for recovery of
   property.

MAINE

SMALL CLAIMS (DISTRICT
   COURT)
Maximum dollar amount: $1,400.
Where to file suit: Where
   defendant resides or has a
   place of business where
   transaction occurred or
   where registered agent
   resides if corporation.

MARYLAND

SMALL CLAIMS (DISTRICT
   COURT)
Maximum dollar amount: $2,500.
Where to file suit: County in

which defendant resides, is
employed or does business,
or where injury occurred.
Corporation may be sued
where it maintains principal
office.

MASSACHUSETTS

SMALL CLAIMS (BOSTON—
   MUNICIPAL COURT;
   ELSEWHERE DISTRICT
   COURT)
Maximum dollar amount: $1,500.
   No limit for property
   damage caused by a motor
   vehicle.
Where to file suit: Judicial district
   in which plaintiff or
   defendant resides or where
   the defendant is employed
   or does business. In the case
   of landlord-tenant cases,
   where the property is
   located.

MICHIGAN

SMALL CLAIMS DIVISION
   (DISTRICT COURT)
Maximum dollar amount: $1,500.
Where to file suit: County where
   defendant resides or where
   act or omission occurred.

defendant resides, has a place of business, or obligation occurred. Corporation resides where it has principal place of business or an agent.

OKLAHOMA

SMALL CLAIMS (DISTRICT COURT)

Maximum dollar amount: $2,500.

Where to file suit: County where defendant resides or obligation was entered into. A corporation may be sued where principal office is or where the injury occurred.

OREGON

SMALL CLAIMS (DISTRICT OR JUSTICE COURT)

Maximum dollar amount: $2,500.

Where to file suit: Where defendant resides or can be found or where injury occurred. Contract cases where performance was expected.

PENNSYLVANIA

NO SMALL CLAIMS PROCESS. PHILADELPHIA— MUNICIPAL COURT; OTHER PLACES WITHIN

THE STATE—DISTRICT OR JUSTICE COURT

Maximum dollar amount: $5,000 (municipal court); $4,000 (district or justice court).

Where to file suit: Where defendant resides or can be served. Corporation or partnership resides where it has principal place of business.

PUERTO RICO

NO SMALL CLAIMS PROCESS (DISTRICT COURT)

Maximum dollar amount: $500.

Where to file suit: Where defendant resides. If corporation, where it does business or where obligation incurred.

RHODE ISLAND

SMALL CLAIMS (DISTRICT COURT)

Maximum dollar amount: $1,500.

Where to file suit: Where either party resides. Corporation resides where it does business.

SOUTH CAROLINA

NO SMALL CLAIMS PROCEDURE (MAGISTRATE'S COURT)

Maximum dollar amount: $2,500.
Where to file suit: Where
  defendant resides. A
  corporation resides where it
  does business.

SOUTH DAKOTA

SMALL CLAIMS PROCEDURE
  (CIRCUIT OR
  MAGISTRATE COURT)
Maximum dollar amount: $2,000.
Where to file suit: County whose
  defendant resides or injury
  or property damage
  occurred. Corporation
  resides at its principal place
  of business.

TENNESSEE

NO SPECIFIC SMALL
  CLAIMS PROCEDURE
  (COURT OF GENERAL
  SESSIONS)
Maximum dollar amount:
  $10,000; $15,000 if county
  population is more than
  700,000.
Where to file suit: Where
  defendant resides.
  Corporation resides where it
  maintains an office.

TEXAS

SMALL CLAIMS (JUSTICE
  COURT)

Maximum dollar amount: $2,500.
Where to file suit: Where
  defendant resides or
  obligation was to be
  performed.

UTAH

SMALL CLAIMS (CIRCUIT
  OR JUSTICE COURT)
Maximum dollar amount: $2,000.
Where to file suit: County in which
  the defendant resides or
  breach or injury occurred.

VERMONT

SMALL CLAIMS (DISTRICT
  COURT)
Maximum dollar amount: $2,000.
Where to file suit: Where
  defendant or plaintiff
  resides or injury occurred.

VIRGINIA

SMALL CLAIMS (IN EVERY
  COUNTY WITH MORE
  THAN 300,000 RESIDENTS)
Maximum dollar amount: $1,000.
Where to file suit: Where
  defendant resides, is
  employed, or regularly
  conducts business, where
  breach or injury occurred or
  where property is located.

WASHINGTON

SMALL CLAIMS
   DEPARTMENT (DISTRICT
   COURT)
Maximum dollar amount: $2,000.
Where to file suit: County where
   defendant resides.
   Corporation resides where it
   does business or has an
   office.

WEST VIRGINIA

MAGISTRATE COURT (NO
   SMALL CLAIMS PROCESS)
Maximum dollar amount: $3,000.
Where to file suit: Where
   defendant resides or where
   breach or injury occurred;
   or, if corporations, where
   they do business.

WISCONSIN

SMALL CLAIMS (CIRCUIT
   COURT)
Maximum dollar amount: $2,000;
   no limit in eviction cases.
Where to file suit: County where
   defendant resides or does
   substantial business or
   where claim arose.
   Corporation resides where it
   has principal office or where
   it does business.

WYOMING

COUNTY COURT OR
   JUSTICE OF THE PEACE
   COURT
Maximum dollar amount: $2,000.
Where to file suit: County where
   the defendant resides or if
   corporation, has principal
   office or place of business.
   Resident corporation where
   breach or injury occurred.

Bibliography

Your Home and Property

Chapter 1 (Contracts)

Drafting Contracts, Scott J. Burnham (The Michie Company, 1987)

Simple Contracts for Personal Use, Stephen Elias and Marcia Stewart (Nolo Press, 1991)

The Copyright Handbook: How to Protect and Use Written Works, Stephen Fishman (Nolo Press, 1992)

Chapter 2 (Landlords and Tenants)

Tenants' Rights, Myron Moskovitz and Ralph Warner (Nolo Press, 1992)

The Landlord's Law Book, David Brown and Ralph Warner (Nolo Press, 1991)

Chapter 3 (Buying and Selling a House)

For Sale by Owner, George Devine (Nolo Press, 1992)
The Deeds Book, Mary Randolph (Nolo Press, 1992)

Chapter 4 (Defective Products)

Blashfield Automobile Law and Practice (West, 1969)
The American Trial Lawyer's Association publishes various materials on product safety. Write to the Public Interest Programs Department, ATLA, 1050 31st St., N.W., Washington, DC 20007, or call (toll-free) 1-800-424-2725, extension 380.

Chapter 5 (Debtors and Creditors)

Money Troubles: Legal Strategies to Cope with Your Debts, Robin Leonard (Nolo Press, 1991)
How to File for Bankruptcy, Robin Leonard (Nolo Press, 1991)

Your Family

Chapter 6 (Marriage and Divorce)

How to Do Your Own Divorce in California, Charles Sherman (Nolo Occidental, 1994)
Divorce and Money: Everything You Need to Know about Dividing Property, Violet Woodhouse and Victoria Felton-Collins with M.C. Blakeman (Nolo Press, 1993)
Practical Divorce Solutions, Charles Ed Sherman (Nolo Occidental, 1994)
Family Law in a Nutshell, Harry D. Krause (West, 1986)
Sharing the Children: How to Resolve Custody Problems and Get on with Your Life, Robert E. Adler (Adler & Adler, 1988)

Chapter 7 (Adoption and Name Changes)

How to Adopt Your Stepchild in California, Frank Zagone and Mary Randolph (Nolo Press, 1990)

How to Change Your Name, David Ventura Loeb and David W. Brown (Nolo Press, 1990)

Chapter 8 (Guardianships and Powers of Attorney)

The Power of Attorney Book, Denis Clifford (Nolo Press, 1991)

Chapter 9 (Health Matters)

The Consumer's Legal Guide to Today's Health Care, Stephen L. Isaacs and Ava C. Swartz (Houghton Mifflin, 1992)

Elder Care—Choosing and Financing Long-term Care, Joseph Matthews (Nolo Press, 1990)

Social Security, Medicare and Pensions: The Sourcebook for Older Americans, Joseph L. Matthews (Nolo Press, 1990)

Medical Records: Getting Yours, Bruce Samuel and Sidney M. Wolfe (Public Citizen's Health Research Group, 1992)

The Medicare 1992 Handbook (U.S. Department of Health and Human Services Health Care Financing Administration)

Insurance Law and Practice, John Alan Appleman and Jean Appleman (West, 1966)

For free publications, write to Consumer Information Center, Department 59, Pueblo, CO 81009.

Chapter 10 (Wills and Probate)

Probate—Settling an Estate: A Step-by-Step Guide, Kay Ostberg (Random House, 1990)

Nolo's Simple Will Book, Denis Clifford (Nolo Press, 1989)

Your Work

Chapter 11 (Employees' Rights)

Your Rights in the Workplace, Dan Lacey (Nolo Press, 1991)

Chapter 12 (Starting a Business)

The Legal Guide for Starting and Running a Small Business, Fred S. Steingold (Nolo Press, 1992)

How to Form a Nonprofit Corporation, Anthony Mancuso (Nolo Press, 1992)

How to Form Your Own Corporation, Anthony Mancuso (Nolo Press, 1992)

Your Rights

Chapter 13 (Alternative Dispute Resolution)

Ending It: Dispute Resolution in America, Susan M. Leeson and Bryan M. Johnston (Anderson, 1988)

Getting Apart Together, Martin A. Kranitz (Impact, 1987)

Chapter 14 (Small Claims)

Small Claims Court: Making Your Way Through the System, Theresa Meehan Rudy (Random House, 1990)

Neighbor Law: Fences, Trees, Boundaries and Noise, Cora Jordan (Nolo Press, 1991)

How to Win Your Personal Injury Claim, Joseph L. Matthews (Nolo Press, 1992)

Everybody's Guide to Small Claims Court, Ralph Warner (Addison-Wesley, 1980)

Everybody's Guide to Municipal Court, Roderic Duncan (Nolo Press, 1991)

Chapter 15 (Traffic Violations)

Traffic Court: How to Win, James Glass (Allenby Press, 1988)

Fight Your Ticket, David W. Brown (Nolo Press, 1992)

Chapter 16 (Personal Rights and Liberties)

The Bill of Rights for All Americans, Ira Glasser (Arcade, 1991)
The American Civil Liberties Union publishes a number of

books and pamphlets concerning the rights of specific groups—including those of aliens, authors, crime victims, employees, older persons, parents, patients, prisoners, protesters, students, teachers, and women. For a complete list of ACLU publications, write to ACLU Department of Public Education, 132 West 43rd St., New York, NY 10036, or telephone (212) 944-9800.

Chapter 17 (Getting the Most Out of Washington)

Getting the Most Out of Washington: Using Congress to Move the Federal Bureaucracy, Senator William S. Cohen and Kenneth Lasson (Facts on File Publications, 1982)

Litigation under the Federal Open Government Laws, Allan Robert Adler (American Civil Liberties Union Foundation, 1991)

Chapter 18 (Hiring a Lawyer)

You and the Law [Chapter 1, "When and How to Use a Lawyer"] (American Bar Association, 1990)

General Reference

You and the Law (American Bar Association, 1990)

Law and Legal Information Directory (Gale Research, Inc., 1993)

Prosser and Keeton on Torts, Fifth Ed., W. Page Keeton, Dan B. Dobbs, Robert E. Keeton, David G. Owen (West, 1984)

Nolo Press publishes numerous self-help books on legal matters. Its general information telephone number is (510) 549-1976; toll-free orders can be made by dialing 1-800-992-6656 (fax 1-800-645-0895).

℗ **PLUME**

LEGAL EASE

☐ **REPRESENTING YOURSELF** *What You Can Do Without a Lawyer.* **Second Edition. by Kenneth Lasson with Alan B. Morison and the Public Citizen Litigation Group.** With lawyers' hourly fees soaring, more Americans are wondering if there is an alternative to seeking an attorney when they're faced with legal problems. This uniquely practical guide is the consumer's answer to questions about law from the commonplace to the complex. (274516—$12.95)

☐ **WINNING YOUR DIVORCE** *A Man's Survival Guide.* **by Timothy J. Horgan.** This essential book of strategy deals with the legal aspects of divorce, and is the only up-to-date book of its kind for men. It offers practical, straightforward, professional advice that arms you with knowledge and forewarns you about the likely tactics of your wife's lawyer. Included, too, are real-life scenarios that illustrate costly mistakes to avoid. (273730—$10.95)

☐ **MAKING IT IN THE MUSIC BUSINESS.** *A Business and Legal Guide for Songwriters and Performers.* **by Lee Wilson.** This invaluable guide gives beginning songwriters and performers a working knowledge of music law and music industry business practices. Included here are discussions of the contracts that songwriters and performers encounter, an appendix that reproduces some of the documents discussed, a glossary of technical and legal terms, a resources section that lists helpful books, free publications, and music industry organizations. (268486—$12.95)

Prices slightly higher in Canada.

Visa and Mastercard holders can order Plume, Meridian, and Dutton books by calling
1-800-253-6476.
They are also available at your local bookstore. Allow 4-6 weeks for delivery.
This offer is subject to change without notice.